CAMBRIDGE STUDIES IN LINGUISTICS

Parallel structures in syntax

In this series

1 DAVID CRYSTAL: *Prosodic systems and intonation in English**
4 JOHN M. ANDERSON: *The grammar of case**
5 M. L. SAMUELS: *Linguistic evolution**
6 P. H. MATTHEWS: *Inflectional morphology**
7 GILLIAN BROWN: *Phonological rules and dialect variation**
8 BRIAN NEWTON: *The generative interpretation of dialect**
9 R. M. W. DIXON: *The Dyirbal language of North Queensland**
11 MELISSA BOWERMAN: *Early syntactic development**
12 W. SIDNEY ALLEN: *Accent and rhythm*
13 PETER TRUDGILL: *The social differentiation of English in Norwich**
14 ROGER LASS and JOHN M. ANDERSON: *Old English phonology*
15 RUTH M. KEMPSON: *Presupposition and the delineation of semantics**
16 JAMES R. HURFORD: *The linguistic theory of numerals*
17 ROGER LASS: *English phonology and phonological theory*
18 G. M. AWBERY: *The syntax of Welsh*
19 R. M. W. DIXON: *A grammar of Yidiɲ*
20 JAMES FOLEY: *Foundations of theoretical phonology*
21 A. RADFORD: *Italian syntax: transformational and relational grammar*
22 DIETER WUNDERLICH: *Foundations of linguistics**
23 DAVID W. LIGHTFOOT: *Principles of diachronic syntax**
24 ANNETTE KARMILOFF-SMITH: *A functional approach to child language**
25 PER LINELL: *Psychological reality in phonology*
26 CHRISTINE TANZ: *Studies in the acquisition of deictic terms*
28 TORBEN THRANE: *Referential-semantic analysis*
29 TAMSIN DONALDSON: *Ngiyambaa*
30 KRISTJÁN ÁRNASON: *Quality in historical phonology*
31 JOHN LAVER: *The phonetic description of voice quality*
32 PETER AUSTIN: *A grammar of Diyari, South Australia*
33 ALICE C. HARRIS: *Georgian syntax*
34 SUZANNE ROMAINE: *Socio-historical linguistics*
35 MARTIN ATKINSON: *Explanations in the study of child language development**
36 SUZANNE FLEISCHMAN: *The future in thought and language*
37 JENNY CHESHIRE: *Variation in an English dialect*
38 WILLIAM A. FOLEY and ROBERT D. VAN VALIN JR: *Functional syntax and universal grammar**
39 MICHAEL A. COVINGTON: *Syntactic theory in the High Middle Ages*
40 KENNETH J. SAFIR: *Syntactic chains*
41 J. MILLER: *Semantics and syntax*
42 H. C. BUNT: *Mass terms and model-theoretic semantics*
43 HEINZ J. GIEGERICH: *Metrical phonology and phonological structure*
44 JOHN HAIMAN: *Natural syntax*
45 BARBARA M. HORVATH: *Variation in Australian English: the sociolects of Sydney*
46 GRANT GOODALL: *Parallel structures in syntax: coordination, causatives, and restructuring*

Supplementary Volumes

BRIAN D. JOSEPH: *The synchrony and diachrony of the Balkan infinitive*
ANNETTE SCHMIDT: *Young people's Dyirbal: an example of language death from Australia*
JOHN HARRIS: *Phonological variation and change: studies in Hiberno-English*
TERENCE MCKAY: *Infinitival complements in German*
STELLA MARIS BORTONI-RICARDO: *The urbanization of rural dialect speakers: a socio-linguistic study in Brazil*

* *Issued in hard covers and as a paperback*

PARALLEL STRUCTURES IN SYNTAX

Coordination, causatives, and restructuring

GRANT GOODALL

Department of Linguistics
University of Texas at El Paso

CAMBRIDGE UNIVERSITY PRESS

CAMBRIDGE

NEW YORK   PORT CHESTER

MELBOURNE   SYDNEY

CAMBRIDGE UNIVERSITY PRESS
Cambridge, New York, Melbourne, Madrid, Cape Town, Singapore, São Paulo, Delhi

Cambridge University Press
The Edinburgh Building, Cambridge CB2 8RU, UK

Published in the United States of America by Cambridge University Press, New York

www.cambridge.org
Information on this title: www.cambridge.org/9780521109161

First published 1987
Reprinted 1989
This digitally printed version 2009

A catalogue record for this publication is available from the British Library

Library of Congress Cataloguing in Publication data

Goodall, Grant.
Parallel structures in syntax.
(Cambridge studies in linguistics; 46)
Bibliography.
Includes index.
1. Grammar, Comparative and general – Syntax.
2. Parallelism (Linguistics) 3. Generative grammar.
4. Grammar, Comparative and general – Coordinate constructions.
5. Causative (Linguistics) I. Title. II. Series.
P291.G66 1987 415 86-20790

ISBN 978-0-521-32307-9 hardback
ISBN 978-0-521-10916-1 paperback

To my PARENTS *and* GRANDPARENTS

Contents

Preface

Most of the research in transformational syntax over the last thirty years has dealt with well-formedness conditions of one sort or another on phrase markers. Such major themes in syntactic theory as constraints on transformations, $\bar{X}$-theory, and binding conditions are good examples of this. This research program has assumed, for the most part, that it is reasonably clear what a phrase marker is. The most pressing task at hand, after all, is to construct a grammar which will correctly distinguish between those phrase markers which are allowed in the given language and those which are not, as well as a theory of such grammars.

During the last five to ten years, as syntactic theory has become noticeably more sophisticated, there has been an increasing number of allusions in the literature to the possibility that it is, in fact, not so clear what a phrase marker is, and that perhaps our usual conception of these objects is wrong. This has led to some healthy rethinking about how phrase markers are to be defined and what the empirical consequences of these definitions might be. Still, most of this rethinking has been highly speculative and programmatic, and there is now little, if any, consensus on what the conclusions are.

This book attempts to tackle these issues head-on, by giving a detailed formalization of a revised definition of phrase markers. This revision allows phrase markers to contain "parallel structures" of a type not countenanced in customary definitions.

The bulk of the book consists of extended empirical justification for the introduction of these parallel structures into syntactic theory. Not by coincidence, the areas of data where I look for this justification are themselves sources of vigorous controversy and debate, independently of the question of the nature of phrase markers. The first area, coordination, has recently returned from a decade or two of obscurity to take its place alongside subordination as one of the most satisfyingly complex domains of syntactic investigation, thanks in large measure to the intriguing work of

Gerald Gazdar, David Pesetsky, and others. It currently enjoys special prominence in the debate about the role (or existence) of phrase structure rules in grammar. The second main area, causative and Restructuring verbs in Romance, has been a constant on the theoretical scene since it first began to be investigated in generative terms in the mid-60's. In recent years it has played a critical role in discussions about admissible rule types, the status of grammatical relations, and constraints on movement, among other things.

This book will be of use, then, both to scholars interested in the formal characterization of phrase markers and to those interested in coordination, causatives, Restructuring, and the theoretical issues they intersect with. It is hoped that the discussion of the rather complex data in each area is detailed enough to make the book useful even beyond the period of its theoretical immediacy.

Sections 1 and 2 of chapter 1 are intended as a brief review and reference for readers who are not in full command of the central concepts of government–binding theory, the version of transformational grammar assumed throughout. More experienced readers may skip on to section 3 of chapter 1, where the basic proposal about phrase markers is introduced and discussed. Since a knowledge of the formalism presented there is presupposed in the rest of the book, it is advisable to give that section at least a preliminary reading before beginning any of the subsequent chapters.

Coordination, causatives, and Restructuring are analyzed in chapters 2, 3, and 4, respectively. Chapter 4 depends a fair amount on chapter 3, but otherwise these chapters may be read in any order without serious problems. Parts of the analysis are discussed further in chapter 5, where final conclusions are drawn.

This book began as my 1984 Ph.D. dissertation at the University of California, San Diego. I am extremely grateful to Sandy Chung and Yuki Kuroda, who together chaired my committee, and to Noam Chomsky, who first launched me on this project and helped me with much of it. All three had a profound influence on the ideas developed here. Sandy Chung merits special thanks for her meticulous and insightful comments on virtually every page of the many drafts and for her careful shepherding of the finished dissertation through the lengthy process of revision into its present form. I am also grateful to the other members of my committee, Ed Klima, Steve Anderson, Zeno Vendler, and Walt Savitch, for their valuable help.

While researching and writing this book I have been in residence at the

University of California, San Diego, the Massachusetts Institute of Technology, and the University of Texas at El Paso. I am very thankful for the encouragement and support from my friends and colleagues at each of these institutions.

Several individuals read and/or listened to parts of earlier versions of this book and provided much helpful advice and discussion. They include Isabelle Haïk, Robert Chametzky, Luigi Rizzi, Carol Georgopoulos, Leslie Saxon, Tim Stowell, David Pesetsky, Osvaldo Jaeggli, Hagit Borer, Joseph Aoun, Ian Roberts, Mary Ellen Ryder, Eduardo Raposo, Guy Carden, Geoff Pullum, and Tom Wasow.

Finally, I must express my gratitude to the Great Chihuahua Desert, whose beauty, elegance, and overwhelming power have provided an unusually appropriate backdrop for the study of natural language syntax.

GRANT GOODALL
June 1986

1 *Introduction*

1.1 Preliminaries

One of the things which speakers know about their language is that strings of words which make up a sentence may be grouped into significant sub-strings or "phrases." Speakers of English, for example, know that in a sentence such as (1):

(1) A woman with a big hat stepped on the grass

sub-strings like *a woman, a big hat, the grass, with a big hat, on the grass, a woman with a big hat*, and *stepped on the grass* form phrases, but that sub-strings like *womam with, big hat stepped*, and *with a big* do not.

Our knowledge of English also tells us how these phrases are related to each other. We know, for instance, that the phrase *a woman with a big hat* is composed of two smaller phrases, *a woman* and *with a big hat*. In addition, we known that the phrase *a woman* linearly precedes the phrase *with a big hat*.

The collection of statements about the phrase structure of a sentence, a "phrase marker," constitutes the fundamental object in the theory of syntax. In this study I examine the form that these phrase markers take. The general questions which I will be concerned with are the following. What relations must hold among the various phrases in a sentence? To what extent does the linear ordering of phrases reflect the linear ordering of words in the spoken sentence? What predictions does the choice of a particular type of phrase marker make about the kinds of sentences which are possible in natural language?

The answers to these questions are to be taken as claims about the structure of our knowledge of language, that is, about the way in which language is represented in the mind. Since the form of mental representation is presumably determined in large measure by the particular structure of the human brain, these are ultimately claims about the effects of brain physiology on grammar. Our current understanding of how this works is at a relatively primitive level, so in what follows my attention will necessarily be devoted solely to formal, rather than neurological, representations.

In pursuing this course of inquiry, I will make no systematic attempt to include, or even sample, all of the currently existing varieties of human language; I will, instead, focus on a very small number of them. This will allow me to formulate detailed hypotheses about the organization of the grammars of these languages. Since, as stated above, these are hypotheses about the functioning of the brain, and since this is presumably uniform across the species, it follows that a claim about the fundamental structure of one language will be a claim about the structure of human language in general. Claims that the grammars of two languages are different are only plausible when it can be shown (as it often may) that the child learning the language has access to relevant evidence.

Before proceeding to the core of this study, I present a brief overview of the grammatical framework assumed.

1.2 Background assumptions

1.2.1 The organization of the grammar

I will assume here the version of transformational generative grammar presented in Chomsky (1981, 1982), known as government–binding theory. In this framework, sentences are assigned four distinct levels of representation, listed in (2):

(2) D-structure
S-structure
Phonetic Form (PF)
Logical Form (LF)

These levels are related by mapping operations, organized as in (3):

(3) 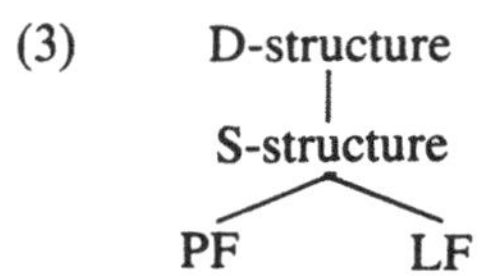

As indicated, the relations between D-structure, PF, and LF are mediated by the level S-structure. The general mapping operation is characterized as

"Move α", where α is any category. D-structure is determined by properties of lexical items; PF and LF are the phonetic and logical representations, respectively, of the sentence.

These levels are constrained by several subsystems of the grammar, listed in (4):

(4) a. $\overline{X}$-theory
b. θ-theory
c. Government theory
d. Case theory
e. Binding theory
f. Bounding theory
g. Control theory

(4) a–e will be directly relevant to much of our subsequent discussion. In the rest of this section, I give a brief introduction to these five subsystems.

1.2.2 $\overline{X}$-theory

The central idea of $\overline{X}$-theory is that phrases are projections of lexical categories. That is to say, given a lexical category X, X is dominated by a phrasal node XP (i.e. a phrasal node of the same category type). X is referred to as the "head" of XP, and XP is the "maximal projection" of X. Complements of X are always maximal projections. The linear position of the head relative to its complements must be specified for each language.

1.2.3 θ-theory

θ-theory deals with the arguments taken by predicates. Predicates assign thematic roles (henceforth θ-roles) to their arguments. The number and type of θ-roles assigned by the predicate is determined lexically. θ-roles may be assigned only to a subject or complement of the predicate. These are called "A-positions." Other positions are "$\overline{A}$-positions." Those A-positions which receive a θ-role are "θ-positions"; those which do not are "$\overline{\theta}$-positions."

The basic principle of θ-theory is the θ-criterion, given in (5):

(5) *θ-criterion*
Each argument receives one and only one θ-role, and each θ-role is assigned to one and only one argument.

The θ-criterion is assumed to hold at LF, but the "Projection Principle," given here in (6), extends it into S-structure and D-structure:

(6) *Projection Principle*
The θ-marking properties of each lexical item must be represented categorically at each syntactic level (i.e. D-structure, S-structure and LF).

Thus if a verb assigns a θ-role to a complement, that complement will be present and θ-marked at every syntactic level. Moreover, by the θ-criterion, the complement position must contain an argument.

We may now give a more precise definition of D-structure: it is the level where all θ-positions are filled by arguments. It follows from this that in the mapping from D-structure to S-structure (by Move α), arguments may move only to $\bar{\theta}$-positions. If they moved to a θ-position, the θ-criterion would be violated, since a single argument would receive two θ-roles. By the Projection Principle, a (empty) category ("trace") is present in the θ-position even when the argument has moved to a $\bar{\theta}$-position. In order for the θ-criterion to be satisfied, this moved argument must be coindexed with the trace in its D-structure θ-position.

1.2.4 Government theory

The relation "government" plays an important role in many of the subsystems of grammar. In essence, government is the relation between a head and its complements. Consider then a structure such as (7):

(7)

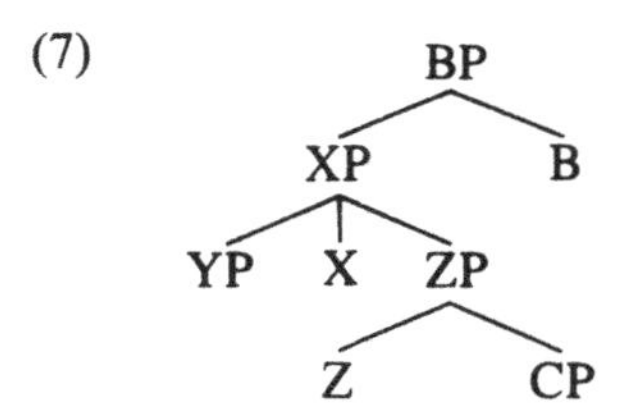

In accordance with $\bar{X}$-theory, X is the head of XP, and its complements are maximal projections (i.e. YP and ZP). X "governs" YP and ZP in this configuration. X does not govern BP or CP.

More precisely, we can say that *x* "governs" *y* when *x* c-commands *y* and when there is no maximal projection which dominates *y* and does not dominate *x*. Node *x* "c-commands" *y* when the first maximal projection above *x* also dominates *y*.

1.2.5 Case theory

Case theory regulates the distribution of phonetically realized NP's via the assignment of abstract case. In a structure like (8), V assigns abstract Case to its NP complement, and INFL, when the clause is tensed, assigns abstract Case to the NP subject:

(8)

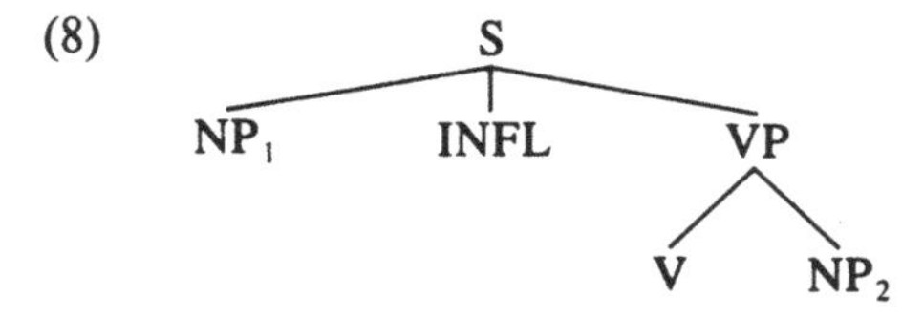

Case is assigned under government; potential Case-assigners are V and INFL, as in (8), and P. Notice that in (8), V governs NP_2 and INFL governs NP_1. When the clause is non-finite, INFL does not assign Case. In much of the subsequent discussion, we will assume the presence of INFL without representing it overtly in tree diagrams.

The main regulating mechanism of Case theory is the Case Filter, given in (9):

(9) *Case Filter*
* NP, where NP has a phonetic matrix and is not Case-marked.

This requires that overt NP's appear in positions which are assigned Case. We may assume that the Case Filter applies at S-structure. The relation between S-structure and D-structure now becomes clearer. At D-structure, arguments must appear in θ-marked positions. At S-structure, those arguments which are phonetically realized NP's must appear in Case-marked positions. Move α assures that both of these conditions are satisfied.

The lexical entry of the verb specifies whether or not the verb assigns Case and, if so, which Case(s). In general, the NP must be adjacent to its Case-assigner, thus determining the order of complements in the phrase.

We have seen, then, that a verb may have a set of θ-roles to assign and a set of Cases to assign. These do not always match up, however. An NP position may be θ-marked but not Case-marked, or Case-marked but not θ-marked. For example, verbs such as *arrive* (called "unaccusative" or "ergative" verbs) appear to assign a θ-role to the object, but no Case. The D-structure representation is thus as in (10):

(10) $[_{NP}$e$]$ $[_{VP}$ has arrived $[_{NP}$ John$]]$

As an S-structure, (10) would violate the Case Filter, so *John* is moved into subject position, which receives Case from INFL. The S-structure representation is thus as in (11):

(11) $[_{NP}$ John$_i]$ $[_{VP}$ has arrived $[_{NP} t_i]]$

Per the Projection Principle, the θ-marked NP object of *has arrived* is present here. *John* and its trace are coindexed, thus satisfying the θ-criterion.

1.2.6 Binding theory

Binding theory imposes further constraints on the distribution of NP's. Depending on inherent features of the NP, it must be either free or bound within a certain domain. We say that x "binds" y when x is coindexed with y and x c-commands y. "Free" means "not bound." We shall also use terms such as "A-bound," which means "bound by an NP in an A-position."

The relevant domain for binding theory is the "governing category." The governing category for NP y may be defined as the first NP or S which contains y and a governor of y.

NP's are divided into three classes: anaphors (reflexives, reciprocals, NP-traces), pronouns, and R-expressions (names, *wh*-traces). The conditions imposed on these by binding theory are as follows:

(12) *Binding theory*
A. An anaphor must be A-bound in its governing category.
B. A pronoun must be A-free in its governing category.
C. An R-expression must be A-free.

One further type of NP is PRO, an empty pronominal anaphor. I will assume that PRO must be ungoverned.

1.3 The theory of phrase markers

1.3.1 The definition of Reduced Phrase Markers

The rest of this study will assume the theory of syntax outlined in the previous section. Our fundamental object of inquiry, however, will be not the subsystems of grammar just described, but rather something which underlies all of these subsystems: the nature of phrase structure.

We stated in (2) that sentences are assigned four levels of representation. The grammar specifies what properties these levels must observe, and how they are interrelated. Although the properties required of each syntactic level are different, the general form of sentences at these levels is identical.

Each representation of a sentence is expressed as a phrase marker, on which the various subsystems operate. Our focus here, then, will be on the notion "phrase marker."

I take as my starting point the restrictive theory of phrase markers in Lasnik and Kupin (1977) (henceforth just Lasnik and Kupin), where phrase markers are represented as sets of strings. The vocabulary and conventions used in their system, which I will adopt here, are given in (13):

(13)

N	set of non-terminals
Σ	set of terminals
a, b, c...	single terminals (elements of Σ)
...x, y, z	strings of terminals (elements*)
A, B, C...	single non-terminals (elements of N)
...X, Y, Z	strings of non-terminals (elements of N*)
$\alpha, \beta, \gamma \ldots$	single symbols (elements of $\Sigma \cup$ N)
$\ldots \chi, \psi, \omega$	strings of symbols (elements of $(\Sigma \cup N)^*$)
A, *B*, *C*...	arbitrary sets

The type of phrase marker allowed by Lasnik and Kupin is called a "Reduced Phrase Marker" (RPM), which we will define below.

RPM's may be thought of as sets consisting of a string of terminals and "monostrings," where these are defined as in (14):

(14) φ is a *monostring* with respect to the sets Σ and N if $\varphi \in \Sigma^* \cdot N \cdot \Sigma^*$

A monostring thus contains one non-terminal surrounded by strings of terminals. In the definitions to follow, monostrings will be used to identify particular non-terminals. Thus when we say that monostring φ *precedes* monostring ψ, for instance, we mean, in ordinary terms, that the non-terminal in φ precedes the non-terminal in ψ.

Lasnik and Kupin's definition of RPM's makes use of the following predicates (let φ = xAz, $\varphi \in P$, $\psi \in P$, where P is an arbitrary set):

(15) y *is a** φ *in P* if xyz $\in P$

(16) φ *dominates* ψ *in P* if $\psi = x\chi z, \chi \neq \varnothing, \chi \neq A$

(17) φ *precedes* ψ *in P* if y *is a** φ *in P* and $\psi = xy\chi, \chi \neq z$

In (15), saying that y *is a** φ, where φ = xAz, means that y is an A. Statement (15) ensures that the terminals which surround the non-terminal in a monostring will be exactly those which the non-terminal does not dominate. Thus, comparing a monostring with the string of terminals in a set tells us which terminals bear the "is a" relationship to the non-terminal of the monostring.

In (16), we see that φ *dominates* ψ if the terminals in φ are a subset of those in ψ. That is to say, if the non-terminal in ψ dominates a subset of the terminals dominated by the non-terminal in φ, then we know that the non-terminal in φ dominates the non-terminal in ψ.

In (17), φ *precedes* ψ if the non-terminal in φ dominates terminals which are to the left of, and distinct from, the terminals dominated by the non-terminal in ψ.

RPM's may now be defined as in (18):

(18) P is an RPM if there exist A and z such that $A \in P$ and $z \in P$; and if $\{\psi, \varphi\} \subseteq P$,
either ψ *dominates* φ *in P*
or φ *dominates* ψ *in P*
or ψ *precedes* φ *in P*
or φ *precedes* ψ *in P.*

There are thus two requirements on RPM's. One is that they must minimally contain a single non-terminal and a string of terminals. The second is that every pair of distinct strings in the RPM must satisfy either *dominates* or *precedes.*

Consider, for example, the set in (19):

(19) {A, Bbc, aC, aDc, abE, abc}

This satisfies the first requirement that the set contain a single non-terminal (A) and a string of terminals (abc). We must now see whether each pair of strings satisfies *precedes* or *dominates.* The pairs are listed in (20):

(20)					
a.	A	Bbc	i.	Bbc	abc
b.	A	aC	j.	aC	aDc
c.	A	aDc	k.	aC	abE
d.	A	abE	l.	aC	abc
e.	A	abc	m.	aDc	abE
f.	Bbc	aC	n.	aDc	abc
g.	Bbc	aDc	o.	abE	abc
h.	Bbc	abE			

Pairs (a–e), (i–l), (n), and (o) satisfy *dominates,* whereas (f–h) and (m) satisfy *precedes.* This means that A dominates B, C, D, and E, that C dominates D and E, and each non-terminal dominates portions of the terminal string. In addition, B precedes C, D, and E, and D precedes E. As a tree diagram, this may be represented as in (21):

(21)

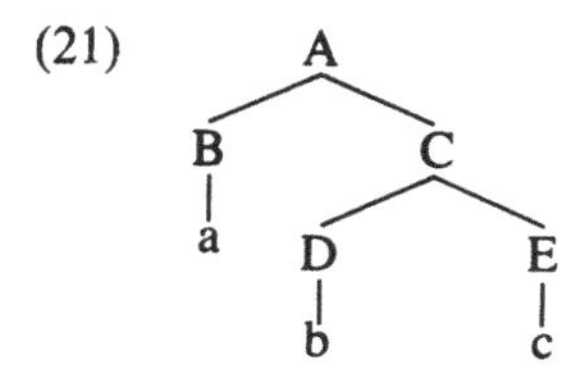

(21) is "rooted," i.e. there is a single node dominating all others, and it has a terminal string. Moreover, for any pair of nodes in (21), one member of the pair dominates or precedes the other. Intuitively, these descriptions of (21) embody the definition of RPM's in (18).

There are of course many kinds of sets which do not qualify as RPM's under (18). Consider (22), for instance:

(22) {Bbc, aC, aDc, abE, abc}

Set (22) violates the requirement that one of the elements of the set be a single non-terminal. Similarly in (23), there is no terminal string, contrary to the definition in (18):

(23) {A, Bbc, aC}

Sets (22) and (23) thus demonstrate violations of the first requirement on RPM's imposed in (18).

The second requirement, that each pair of elements satisfy *dominates* or *precedes*, is violated in sets such as (24):

(24) {A, Bbc, aC, aDc, abE, Fc, abc}

The string Fc in (24) does not satisfy *dominates* or *precedes* with the string aC.

RPM's as defined in (18) are only partially equivalent to the syntactic trees customarily employed by linguists.[1] Specifically, the set of RPM's is a proper subset of the set of phrase markers characterizable as trees. Loosely speaking, then, there are trees which are not possible RPM's, but there are no RPM's which are not possible trees.

The sets which we just saw in (22)–(24), for instance, are examples of objects which are neither trees nor RPM's. The diagram associated with (22) is given in (25):

(25)

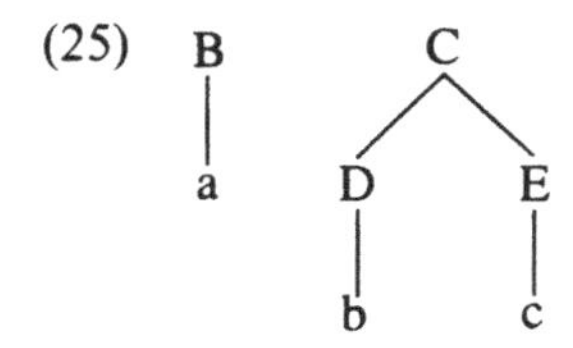

The structure in (25) is not "rooted" in the sense described above, and hence is not a well-formed tree.

(23) is equivalent to the diagram in (26):

(26)

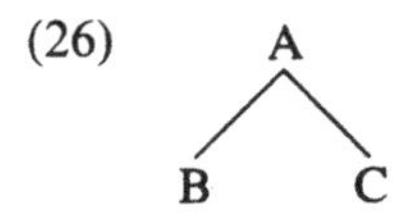

The fact that (26) contains no terminal nodes disqualifies it as a well-formed tree structure.

Although (25) and (26) are not trees, they are at least representable as something like trees, i.e. as diagrams showing the dominance and precedence relations among nodes. This is not so in (24), since there the dominance–precedence relations are not fully specified. Node C neither dominates nor precedes F, and *vice versa*. I indicate this as F/C in the following diagram:

(27)

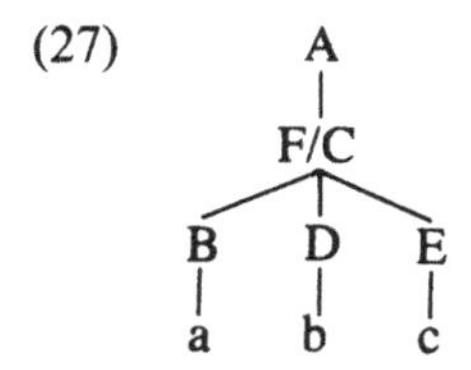

Notice that (27) is not equivalent to (28):

(28)

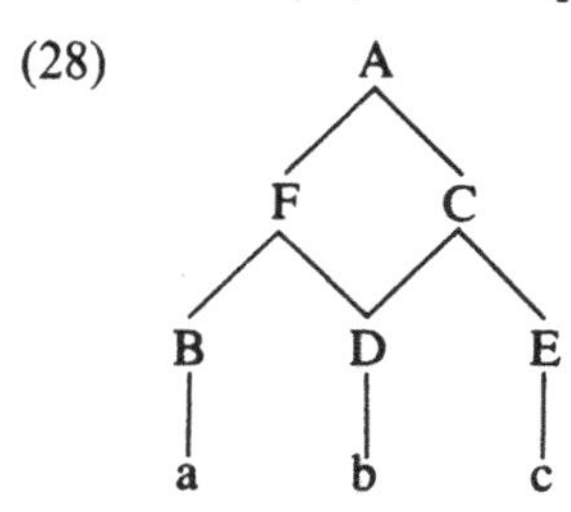

In (28), F precedes C, contrary to the information given in the set (24). In any event, neither (27) nor (28) are well-formed trees: (27) is out because, as just mentioned, neither dominance nor precedence holds between F and C; (28) is out because the nodes F and C "overlap" at node D.

Structures (22)–(28), then, are neither trees nor RPM's. We now turn to objects which are trees, but which are not RPM's. Consider first the trees in (29) and (30):

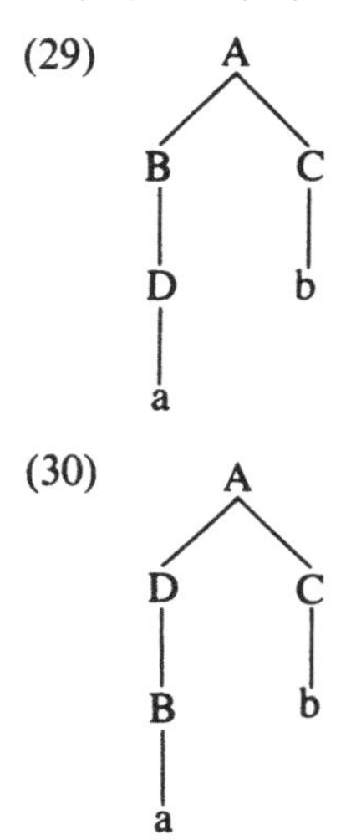

Both (29) and (30) are well-formed, but the difference between them cannot be expressed in terms of RPM's. Both trees are associated with the RPM in (31):

(31) {A, Bb, aC, Db, ab}

In (31), Bb *dominates* Db and Db *dominates* Bb.[2] We are unable to construct an RPM in which only one of these holds; that is to say, there is no RPM in which B dominates D, but D does not dominate B (as in (29)), or in which D dominates B, but B does not dominate D (as in (30)). In this sense, RPM's are more restrictive than trees.

Similarly, RPM's are incapable of representing structures such as (32):

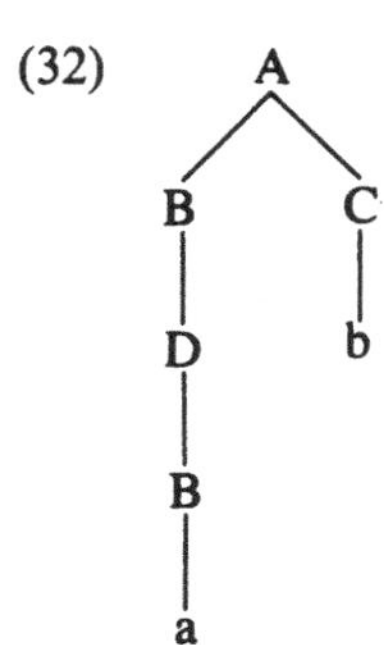

(32) states that a is a B twice, but this cannot be stated in terms of an RPM. A set such as (33) is equivalent to (31):

(33) {A, Bb, Bb, aC, Db, ab}

The fact that there is a second occurrence of Bb in (33) adds no information which does not already appear in (31). The tree in (32), on the other hand, is distinct from both (29) and (30). Again, we see here how structures which are well-formed as trees are not expressible as RPM's.

In summary, the set of possible RPM's is a proper subset of the set of possible trees. We have seen examples of objects which are neither trees nor RPM's, and of objects which are trees, but not RPM's. There are also, of course, objects which are both trees and RPM's, as in (21).

Lasnik and Kupin (1977) and Kupin (1978) have argued that RPM's are empirically adequate for linguistic description and hence are to be preferred over the less restrictive notion of tree. I will adopt this result here without further discussion. My concern below, though, will be formal objects which are neither trees nor RPM's. Any modifications which I make in the definition of RPM's will thus also require modifications to a theory in which phrase markers are equivalent to trees.

1.3.2 Reconsidering *dominates* and *precedes*

The definition of RPM's in (18) thus defines the class of objects which potentially may exist as representations in the three syntactic levels of the grammar. The various modules of the grammar act to allow some RPM's and exclude others, but it is always RPM's which are operated on.

It is worth asking at this point whether the notion RPM as in (18) is correct, that is, whether RPM's are the relevant structures for the operation of grammatical principles. This of course is an empirical question, and one to which the rest of this study will be addressed. In this section, I will examine some of the available possibilities and present the hypothesis which will be argued for in subsequent chapters.

Let us begin by considering the first requirement on RPM's in (18), that they contain a single non-terminal and a string of terminals. These would seem to be the minimal stipulations for any reasonable definition of phrase markers. To say that one element in the set must be a single non-terminal is to say that the sentence is a significant object in linguistic description. Similarly, the requirement that there be a string of terminals follows from the assumption that phrase markers interact with or are projected from lexical properties. In the model of grammar adopted here, it makes no sense to think of a phrase marker without lexical items. I will assume, then, that this first requirement on RPM's is correct. The entire phrase marker must be a constituent and it must dominate lexical items.

We now consider the second requirement on RPM's in (18), that each pair of distinct elements satisfy *dominates* or *precedes*. In more ordinary terms, this means that for each pair of non-terminal nodes in the phrase marker, one member of the pair must either dominate or precede the other. We should now ask whether this is correct. At an impressionistic level, it would seem that it would have to be. When we hear sentences, they are spoken in linear time. It thus seems to make sense to represent them, minimally, as an ordered sequence of morphemes in which a precedence relation is specified for each pair. From traditional grammar we know that sentences may be given a hierarchical structure. The string is thus divided into discrete phrases, these phrases form higher-level phrases, and so on. If we represent this intuitive idea as a phrase marker, the nodes will always dominate or precede one another.

From the standpoint of generative grammar, however, this conclusion is not necessary. Whatever intuitive appeal the traditional conception of phrase structure may have, there is no reason to assume that it is correct *a priori*. The fact that the surface strings which we are exposed to may be conveniently analyzed in terms of dominance and precedence does not guarantee that the syntactic structure of these sentences is so represented.

The question, then, is whether there is empirical evidence for or against the *dominates–precedes* requirement on phrase markers. Notice that such evidence is not likely to be immediately available from surface data. Suppose, for example, that sets such as (24) are allowable phrase markers. The terminal string in a set such as (24), which does not satisfy *dominates* or *precedes*, is identical to the terminal string in a set such as (19), which does satisfy (18). The PF interpretation of these phrase markers (i.e. what we hear when the structure is pronounced) might then also be identical. This holds true even when the terminal string is what violates (18). Consider a set such as (34):

(34) {A, Bbc, aC, aDc, abE, abc, def}

Here there are two terminal strings, and neither one *dominates* or *precedes* the other. In PF, this structure would have to be linearized, with the result that (34) might be phonetically indistinguishable from a phrase marker with a single terminal string, such as abcdef. Thus although phrase markers like (24) and (34) may appear "exotic" syntactically, it is unlikely that they would appear so based on the unanalyzed surface string. Relevant evidence, if it is available, will have to come from a detailed analysis of the syntax.

The central purpose of the present study is to show that there is evidence for the existence of phrase markers in which *dominates* and *precedes* are not satisfied. I replace (18) with the definition in (35):

(35) P is an RPM if there exist A and z such that $A \in P$ and $z \in P$; and if for φ, $\varphi \in P$, $\varphi \notin \Sigma^*$, there exists y, such that y *is a* φ in P*.

The first part of this definition is the same as (18). The entire phrase marker must be dominated by a single non-terminal and there must exist a terminal string. The second part states that some portion of the terminal string must bear the *is a** relationship to each monostring. In other words, the structure will be ruled out if there is a non-terminal which does not dominate any part of the terminal string. This preserves the spirit of the original definition in (18), which requires non-terminals to dominate terminals. In addition, it has the effect of requiring all members of the set which are not terminal strings to be monostrings. If they are not monostrings, they will not be able to act as φ in the definition of the *is a** predicate in (15) (where $\varphi = \text{xAz}$). Notice that the *dominates–precedes* requirement in (18) also had this effect. Thus in both (18) and (35), elements of $(\Sigma \cup N)^*$ in the set must be monostrings. This means that pairs of strings in sets defined by (35) may satisfy *dominates* or *precedes*, although they are not required to. In fact, each monostring will at least be dominated by A. Thus each non-terminal node in the structure is dominated by the root node and dominates some part of the terminal string. In addition, it may enter into dominance or precedence relations with other non-terminals in the structure.

The definition in (35) includes all of the objects defined by (18). The set (19), for example, satisfies (18), as we saw earlier. It also satisfies (35), in that for each monostring in (19), there is a portion of the terminal string abc which bears the *is a** relationship to it.

(35) is less restrictive than (18), though, since some sets which violate the latter satisfy the former. Consider the set (24), for example. We saw above that it violates (18), because the pair Fc-aC does not satisfy either *dominates* or *precedes*. Set (24) is well-formed according to (35), however: each monostring bears the appropriate relation (*is a**) to a portion of the terminal string.

Finally, of course, there are sets which are disallowed by both (18) and (35). First, structures such as (29), (30) and (32) are equally unrepresentable with either definition of RPM's, since the definition of the predicate *is a** remains unchanged. The structure in (28) is disallowed for essentially the same reason. Our definition of *is a** and *precedes* do not permit "overlapping" constituents such as F and C in (28). If a and b "is a" F, and b and c "is a" C, then F does not precede C with the Lasnik and Kupin definition of *precedes*. (35) does not require that F precede C, but F may precede C if the Lasnik and Kupin definition of *precedes* in (17) is satisfied. A configuration such as (28) is thus disallowed regardless of whether we adopt (18) or (35) as our definition of RPM's.

"Discontinuous" constituents, as in (36), are also prohibited.[3]

(36)

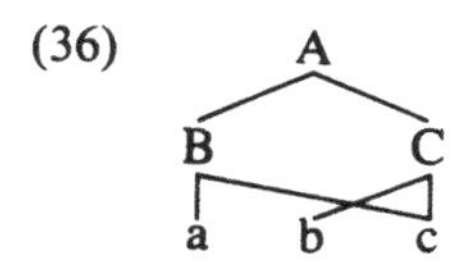

Again, the definition of *is a** does not permit a configuration like (36), in which ac "is a" B.

In summary, the set of all RPM's defined as in (18) is a proper subset of the set of all RPM's defined as in (35). This proper subset is also the intersection of (35) and traditional trees, as may be seen in the Venn diagram in (37).

(37)

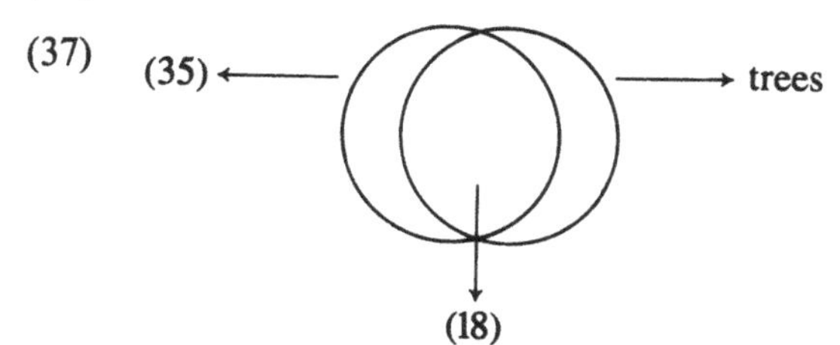

In other words, our new definition of RPM's in (35) maintains the restrictiveness of the older version in (18) *vis-à-vis* trees, but it decreases it *vis-à-vis* non-trees.

What will be of interest here are those non-trees which are allowed by (35). They are distinguished from ordinary trees by the fact that they contain pairs of nodes for which neither dominance nor precedence obtains – as we have seen, for instance, in examples (24) and (34). These nodes bear relations with other nodes in the phrase marker but they themselves neither dominate nor precede one another. In a sense, then, they exist in "parallel planes" within the same phrase marker. In (24) both C and F are dominated by A, and both dominate the terminal string abc, yet neither one dominates or precedes the other. Similarly in (34), no relation obtains between abc and def, but both are dominated by the non-terminal A. I shall refer to pairs of nodes such as these as "parallel structures."

My claim, in essence, is that the set of objects upon which the grammar operates is characterized by the definition in (35). Phrase markers, in this view, are not always representable as tree diagrams, the traditional format for displaying precedence and dominance relations.

Evidence for this position will come from two primary domains of data, both of which have a long history of study in generative grammar. The first is coordination, for which the phrase marker consists of two or more independently well-formed phrase markers. The structure may then contain two or more distinct terminal strings. I will refer to this as the "union of phrase markers," thus indicating that the larger set may be usefully thought of as the union of two or more smaller sets, all of which satisfy (35). Each of the smaller sets form parallel structures, in the sense defined above, in the larger set.

The second area of evidence for the desirability of (35) over (18) comes from some infinitival complement constructions in the Romance languages. Here the phrase marker contains only a single terminal string, but some of the non-terminal nodes neither dominate nor precede one another. Parallel structures in this case are thus found in the hierarchical structure, and not, as is necessary in coordination, in the terminal string.

My strategy throughout will be to hold constant the grammar outlined in section 1.1. That is, I alter the formal object to which the subsystems of grammar apply, but significant revisions in the subsystems of grammar themselves will not be necessary. We shall see that allowing for phrase markers as defined in (35) will be sufficient for certain, otherwise apparently intractable, problems in grammatical description to be solved in a very plausible fashion. This will justify the move from (18) to (35).

The rest of this study is organized as follows. The main empirical evidence in favor of (35) is presented in chapters 2, 3, and 4. Chapter 5 concludes with some further remarks on the implications of parallel structures for grammatical theory.

2 Coordination

2.1 Introduction

2.1.1 A short conceptual history of the study of coordination

In this chapter I take the position that coordination is the result of union of phrase markers, and I will argue that this formulation allows for a particularly insightful analysis of coordination.[1] This proposal stands in sharp contrast to the major previous approaches to coordination, which have assumed a more traditional conception of phrase structure. In what follows below I will briefly examine these approaches before outlining the system to be developed here.[2]

A small sample of the kind of data a theory of coordination is usually expected to account for is shown in (1):

(1) a. Louise and George rode bicycles
  b. Mary reads and writes books in French
  c. The old man fed the birds and the squirrels
  d. Tom and Jane eat bread and crackers (respectively)

It is not especially difficult to devise a system which will generate (1) and many similar sentence types. What is challenging is to come up with a system which at the same time may be plausibly embedded in a relatively comprehensive grammar. It is clear that coordinate sentences exhibit properties which appear different from those of other kinds of sentences, but it seems equally clear that we don't want the grammar to contain a large set of principles which pertain exclusively to coordination or types of rules which are considerably more powerful than what is needed in the rest of the grammar. The tension between the need, on the one hand, to describe the sentence patterns of coordination and, on the other, to relate this description to the general theory of grammar has made the study of coordination a lively source of controversy throughout the history of generative grammar.

One of the earliest approaches to coordination was what is often called "derived conjunction" (Gleitman 1965 is a good example of this). Under this view, the grammar contains a rule which conjoins sentences and a rule or set of rules which deletes identical elements of the conjoined sentences and regroups what is left. The sentences in (1), for example, would be derived from underlying sources as in (2):

(2) a. Louise rode bicycle(s) and George rode bicycle(s)
b. Mary reads books in French and Mary writes books in French
c. The old man fed the birds and the old man fed the squirrels
d. Tom eats bread and Jane eats crackers

In (2a), *rode bicycle(s)* in the first sentence is deleted, and *Louise and George* is grouped together to form one NP. In the (b) example, the first sentence again has material deleted (*books in French*), while in the second sentence, *Mary* is deleted. The verbs *reads* and *writes* are then grouped into a single constituent. In (2c), *the old man fed* in the second sentence is deleted, and *the birds* and *the squirrels* are then grouped together. The most elaborate case is (2d), where *eats* is deleted and there is regrouping to make constituents out of *Tom and Jane* and *bread and crackers.*

Notice that no matter how we formulate the deletion rule needed to derive the sentences in (2), it will have important properties which are not utilized in deletion rules in other areas of the grammar. First, it must delete non-constituents, as in (2c) (*the old man fed*). Second, it must apply bidirectionally. In (2a) it deletes elements in the left-hand conjunct, while in (2b) and (2c) it does so in the right-hand conjunct. In addition, the regrouping process in (2d) appears suspect, in that it has no known correlate in the rest of the grammar. These factors detract from the desirability of this solution.

Given certain assumptions which were prevalent at the time it was developed, the derived conjunction analysis also makes some incorrect empirical predictions. Consider a sentence like (3):

(3) John and Bill met in the park

which must be derived from (4):

(4) John met in the park and Bill met in the park

If we assume that the underlying structure is the sole input to semantic interpretation, then this sentence presents a problem. As has been widely observed, (4) is semantically deviant (*meet* here requires a plural subject), and we should then expect, contrary to fact, that (3) would be also. Accounts have been devised to allow for (3) while conserving the general approach, but the fact that additional statements need to be made for these sentences takes us even further from the ideal solution.[3]

Another approach to coordination, which attempts to avoid the difficulties of the derived conjunction analysis, generates the sentences in (1) directly, through phrase structure rules, without any need for deletion.[4] In (1a), for example, there is only a single S. The subject NP node is expanded to form the conjunct *Louise and George*. This sort of analysis, usually called "phrasal conjunction," requires a set of rules like those in (5):

(5) a. NP → NP and NP
 b. V → V and V

The two rules given here allow us to generate the sentences in (1) (although there will be no distinction between the derivation of (1d) and the homophonous sentence with the collective meaning). No deletion or regrouping is required; what makes up for this is a set of phrase structure rules of the type shown in (5), perhaps collapsed into a single rule using $\bar{X}$-notation. (3) may now be generated, since under this analysis *meet* has a plural subject in all stages of the derivation.

The phrasal conjunction analysis avoids the problem of expanding the power of the transformational component, since no special transformational rules seem to be necessary at all. On the other hand, the phrase structure component must incorporate a new type of rule, one which violates the $\bar{X}$ convention by not including a unique head in the expansion of a node. A rule of this form was also needed in the derived conjunction analysis, but only to conjoin clauses.

The phrasal conjunction analysis also runs into a serious empirical problem. Observe the following sentence:

(6) John hunted tigers and was killed by snakes

In this analysis, sentence (6) must be the result of conjoining the VP's listed in (7):

(7) a. hunted tigers
 b. was killed by snakes

(7b), however, is not a deep structure VP and thus may not be conjoined in this form in the base. Under standard assumptions, the string in (7b) is derived transformationally. *John* is moved out of the object position of *was killed* and into subject position.[5] The subject position, however, is already occupied by the subject of *hunted tigers*. Thus in order to derive (6), we need to conjoin sentences rather than VP's, but by conjoining sentences we have arrived back at the derived conjunction solution.

Thus we have seen that both derived and phrasal conjunction appear to be unable to account for some of the facts of coordination. It might be possible, however, to account for all of the data in question by utilizing both analyses (this position has been taken in, for example, Lakoff and Peters 1966). This leads to considerable overlap in coverage, of course, in the sense that most sentences will be derivationally ambiguous. As has often been pointed out, this derivational ambiguity does not always correspond to semantic ambiguity, a fact which might arouse suspicion. Quite apart from this, however, it is clear that with respect to the problem mentioned earlier, of integrating coordination with the rest of the grammar, this combined analysis is disastrous. Instead of keeping the additional apparatus necessary for coordination to a minimum, we have now expanded it enormously with both a new kind of phrase structure rule and a new kind of transformation.

2.1.2 Union of phrase markers

In the treatment proposed here, I essentially abandon the approaches discussed in the previous section (which constitute the main contribution of standard transformational grammar to this problem), and adopt instead an analysis wherein coordination is represented as a union of phrase markers. The technical details of this will be discussed later. For most of our discussion it will suffice to think of it in tree terms as a "pasting together," one on top of the other, of two trees, with any identical nodes merging together.

Now assuming that a union of phrase markers is well-formed, it is not immediately obvious how this structure is to be interpreted in PF and LF, since certain of the elements will be in the same linear position. This seems especially problematic for PF interpretation, since it is apparent that all elements of the sentence must be linearly ordered for the sentence to be utterable. I will show, however, that the correct PF and LF representations of coordinate structures may be derived with only trivial modifications to the grammar.

Notice that, in a sense, this union of phrase markers treatment of coordination is closely related to the derived conjunction analysis discussed above in that under both approaches sentences like those in (1) are underlyingly made up of more than one sentence. The difference is that with derived conjunction these underlying sentences are sisters in a phrase marker, whereas in the approach to be developed here they are components of a union of phrase markers. In other words, with derived conjunction the underlying sentences are linearly ordered with respect to each other, while in a union of phrase markers they are not. Both of these approaches contrast with the phrasal conjunction analysis, in which no such underlying sentences are posited.[6]

In the rest of this chapter I will explain how this system works in greater detail, and I will argue that in exchange for admitting union of phrase markers as a possible syntactic configuration, a much improved empirical account of coordination follows. I claim that this brings us much closer than has previously been possible to an optimal theory of coordination.

Before we proceed, a brief methodological note is in order. I have thus far not given any definition of what I consider coordination to include, beyond the few examples in (1). This has been intentional. As a preliminary characterization I will assume the traditional distinction between clauses and other entities conjoined with *and*, *or*, or *but*, and those conjoined with *while*, *after*, *whereas*, etc. Although I believe there to be a true structural distinction between these cases, I do not think that all sentences containing a conjunction (*and*, *or*, or *but*) form a natural class. More specifically, we will observe some constructions containing *and* which appear to have properties radically different from the central cases of coordination. For this reason, I choose to leave the "borders" of coordination flexible for now, defining them more carefully as we proceed. This move, which goes back at least to Ross (1967), will have consequences in much of the subsequent analysis.

The organization of this chapter is as follows. Section 2.2 contains a discussion of the linearization rule which produces the surface structure order of elements in coordinate structure. Section 2.3 discusses the formal properties of phrase markers in connection with the well-known parallelism requirement on conjuncts. In section 2.4 I treat the question of LF interpretation and I present a solution to the problem of sentences like (3) and (6) above. In section 2.5 I derive the Coordinate Structure Constraint and the Across-the-Board principle. An analysis of Gapping is presented in section 2.6, where I show that some significant properties of Gapping may be derived from more general properties of union of phrase markers. Section 2.7 treats the operation of subject–verb agreement in coordinate structures. Right Node Raising is discussed briefly in section 2.8, and the chapter is summarized in section 2.9.

2.2 Linearization

2.2.1 Linearization derived

In this section I address the question of how PF interprets coordinate structure, which I am assuming to be the result of union of phrase markers. In answering this question I will be pursuing two simultaneous goals: one is to generate all and only the surface patterns of coordination found in English; the second is to do this with as few stipulations as possible.

Let us begin by considering the union of phrase markers for the sentences in (8), given in (9):

(8) a. Jane saw Bill
b. Alice saw Bill

(9) {S, NP_1 saw Bill, Jane VP, Jane V Bill, Jane saw NP, Jane saw Bill, NP_2 saw Bill, Alice VP, Alice V Bill, Alice saw NP, Alice saw Bill}

This can be represented as something like the tree diagram in (10):

(10)

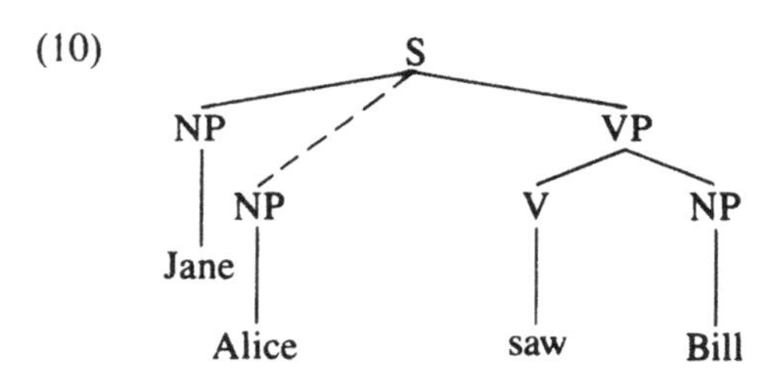

where neither the NP *Jane* nor the NP *Alice* dominates or precedes the other. Our question, then, is how structures such as (9) are converted into a surface string.

Notice that this is a question only because not all of the precedence relations between terminal elements are specified in (9). The two terminal strings indicate that *saw* precedes *Bill* and that both *Jane* and *Alice* precede *saw*, but *Jane* and *Alice* themselves are unordered (i.e. no precedence relation is given). This is shown in the diagram in (11), where only the precedence relations are displayed:

(11) 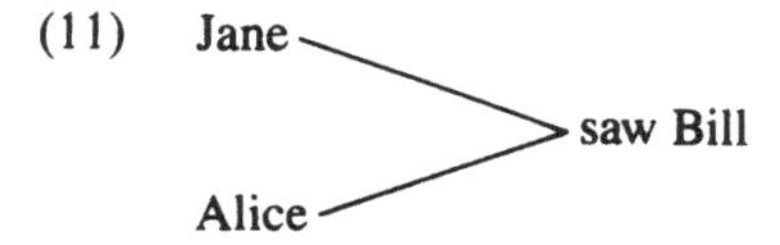

Ideally, all we should have to say about these structures is that they must be linearized. In other words, a precedence relation must be established between those elements of the tree which are otherwise not ordered with respect to each other. This is the effect of the linearization principle in (12):[7]

(12) Given an RPM containing distinct terminal strings $x_1, x_2, \ldots, x_n$, for each element y_i of x_i, y_i not an element of x_{i+1}, there is an element y_{i+1} of x_{i+1}, y_{i+1} not an element of x_i, such that y_i precedes y_{i+1}.

(12) says, essentially, that when there are two distinct elements from two different strings, one of these must precede the other. The placement of these elements then follows from the effect of (12) combined with the precedence relations already established in the RPM. (12) does not change precedence relations in the RPM; it merely supplies a relation where none would exist otherwise. For example, consider an RPM containing the terminal strings abcde and afcge. If we take abcde to be x_1 in (12), and afcge to be x_2, then b precedes f and d precedes g.[8] We already know (from the terminal strings themselves) that both b and f are preceded by a and precede c, and that both d and g are preceded by c and precede e. The only linearization consistent with these facts, then, is abfcdge.

In our example in (9), we can take *Jane saw Bill* to be x_1, and *Alice saw Bill* to be x_2. *Jane* is then y_1 and *Alice* is y_2. *Jane* thus precedes *Alice*. As we saw in (11), both of these precede *saw Bill*. This gives us the grammatical surface string in (13).[9]

(13) Jane and Alice saw Bill

Both *Jane* and *Alice* continue to precede *saw*, as required by (9).

Other conceivable linearizations are not allowed by (12). Consider (14), for example:

(14) a. Jane saw and Alice Bill
b. Jane saw Bill and Alice

Neither one of these sentences is derivable with (12), since in both cases the precedence relations differ from what is indicated in (9). *Saw* precedes *Alice* in (14), contrary to the ordering in (9).

The linearization principle in (12) thus enables us to derive the correct string in (13), while avoiding such incorrect strings as those in (14). This is the result we should hope for, since (12) embodies the minimal assumptions about how structures such as (9) are linearized. Additional assumptions appear to be unnecessary.

Examining some other simple cases, we see that (12) continues to yield the correct results:

(15)

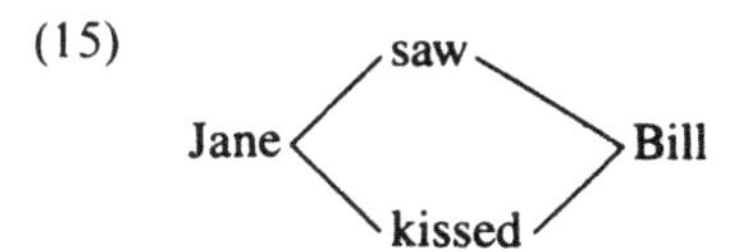

Jane saw and kissed Bill

(16)

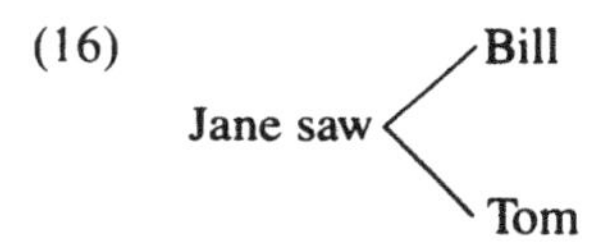

Jane saw Bill and Tom

(17)

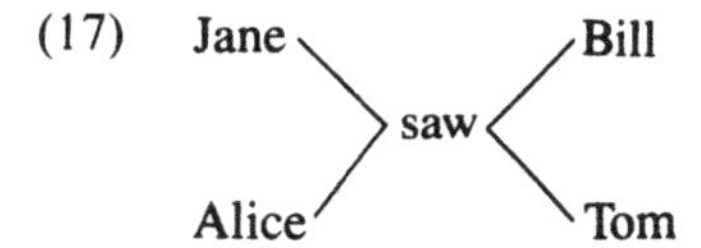

Jane and Alice saw Bill and Tom

In each of these structures, there are pairs of words which are mutually unordered. By imposing an order on these pairs we obtain the grammatical strings given.

Notice that the sentence in (17) is ambiguous between the *respectively* reading (where Jane sees Bill and Alice sees Tom) and the collective one (where Jane and Alice see both Bill and Tom). As will become clear in section 2.4, these two readings have distinct sources: the *respectively* sense stems from the union of phrase markers represented by the sentences in (18), and the collective sense from the union of phrase markers represented by the sentences in (19).

(18) Jane saw Bill
Alice saw Tom

(19) Jane saw Bill
Jane saw Tom
Alice saw Bill
Alice saw Tom

Although (18) and (19) are clearly different, the sequential order relations are identical, hence the identical output.[10] This is not a trivial result. As we saw in example (1d), the derivation of the *respectively* reading is especially problematic for the derived conjunction analysis. The phrasal conjunction analysis can generate the sentence in (17), but it is not clear how it would assign it the *respectively* reading. It is thus significant that (17) falls into place with the other examples under the system developed here.

In the examples we have seen so far, the pairs of mutually unordered elements have been pairs of single words. We now consider cases where the pairs consist of two words each, as in (20)–(22):

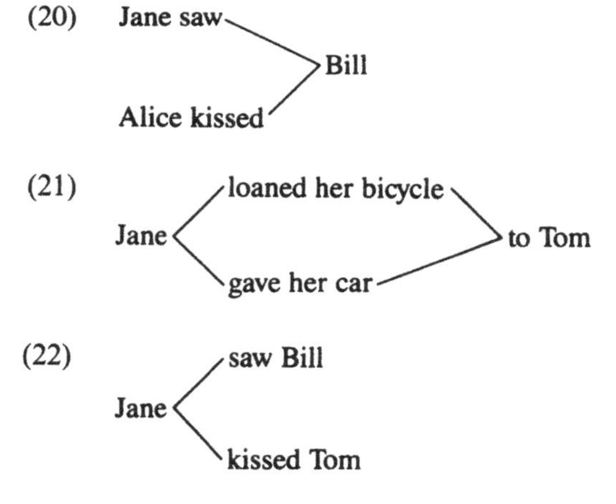

Let us begin with (20), considering first the reading in which the union of phrase markers consists of the sentences in (23):

(23) a. Jane saw Bill
b. Alice kissed Bill

(12) does not yield a unique result here. The diagram in (20) indicates that *Jane* precedes *saw* and that *Alice* precedes *kissed*, and that all of these precede *Bill*. However *Jane* is unordered with respect to *Alice* and *kissed*, *Alice* is unordered with respect to *Jane* and *saw*, etc. By (12) we must state that elements of one string, let us say (23a), precede those of the other,

(23b). Depending on whether we take y_i/y_{i+1} in (12) to be *Jane/Alice* and *saw/kissed*, or *Jane saw/Alice kissed*, the result will be either that *Jane* precedes *Alice* and *saw* precedes *kissed*, or that *Jane saw* precedes *Alice kissed*. This ambiguity in the application of (12) gives us (24a) and (24b).[11]

(24) a. Jane saw and Alice kissed Bill
b. Jane and Alice saw and kissed Bill

These are exactly the grammatical strings we desire.

Sentence (24b) is ambiguous between the reading just discussed and that derived from the union of phrase markers for the sentences in (25):

(25) Jane saw Bill
Jane kissed Bill
Alice saw Bill
Alice kissed Bill

(24b) is a well-formed linearization of (25), but (24a), for example, is not. Notice that *Alice* precedes *saw* in (25) but does not in (24a). Since linearization cannot change precedence relations in this way, (24a) is not a possible output for (25). (24b) is, however, and hence it is ambiguous between (25) and (23).

Examples (21) and (22) work in essentially the same way as (20). The terminal strings for (21) may be either as in (26) or (27):

(26) Jane loaned her bicycle to Tom
Jane gave her car to Tom

(27) Jane loaned her bicycle to Tom
Jane gave her bicycle to Tom
Jane loaned her car to Tom
Jane gave her car to Tom

(26) receives either linearization (28a) or (28b), whereas (27) (the contradictory reading) may only be linearized as (28b):

(28) a. Jane loaned her bicycle and gave her car to Tom
b. Jane loaned and gave her bicycle and her car to Tom

The same holds for (29)–(31) with respect to (22):

(29) Jane saw Bill
Jane kissed Tom

(30) Jane saw Bill
Jane saw Tom
Jane kissed Bill
Jane kissed Tom

(31) a. Jane saw Bill and kissed Tom
b. Jane saw and kissed Bill and Tom

Again we see that facts of some complexity are neatly accounted for with the formulation in (12).

Returning to the discussion at the beginning of this section, we are now in a position to answer our original question of how PF interprets coordinate structure. As we have seen, PF has no special provisions for the interpretation of this type of structure beyond the requirement that it be converted to a linear format. From this minimal assumption, a restricted number of possible linearizations for a given coordinate structure results. It is interesting, then, that these linearizations seem to correspond exactly to the surface patterns of coordination in English.

As mentioned earlier, one of our goals here has been to provide an empirically adequate account of these patterns, and we have seen that this is possible. Our treatment of *respectively*-type constructions in particular, as in (18), (23), (26) and (29), is a considerable improvement over previous attempts.

Our second goal has been to show that such an empirically adequate account can be had at no cost. This also seems to be possible, in that the linearization procedure we have adopted is essentially the null hypothesis. Notice that the same can not be said for many other approaches to coordination. In the derived conjunction analysis, for instance, specific deletion rules need to be formulated which are, in an important sense, arbitrary. Similarly with phrasal conjunction, special provisions must be made to allow *respectively*-constructions. In the present theory, all of this follows immediately from the representation we have adopted. That is, union of phrase markers predicts in a principled way the actual surface patterns of coordination.

2.2.2 Apparent counterexamples

As we have just seen, the system developed here makes testable predictions about possible coordinate sentences. I will now examine some apparent counterexamples to these predictions, first to demonstrate the restrictiveness of the present theory, and second to show how I propose to handle these cases.

Sjoblom (1980) counts the following type of sentence as grammatical:

(32) John ran and Mary

In my system, this would be derived from the union of the phrase markers for the sentences in (33):

(33) John ran
Mary ran

Notice, however, that linearization cannot derive (32) from (33), since *Mary* precedes *ran* in (33), but follows it in (32). This is a desirable result, I believe, because almost all speakers judge (32) to be ungrammatical. It is, of course, very close to the completely grammatical sentences in (34):

(34) a. John ran and Mary too
b. John ran, but not Mary

The obligatory presence of *too* and *not* here is significant. They appear to be used in an anaphoric sense, in that they refer back to the VP *ran*. If this is correct, then these sentences are not derived from (33), but rather from something like (35):

(35) a. John ran
Mary too
b. John ran
Not Mary

Linearization may then proceed as normal to produce (34).

Another type of apparent counterexample is shown in (36):

(36) Mary eats apples and John oranges

This, of course, is an example of what has traditionally been called "Gapping." If (36) comes from (37):

(37) Mary eats apples
John eats oranges

then it cannot be derived by linearization, since elements like *John* are reordered in a way which (12) does not allow. I postpone discussion of Gapping until section 2.6, where I propose a special rule which will allow the linearization of (37) as (36). Many of the properties of Gapping which have previously been thought to be arbitrary may be seen as a consequence of this rule.

Another apparent counterexample may be seen in (38):

(38) John rode his bike to Albuquerque and Mary took the train

under the reading where Mary took the train to Albuquerque. This reading should be derived from the union of the phrase markers for the sentences in (39):

(39) John rode his bike to Albuquerque
Mary took the train to Albuquerque

Linearizing (39), we get (40), synonymous with our reading of (38):

(40) John rode his bike and Mary took the train to Albuquerque

Crucially, we cannot derive (38) from (39). This is a desirable result, since sentences like (38) exhibit properties quite different from the usual cases of coordination.

First, notice that whatever truncation process is responsible for (38) works not just with the conjunctions *and*, *or*, or *but*, but also with *while* and *whereas*:

(41) a. John rode his bike to Albuquerque, while Mary took the train
b. Mary went to the Bahamas last year, whereas Jane stayed home

This is not possible with true coordination:

(42) a. *Tom ate an apple, while Jane an orange
b. *George read a magazine, whereas Eleanor a book

Second, truncation does not obey the parallelism requirement on coordinate structure. Compare the grammatical truncation example (43) and the ungrammatical coordination example (44):

(43) John rode his bike to Albuquerque and I read in the paper yesterday that Mary took the train

(44) *[John] and [I read in the paper yesterday that Mary] rode their bikes to Albuquerque

The exact nature of this parallelism requirement will be examined in section 2.3; for now it suffices to say that conjuncts must have the same constituent structure. This is not the case in (43) and (44), as may be seen in the following diagrams:[12]

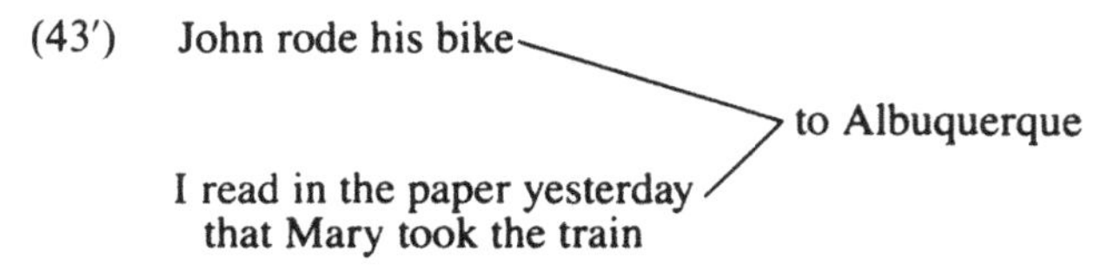

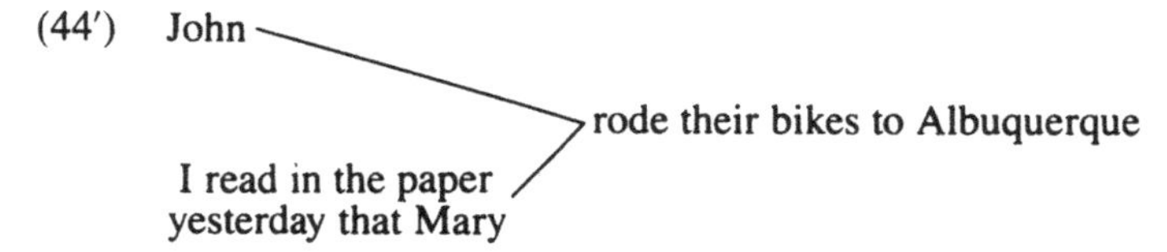

Assuming that the PP *to Albuquerque* is under either S or VP, neither of the pairs of conjuncts shows syntactic parallelism, yet (43) is grammatical. The fact that truncation does not appear to be subject to the parallelism requirement is good evidence that it does not result from the union of phrase markers.

Finally, there is an interesting difference between truncation and true coordination with respect to Across-the-Board *wh*-extraction (in the sense of Ross 1967). As I will show in section 2.5, this phenomenon is possible only with the three-dimensional phrase structure induced by union of phrase markers. We should then not expect to see Across-the-Board movement in truncation sentences. Consider a sentence like (45):

(45) John eats porridge in the winter and Mary cooks bacon

Under the truncation reading, *in the winter* applies both to John's eating porridge and Mary's cooking bacon. Now consider a similar sentence with Across-the-Board *wh*-movement:

(46) ?*What does John eat in the winter and Mary cook?

Judgements are fairly subtle, but (46) appears to be bad either as truncation or as union of phrase markers. When it results from truncation (i.e. when *in the winter* applies both to John's eating and Mary's cooking), Across-the-Board movement should not be possible. When it results from the union of phrase markers (i.e. when *in the winter* applies to John's eating and the time of Mary's cooking is unspecified), (46) violates the parallelism requirement mentioned earlier. Compare (46) with (47), which meets this requirement:

(47) What does John eat in the winter and Mary cook in the summer?

Our analysis predicts, then, that as a truncation sentence (46) should be out, and as an instance of true coordination it should at least be worse than (47). This seems to be correct, thus supporting our view that truncation is not the result of the union of phrase markers.[13]

2.2.3 The order of conjuncts

The linearization principle given in (12) crucially assumes that the terminal strings in a union of phrase markers are ordered with respect to each other. Elements of terminal string x_i, for example, are made to precede their corresponding elements in terminal string x_{i+1}. The precedence relations that are established among the conjuncts thus depend on the ordering of the terminal strings as wholes. Here I will show how this ordering is represented in the union of phrase markers.

Notice first of all that the order of terminal strings, and consequently the order of conjuncts, appears to be of more than phonological import, in that a change in the order may affect the semantic interpretation of the sentence. With *and*, for example, linear precedence sometimes indicates temporal precedence. Thus (48a) is much more felicitous than (48b):

(48) a. John drank the poison and died
b. John died and drank the poison

Ordering also plays a role with *but*; (49a), for instance, means something slightly different from (49b):

(49) a. Mary was poor but honest
b. Mary was honest but poor

Since the order of terminal strings thus has effects both in PF and LF, we must assume that this information is present in the syntax proper.

The terminal strings in a union of phrase markers may now be represented as in (50):

(50) $\{\ldots$ coordination-type $(x_1, x_2, \ldots, x_n) \ldots\}$

That is to say, the terminal strings are represented as an ordered set within the larger (unordered) set. Each ordered set is marked with its coordination-type (i.e. *and*, *or*, or *but*). In this notation, the sentences in (48) and (49) now each have distinct syntactic representations. The terminal strings of (48a) and (48b), for example, are as in (51a) and (51b), respectively:

(51) a. {... and (John drank the poison, John died) ...}
b. {... and (John died, John drank the poison) ...}

The linearization principle in (12) interprets these sets in such a way that (48) is produced.

In the rest of our discussion of coordination, we will not always be directly concerned with the order of conjuncts, and in these cases I will omit the ordering of the terminal strings within the union of phrase markers.

2.2.4 Conjunction-placement

In our discussion of linearization so far, I have not dealt explicitly with the placement of the conjunction (*and*, *or*, *but*). Let us now look at how this can be achieved.

As we have seen, each instance of a union of phrase markers is marked with its coordination-type, i.e. *and*, *or*, or *but*. When the phrase marker is linearized in PF, a phonetic manifestation of the coordination-type is inserted whenever a linear order is imposed between pairs. The conjunction thus serves to mark where linearization has occurred. Consider (52), for example:

(52) 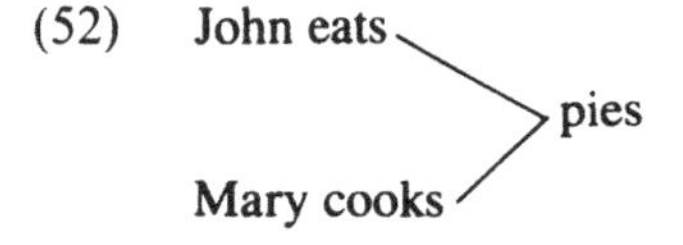

Suppose that (52) is an *and*-type coordination. If it is linearized as (53):

(53) John eats and Mary cooks pies

and is inserted between the two conjuncts *John eats* and *Mary cooks*. As discussed earlier, a structure like (52) may also be linearized as (54):

(54) John and Mary eat and cook pies (respectively)

Although (54) is synonymous with (53) – they are derived from the same S-structure (52) – *and* in this case is inserted twice, since there are two pairs (*John*/*Mary* and *eat*/*cook*) which are ordered by linearization.

If there are more than two words in the same linear position, the conjunction is inserted either before the last member of this set of words or between every member. This may be seen in (56) and (57), both derived from (55).

(55) 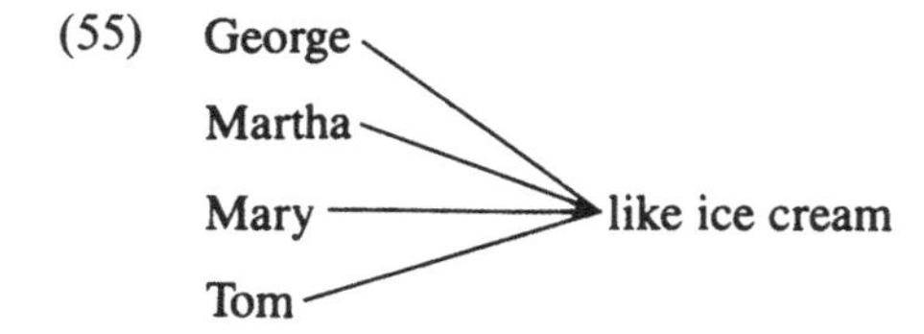

(56) George, Martha, Mary, and Tom like ice cream

(57) George and Martha and Mary and Tom like ice cream

Or works in essentially the same way as *and*, while *but* may only conjoin two conjuncts.

As is well-known, these rules of conjunction-placement vary somewhat cross-linguistically. In Romance languages, for instance, some conjunctions may be redundantly placed to the left of each conjunct, rather than in-between as we have seen in English. In the Dravidian language Malayalam, on the other hand, the conjunction comes at the right of each conjunct (see Archangeli 1983). Mandarin Chinese represents yet another possibility, in which no conjunction element is present at all: the sequence of constituents is sufficient to show that a given sentence is a linearized version of a coordinate structure.

Some sentences will be the result of a union of phrase markers which may be of more than one coordination-type. Consider, for example, (58):

(58) Ann and Fred eat beans or rice

This may be represented as either (59) or (60):

(59) {... and (or (Ann eats beans, Ann eats rice), or (Fred eats beans, Fred eats rice))...}

(60) {... or (and (Ann eats beans, Fred eats beans), and (Ann eats rice, Fred eats rice))...}

Both (59) and (60) are linearized as (58). When the pair *beans/rice* is ordered, *or* is used, and when the pair *Ann/Fred* is ordered, *and* is used.

Two interesting properties have emerged in the system outlined here. First, the synonymy between sentence pairs like (53) and (54) is, as mentioned above, captured directly. Second, the irrelevance of the number of occurrences of the conjunction is mirrored nicely in this analysis. This is an advantage over most phrase structure rule analyses, in which each occurrence of the conjunction is generated by a separate application of the conjunction rule. As Pesetsky (1982) says of these analyses: "the fact that certain instances of [the conjunction] may or must be deleted, given the principle of Recoverability of Deletion, suggests that the separate occurrences of [the conjunction] ... are linked, and perhaps constitute a single discontinuous element." The present analysis postulates this overtly.

2.3 Union of phrase markers and the coordination of likes

In this section I examine an intriguing parallelism constraint on coordinate structures. I begin by presenting the empirical problem of coordination of likes, then I show how a solution may be found in the formalization of union of phrase markers.

2.3.1 The Law of the Coordination of Likes

One important, yet curious, property of coordinate sentences is that the conjuncts must be syntactically parallel, that is, it must be possible to group each conjunct into like categories. This phenomenon is called the Law of the Coordination of Likes (LCL) by Williams (1981a), and for convenience I will adopt his terminology here. Many of the examples in this section are either taken from or inspired by George (1980), one of the few careful studies in this area.

As an illustration of what the LCL refers to, consider examples (61)–(64):[14]

(61) *The bouncer was muscular and a guitarist
(62) *Elaine took Mary to the airport and Jane
(63) *John kissed Louise tenderly and Mary yesterday
(64) *[The boys] and [I believe that the girls] like ice cream

These may be compared with the similar, but grammatical, sentences in (65)–(68):

(65) The bouncer was muscular and was a guitarist
(66) Elaine took Mary to the airport and Jane to the beach
(67) John kissed Louise tenderly and Mary passionately
(68) I know that the boys and I believe that the girls like ice cream

The LCL requires that the conjuncts be composed of like categories. The crucial difference between (61)–(64) and (65)–(68) in this regard may be seen in the diagrams (61′)–(68′):

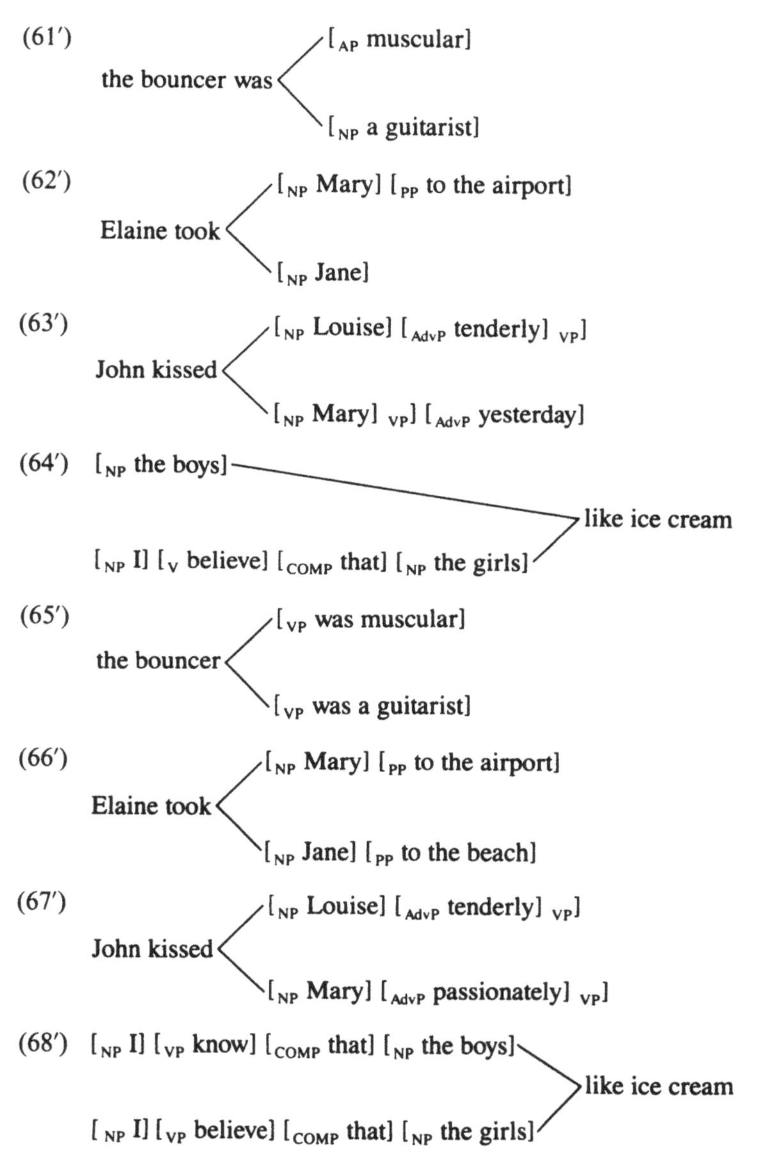

The conjuncts in (65′)–(68′) all contain like categories, but this parallelism does not obtain in (61′)–(64′), hence their ungrammaticality. Notice that the internal structure of the like categories does not appear to be important. In (65′), for instance, one VP contains an AP and the other an NP, but the LCL is satisfied.

Part of the LCL effects are taken care of automatically in a phrasal conjunction analysis, since the phrase structure rules in this case are generally of the form in (69), not (70):

(69) NP → NP and NP
(70) NP → NP and AP

However, the LCL is not limited to constituent coordination, as are rules of the type (69). (66′), for example, shows that it is coordination of likes which is the relevant notion, not coordination of constituents.

2.3.2 Formalizing union of phrase markers

Let us now examine more carefully the structure I am assuming for coordination. As stated earlier, by "union of phrase markers" I mean that the RPM contains at least two discrete subsets, each of which is a sentence. Consider then a sentence such as (71):

(71) John sleeps and eats doughnuts

The phrase marker for this sentence contains two component sentences, given here in (72):

(72) a. John sleeps
b. John eats doughnuts

The phrase marker for (71), given in (73c), is thus the same as the union of the phrase markers for (72a) and (72b), given in (73a) and (73b), respectively:

(73) a. {S, NP sleeps, John VP_1, John sleeps}
b. {S, NP eats doughnuts, John VP_2, John V doughnuts, John eats NP, John eats doughnuts}
c. {S, NP sleeps, John VP_1, John sleeps, S, NP eats doughnuts, John VP_2, John V doughnuts, John eats NP, John eats doughnuts}

Importantly, I will assume that non-terminals which dominate at least some of the same terminals are non-distinct. This is the case here with the two S nodes and the two subject NP nodes. One S dominates *John sleeps* and the other dominates *John eats doughnuts*. Since the two strings both contain *John*, we conclude that the two S nodes are non-distinct. As for the subject NP nodes, both dominate *John*, and thus they too are non-distinct.

Non-terminals which do not share any dominated terminals, on the other hand, will be considered distinct.[15] This is the case with the two VP nodes, where one dominates *sleeps* and the other dominates *eats doughnuts.* Notice that conjoined nodes such as these are not dominated by a superordinate node of the same type, contrary to the configuration in all other analyses of which I am aware.

Every pair of strings in (73a) and (73b) satisfies *dominates* and *precedes,* but those in (73c) do not. These pairs are listed in (74).[16]

(74)			
	a.	S	NP sleeps
	b.	S	John VP_1
	c.	S	John sleeps
	d.	S	NP eats doughnuts
	e.	S	John VP_2
	f.	S	John V doughnuts
	g.	S	John eats NP
	h.	S	John eats doughnuts
	i.	NP sleeps	John VP_1
	j.	NP sleeps	John sleeps
	k.	NP sleeps	NP eats doughnuts
	l.	NP sleeps	John VP_2
	m.	NP sleeps	John V doughnuts
	n.	NP sleeps	John eats NP
	o.	NP sleeps	John eats doughnuts
	p.	John VP_1	John sleeps
	q.	John VP_1	NP eats doughnuts
	r.	John VP_1	John VP_2
	s.	John VP_1	John V doughnuts
	t.	John VP_1	John eats NP
	u.	John VP_1	John eats doughnuts
	v.	John sleeps	NP eats doughnuts
	w.	John sleeps	John VP_2
	x.	John sleeps	John V doughnuts
	y.	John sleeps	John eats NP
	z.	John sleeps	John eats doughnuts
	aa.	NP eats doughnuts	John VP_2
	bb.	NP eats doughnuts	John V doughnuts
	cc.	NP eats doughnuts	John eats NP
	dd.	NP eats doughnuts	John eats doughnuts

ee.	John VP_2	John V doughnuts
ff.	John VP_2	John eats NP
gg.	John VP_2	John eats doughnuts
hh.	John V doughnuts	John eats NP
ii.	John V doughnuts	John eats doughnuts
jj.	John eats NP	John eats doughnuts

The predicate *dominates* is satisfied in (a)–(h), (j), (p), (s)–(u), (w), (dd)–(gg), and (ii)–(jj). *Precedes* is satisfied in (i), (l)–(n), (q), (aa)–(cc), and (hh). Neither predicate is satisfied in (k), (o), (r), (v), and (x)–(z).[17]

These last cases, in which neither predicate is satisfied, are the most interesting. In the pair (k), we have two instances of the same NP (dominating *John*), so, as we expect, there is no dominance or precedence here. This NP does not dominate *John* in (o) and (v), but it does in (j) and (dd). The pairs (r) and (x)–(z) represent the parallel structures, in that here we have distinct nodes which do not dominate or precede one another. Notice that these nodes do bear relations with other nodes in the structure. Thus the NP object of *eats*, for example, is dominated by VP_2 (ff), and is preceded by V (hh) and the subject NP (cc). The only distinguishing characteristic of this NP, then, is that it does not bear a relation with all the nodes in the structure.

2.3.3 The LCL derived

Having now explored some of the formal properties of the phrase marker resulting from the union of phrase markers, let us return to the empirical problem described at the beginning of this section. We shall see that the LCL facts presented there fall out rather neatly from independent properties of phrase markers.

Consider a phrase marker which contains the strings xA, xB, xy, xz. The terminals y and z here may be dominated by either A or B. Following $\bar{X}$-theory, A and B must then be of the right category-type to dominate both y and z. Since the categories which they are required to dominate are the same, it follows that A and B themselves are of the same category. Thus the effects of the LCL follow from the fact that we have two structures coexisting in the same phrase marker.

Let us see how this accounts for our examples in (61)–(68). Consider first (61) and its phrase marker in (75):[18]

(75) {S, NP was muscular, the bouncer VP, the bouncer V muscular, the bouncer was AP, the bouncer was muscular, S, NP was a guitarist, the bouncer VP, the bouncer V a guitarist, the bouncer was NP, the bouncer was a guitarist}

This phrase marker is ruled out straightforwardly. Compare the strings *the bouncer was* AP and *the bouncer was a guitarist. A guitarist is a* the bouncer was* AP here, as *muscular is a* the bouncer was* NP. In tree terms, this means that *a guitarist* is not just an NP, but an AP as well, and that *muscular* also is both an NP and AP. This is a clear violation of $\bar{X}$-theory, which requires that the dominating category for X be XP. We should thus expect this structure to be ungrammatical, and as (61) shows, it is.

Compare this with (65), whose phrase marker is given in (76):

(76) {S, NP was_1 muscular, the bouncer VP, the bouncer V muscular, the bouncer was_1 AP, the bouncer was_1 muscular, S, NP was_2 a guitarist, the bouncer VP, the bouncer V a guitarist, the bouncer was_2 NP, the bouncer was_2 a guitarist}

In (76), unlike (75), there are two separate occurrences of the lexical item *was*, distinguished here by different indices. Thus by comparing *the bouncer* was_1 AP and *the bouncer* was_2 *a guitarist*, we do *not* get the result that *a guitarist* is an AP. $\bar{X}$-theory is satisfied here, and consequently (65) is grammatical.

Next let us consider (62), and its phrase marker (77):

(77) {S, NP took Mary to the airport, Elaine VP, Elaine V Mary to the airport, Elaine took NP to the airport, Elaine took Mary PP, Elaine took Mary P the airport, Elaine took Mary to NP, Elaine took Mary to the airport, S, NP took Jane, Elaine VP, Elaine V Jane, Elaine took NP, Elaine took Jane}

Again, it is easy to see the problem here: since (77) contains the strings *Elaine took* NP and *Elaine took Mary to the airport*, it follows that *Mary to the airport* is an NP. *Mary to the airport* is not a well-formed NP, however, and (62)/(77) is thus ruled out, again by $\bar{X}$-theory.

(66) does not have this defect; its phrase marker is given in (78):

(78) {S, NP took Mary to the airport, Elaine VP, Elaine V Mary to the airport, Elaine took NP to the airport, Elaine took Mary PP, Elaine took Mary P the airport, Elaine took Mary to NP, Elaine

took Mary to the airport, S, NP took Jane to the beach, Elaine VP, Elaine V Jane to the beach, Elaine took NP to the beach, Elaine took Jane PP, Elaine took Jane P the beach, Elaine took Jane to NP, Elaine took Jane to the beach}

In this case the component sentences are completely parallel in structure, thus the anomalies of (77) do not arise. This accounts for the difference in grammaticality between (62) and (66).

We proceed now to (63) and its phrase marker (79):

(79) {S, NP kissed Louise tenderly, John VP, John V Louise tenderly, John kissed NP tenderly, John kissed Louise AdvP, John kissed Louise tenderly, S, NP kissed Mary yesterday, John VP yesterday, John V Mary yesterday, John kissed NP yesterday, John kissed Mary AdvP, John kissed Mary yesterday}

Assuming that manner adverbs like *tenderly* and temporal adverbs like *yesterday* are categorially distinguished in some way (as will be discussed in 2.3.5), (79) is ruled out in the same way as (75) and (77). *Yesterday* is dominated by a manner AdvP and *tenderly* by a temporal AdvP, in violation of $\bar{X}$-theory. Such difficulties are not found in (80), the phrase marker for (67):

(80) {S, NP kissed Louise tenderly, John VP, John V Louise tenderly, John kissed NP tenderly, John kissed Louise AdvP, John kissed Louise tenderly, S, NP kissed Mary passionately, John VP, John V Mary passionately, John kissed NP passionately, John kissed Mary AdvP, John kissed Mary passionately}

Phrase marker (80) is well-formed; both adverbs (*tenderly* and *passionately*) are of the same type.

Finally, let us go on to (64), represented here as (81):

(81) {S, NP like ice cream, the boys VP, the boys V ice cream, the boys like NP, the boys like ice cream, S, NP believe that the girls like ice cream, I VP, I V that the girls like ice cream, I believe $\bar{S}$, I believe COMP the girls like ice cream, I believe that S, I believe that NP like ice cream, I believe that the girls VP, I believe that the girls V ice cream, I believe that the girls like NP, I believe that the girls like ice cream}

Although in this case the conjuncts are on the left periphery of the sentence, (81) leads us to basically the same violations we observed in the previous examples. Comparing NP *like ice cream* with *I believe that the girls like ice cream*, we see that *I believe that the girls* is an NP, contrary of course to what the proper labeling should be. Now look at sentence (68), given here in phrase marker form as (82):

(82) {S, NP know that the boys like ice cream, I VP, I V that the boys like ice cream, I know $\bar{S}$, I know COMP the boys like ice cream, I know that S, I know that NP like ice cream, I know that the boys VP, I know that the boys V ice cream, I know that the boys like NP, I know that the boys like ice cream, S, NP believe that the girls like ice cream, I VP, I V that the girls like ice cream, I believe $\bar{S}$, I believe COMP the girls like ice cream, I believe that S, I believe that NP like ice cream, I believe that the girls VP, I believe that the girls V ice cream, I believe that the girls like NP, I believe that the girls like ice cream}

Again we see here that the component sentences are structurally parallel and that no mislabeling occurs.

Thus we see that the effects of the LCL are derivable by applying $\bar{X}$-theory to the RPM's posited for coordinate structure. It is important to note that the LCL falls out directly from our use of union of phrase markers; only by special stipulation would it be possible to have union of phrase markers without the LCL effects.

This is a significant point, since, as mentioned earlier, every other approach to coordination has had to stipulate the LCL in some way. Phrasal conjunction, for example, must build the LCL into the phrase structure rules which generate coordinate structure. Nothing about phrase structure rules forces this result, though, and it is perfectly possible to write rules which do not have this property. The derived conjunction analysis is even worse in this regard, since although the LCL may be stipulated easily enough, it remains mysterious why it should hold. The fact that the LCL may be derived from intrinsic properties of phrase markers thus represents a strong argument in favor of the analysis proposed here.

2.3.4 Comparison with other versions of the LCL

Although there appears to be universal agreement as to the general spirit of the LCL, the predictions made by the stipulations which have been proposed often differ in detail. Here I would like to see whether the version of the LCL predicted by union of phrase markers is in fact the correct one.

We have already seen that the phrasal conjunction analysis may account for LCL effects with constituent coordination but fails to do so with non-constituent coordination in any straightforward way. The analysis developed here makes no distinction between constituent and non-constituent coordination, and consequently the account of the LCL is exactly the same in both cases. This is preferable, since the LCL generalization similarly appears to make no such distinction.

Another interesting property of our version of the LCL is that it does not differentiate the left and right conjuncts, in that the phrase structure relations which result in the LCL are not dependent on the order of conjuncts. I believe that this is correct, but it is not an uncontroversial position. The version of the LCL in George (1980), for example, *is* sensitive to linear order. He conceives of the LCL as a mapping from one conjunct to another. This mapping is directional, in that the "unreduced" conjunct must match the structure of the "reduced" one, in a sense which he makes precise. I won't go into the details of his analysis here, but merely note some problems with this type of "asymmetric parallelism."

The evidence which George presents in favor of this aspect of his analysis is the contrast between (83) and (84):

(83) Daphne wants the bouncer to rescue, and de la Vain loathes, the Siamese kitten that she treed

(84) De la Vain loathes, and Daphne wants the bouncer to rescue, the Siamese kitten that she treed

(83) is ungrammatical, according to George, while (84) is grammatical. This difference is predicted by his mapping requirement. I agree that there is a contrast between (83) and (84), but I do not think that it is due to the LCL. There is a general preference for the final conjunct to be equal or greater in "heaviness." Notice, for instance, the contrast between (85) and (86), where one conjunct is much heavier than the other:

(85) John likes to eat the fish he catches in San Pablo Bay and toast

(86) John likes to eat toast and the fish he catches in San Pablo Bay

(85), like (83), is quite awkward, although George's formulation does not predict this for (85). The account based on heaviness makes the correct prediction here, since the heavy conjunct is first rather than last: (86), in which the conjuncts are reversed, is much better. The heaviness account thus correctly predicts the contrast in both (83)–(84) and (85)–(86) and, because of this, seems preferable to George's account. Moreover, heaviness is a quite plausible explanation in the theory advanced here. Since linearization occurs in PF, it is not surprising that it should be sensitive to factors such as phonological heaviness. I should emphasize here that I am casting doubt on only one aspect of George's LCL, and not on the rest of it, with which I have no disagreement.[19]

In summary, the LCL which we derive from union of phrase markers differs in detail from both the phrasal conjunction analysis and George (1980). We have seen that the union of phrase markers LCL yields superior results.

2.3.5 Syntactic categories and the LCL

The account of LCL effects discussed above interacts in an interesting way with some issues in the theory of syntactic categories. Notice that all of the examples that we have examined so far involve projections of standard lexical categories, such as NP, AP, etc. It has been proposed (see, e.g., Chomsky 1965: ch. 2), however, that there also exist categories such as Predicate, Manner, Time, etc. which are not projections of lexical categories in the ordinary sense.[20] The adoption of such categories brings with it certain advantages. For example, we can state that a verb such as *word* subcategorizes for the categories NP and Manner and thus we can concisely account for the facts in (87):

(87) a. John worded the letter carefully
b. *John worded the letter suddenly
c. John worded the letter with great care
d. *John worded the letter in his car

Otherwise, the properties of *word* would have to be stated in a somewhat more cumbersome way, by saying that it subcategorizes for NP and either a manner AdvP or a manner PP.

On the other hand, the adoption of categories such as Predicate and Manner leads us into some problems for $\overline{X}$-theory, in that we apparently now have a case where a lexical category is dominated by something other than a projection of that category. In (87a), for example, the adverb *carefully* is dominated by Manner, which appears not to be a projection of Adv. This problem can be solved, however, by defining Manner and the others as "archicategories" which are unspecified or underspecified for lexical category. In addition, we must modify $\overline{X}$-theory in such a way that "projection" is defined as a category that does not conflict in lexical category features with the category that it dominates. That is to say, $\overline{X}$-theory must allow (88a, b and c), but not (88d):

(88)

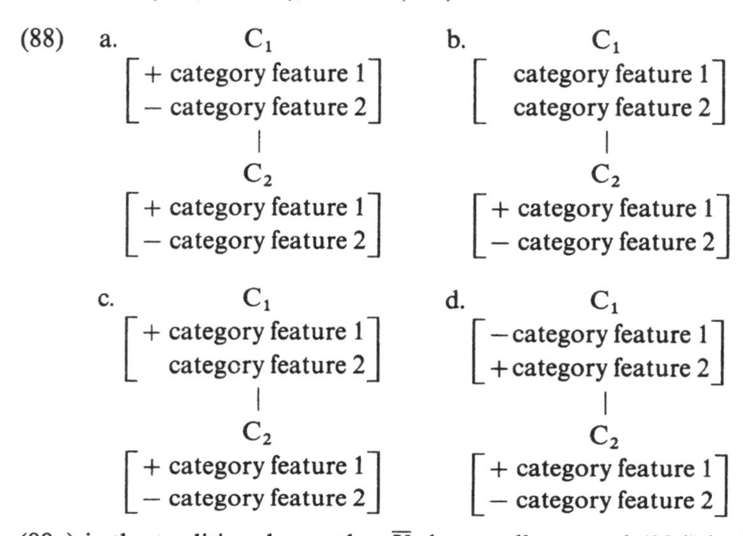

(88a) is the traditional case that $\overline{X}$-theory allows, and (88d) is the traditional case that it disallows. The others are the new cases that I am adding, in which the projection is unspecified, as in (88b), or underspecified, as in (88c), with respect to lexical category features.

Suppose, then, that some such modification of $\overline{X}$-theory is correct.[21] This makes an interesting prediction with regard to the LCL. If phrases belong to the same kind of archicategory, then they should be able to conjoin, regardless of the category-type of the head. This is in fact true, as has been shown in Sag, Gazdar, Wasow and Weisler (1985); some of their examples are given in (89)–(91):

(89) a. Pat is either stupid or a liar
b. Pat is a Republican and proud of it

(90) We walked slowly and with great care

(91) They wanted to leave tomorrow or on Tuesday

In (89) both conjuncts belong to the archicategory Predicate; in (90) they both belong to Manner; and in (91) they both belong to Time. The LCL is thus satisfied.

When the conjuncts belong to different archicategories, the result is ungrammatical, as we would expect:

(92) a. *That stupid and a liar man is my brother
b. *A Republican and proud of it lives next door

(93) *We walked slowly and on Tuesday

(94) *They wanted to leave tomorrow and with great care

Neither NP in (92) is used predicatively, and in (93) and (94) the conjuncts do not match with regard to time and manner.[22] Notice that it is the archicategory which is relevant here, not the category status of the head of the phrase. In a sentence such as (95), for example, both conjuncts are phrases headed by P.

(95) *We walked with great care and on Tuesday

However, *with great care* is of the archicategory Manner, while *on Tuesday* is of the archicategory Time. This violates the LCL and the sentence is predictably ungrammatical.

The way I am using the category labels Manner and Time is fairly straightforward. The archicategory Manner includes those phrases that are usually referred to as manner adverbials and manner PP's. Essentially the same may be said for Time. With the archicategory Predicate, on the other hand, the situation is somewhat more complicated. Chomsky (1965) uses this term to refer to adjectives and predicate nominals, but the definition I need here is more restrictive: that is, the archicategory Predicate must include only those predicate nominals which are able to conjoin with adjectives (which of course will also be members of Predicate). As may be seen in (96), these are a subset of the total set of predicate nominals.

(96)

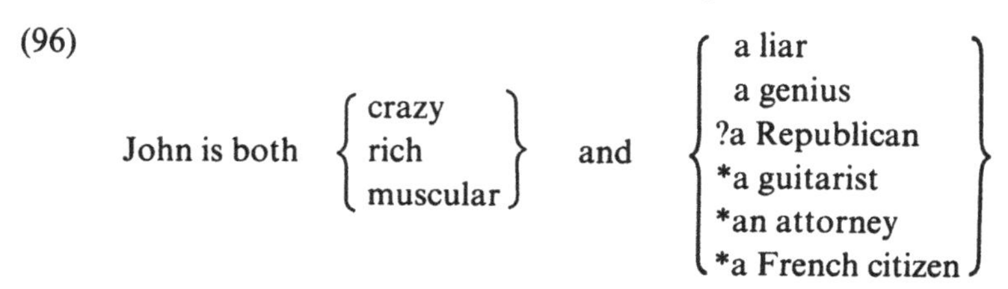

Such a division in the class of predicate nominals is not specific to coordination, however. As Mary Ellen Ryder has pointed out to me, we appear to find exactly the same division when we examine the modification of predicate nominals by *very much*, as seen in (97):

(97) John is very much { a liar / a genius / ?a Republican / *a guitarist / *an attorney / *a French citizen }

Those predicate nominals which may be conjoined with adjectives are precisely those which may be modified by *very much*. The dividing line between the two groups of predicate nominals is by no means clear-cut, but the correlation between (96) and (97) seems to be real. We can thus say that the archicategory Predicate may dominate both adjectives and an independently motivated subset of the predicate nominals.

In summary, we have examined traditional categories such as Manner, Time, and Predicate, and we have seen how they can be incorporated into $\bar{X}$-theory. Given this refinement of the theory, the LCL effects such as those shown in (89)–(96) immediately follow.

2.3.6 Clauses conjoined with NP's

Sag *et al.* (1985) bring to light some interesting sentences in which NP's are conjoined with clauses, as in (98):

(98) a. You can depend on my assistant and that he will be on time
b. We talked about Mr. Colson and that he had worked at the White House
c. Pat was annoyed by the children's noise and that their parents did nothing to stop it

This kind of sentence is of interest for two reasons. First, these are apparent counterexamples to the LCL, in that we seem to have conjoined an NP with an $\bar{S}$. To handle this, we can propose a new archicategory to subsume both NP and $\bar{S}$, in the same way that we used archicategories to account for the data in section 2.3.5.

The second and more problematic point about this kind of sentence is that one of the component sentences is ungrammatical in isolation. Consider, for example, the component sentences in the union of phrase markers underlying (98a), given here in (99):

(99) a. You can depend on my assistant
b. You can depend on that he will be on time

Although (99a) is grammatical, (99b) is not. In general in English, prepositions may not take tensed clauses as objects, as in (99b). This situation is curious, because in all of the examples we have seen until now, a grammatical coordinate structure consists of grammatical component sentences. As will be discussed in section 2.4, this is a general requirement on coordination. How is it that the sentences in (98) are able to escape this requirement?

To begin to answer this question, let us first consider why (99b) is ungrammatical, i.e. why tensed clauses cannot be objects of prepositions. I adopt here the analysis of Stowell (1981), in which this restriction on the distribution of tensed clauses reduces to his Case Resistance Principle, given in (100):

(100) Case may not be assigned to a category bearing a Case-assigning feature.

Stowell argues that tensed clauses bear a Case-assigning feature and thus may not be assigned Case themselves. It then follows that tensed clauses may not appear as objects of prepositions, since in that position they would receive Case.[23]

In order to explain the grammaticality of the sentences in (98) we have two available strategies. First, we could say that in coordinate structures tensed clauses may exceptionally receive Case, contrary to the Case Resistance Principle in (100). Second, we could say that Case is not always assigned to both conjuncts in a coordinate structure. The tensed clauses in (98) could in this way avoid being assigned Case, thus satisfying the Case Resistance Principle.

The first possible strategy appears to be little more than a stipulation, so I will not pursue it here further. The second strategy available to us, on the other hand, does have some plausibility. Assuming that morphological case can give us some clues into the assignment of abstract Case, we shall see that it is quite common for normal Case-assignment to be disrupted in coordinate structures. In the non-clitic pronoun system in Spanish, for example, there is a morphological distinction between object pronouns, used in object positions, and non-object pronouns, used everywhere else. This is shown in (101) for the 1st and 2nd person singular forms:

(101)	*1st person*	*2nd person*	
	yo	tú	*non-object*
	mí	ti	*object*

When the pronoun appears as the object of a preposition, for instance, the objective form is used, as seen in (102):

(102) a. para ti
   'for you'
 b. para mí
   'for me'
 c. *para tú
   'for you'
 d. *para yo
   'for me'

Presumably this is a reflex of the fact that the preposition assigns objective Case to the pronoun. When conjoined pronouns appear as the object of the preposition, however, this Case-assignment seems to be blocked, in that the unmarked non-object forms show up instead of the object ones.[24] This is shown in (103):

(103) a. *para ti y mí
'for you and me'
b. para tú y yo
'for you and me'

Given the facts in (102), this is just the opposite of what we would expect.

English similarly distinguishes between subject pronouns (e.g. *I*, *she*, *he*) and non-subject pronouns (e.g. *me*, *her*, *him*). It is the non-subject pronoun which is unmarked for most forms of English. That is to say, the subject pronouns appear only in subject position, and the non-subject pronouns appear everywhere else, including non-object positions (cf. *It is me*). In sentences such as those in (104), then, only the subject form is allowed:

(104) a. {She / *Her} is going to arrive early
b. {He / *Him} is going to arrive early

We may assume that this is because nominative Case is assigned to the subject position. In one widespread dialect of American English, though, these pronouns exhibit surprising behavior in coordinate structures. When two conjoined pronouns appear in subject position, only the first one is marked nominative, as seen in (105):

(105) {She and him / *Her and he / *Her and him / *She and he} are going to arrive early

The three other logical possibilities are disallowed, including the one that we would expect, *she and he*.[25] It thus appears that Case-assignment to the second conjunct is somehow blocked.

These facts have interesting implications for the issue we set out to address here, i.e. the unexpected grammaticality of the sentences in (98). We saw that the clausal conjunct in those sentences is apparently able to avoid receiving Case and thus does not violate the Case Resistance Principle. The data that we have just examined with pronouns in Spanish and

English give some concrete evidence that Case-assignment may be blocked in coordinate structures. In fact, the pattern of Case-assignment that we saw with the English pronouns in (105) seems to be exactly what occurs with the clausal conjuncts as in (98). In (105) we saw that Case is assigned to the first conjunct, but not to the second; with the type of sentences shown in (98), clauses may appear as the second conjunct, but not as the first. This is seen in the contrast in (106), taken from Sag *et al.* (1985):

(106) a. We talked about the issues we had worked on as students and that our perspectives had changed over the years
b. *We talked about that our perspectives had changed over the years and the issues we had worked on as students

If Case-assignment in (106) proceeds as it does in (105), then in (106b) the clausal conjunct receives Case, whereas in (106a) it does not. This means that in (106b) the Case Resistance Principle will be violated, whereas in (106a) it will not. Thus the independently needed pattern of Case-assignment in coordinate structure that we saw in (105) makes exactly the right predictions with respect to the distribution of clauses conjoined with NP's.

We have now provided a partial solution to the problem of the grammaticality of (98). The Case Resistance Principle, which disallows Case-marked tensed clauses, as in (99b), is circumvented in (98) by the fact that there the tensed clause appears in a coordinate structure and does not receive Case. The idea that normal Case-assignment can be disrupted in coordinate structures was supported by evidence from the pronominal systems of English and Spanish.

Although this analysis gives us an answer to our original question about (98), it also raises several new questions we had not previously considered. The most fundamental of these is why it is that Case-assignment can be blocked in coordination. Similarly, we would want to know how this affects the operation of the Case Filter and the θ-criterion. I do not believe that the model of coordination I am developing here sheds any new light on these questions, so I will simply note that they form an interesting area of investigation that is worth pursuing.

2.3.7 The LCL in Malayalam

In an interesting analysis of coordination in the Dravidian language Malayalam, Archangeli (1983) provides data which argue strongly in favor of the LCL. Some properties of coordination in this language which at first appear quite unexpected may be seen to follow directly from the LCL.

Malayalam is a verb-final language which allows either SOV or OSV order (see Mohanan 1982). I will assume here that SOV sentences are structurally distinct from OSV sentences. For the sake of argument, suppose that SOV sentences are represented as in (107), and that the OSV order is derived from this by object-fronting, as in (108):

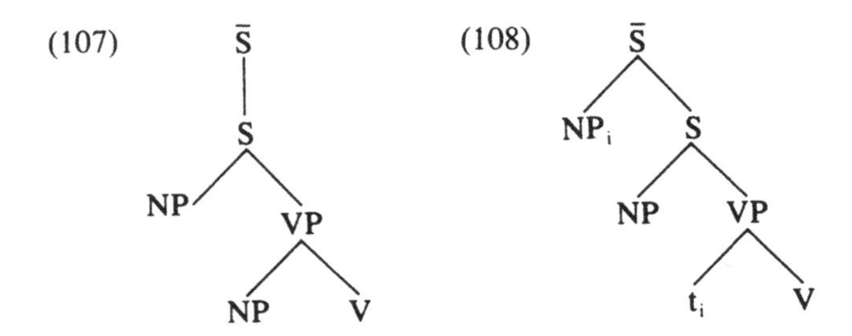

The details here are not important. All that is crucial for what follows is that the SOV and OSV orders are distinguished by their phrase structure configurations.

We can now examine the possibilities for coordination in Malayalam. Consider sentences with conjoined subjects and objects. With Malayalam's verb-final order, these will be instances of backward Gapping (see 2.6 below), equivalent to *John ate the orange and Mary the apple* in English. Given the availability of both SOV and OSV orders, the following four sentence-types should be possible (conjuncts are marked by *-um*):

(109) a. [S O]-um [S O]-um V
b. [O S]-um [O S]-um V
c. [S O]-um [O S]-um V
d. [O S]-um [S O]-um V

However, some of these orders are ruled out by the LCL. Consider the representations in (110):

(110) a. $[_{\bar{S}} [_S [_{NP}$ S$] [_{VP} [_{NP}$ O$]$ ——
V]]]
$[_{\bar{S}} [_S [_{NP}$ S$] [_{VP} [_{NP}$ O$]$ ——

b. $[_{\bar{S}}\ [_{NP}\ \mathrm{O}]\ [_{S}\ [_{NP}\ \mathrm{S}]\ [_{VP}\ [_{NP}\ \mathrm{t}]$

$\qquad\qquad\qquad\qquad\qquad\qquad$ > V]]]

$\quad [_{\bar{S}}\ [_{NP}\ \mathrm{O}]\ [_{S}\ [_{NP}\ \mathrm{S}]\ [_{VP}\ [_{NP}\ \mathrm{t}]$

c. $[_{\bar{S}}\ [_{S}\ [_{NP}\ \mathrm{S}]\ [_{VP}\ [_{NP}\ \mathrm{O}]$

$\qquad\qquad\qquad\qquad\qquad\qquad$ > V]]]

$\quad [_{\bar{S}}\ [_{NP}\ \mathrm{O}]\ [_{S}\ [_{NP}\ \mathrm{S}]\ [_{VP}\ [_{NP}\ \mathrm{t}]$

d. $[_{\bar{S}}\ [_{NP}\ \mathrm{O}]\ [_{S}\ [_{NP}\ \mathrm{S}]\ [_{VP}\ [_{NP}\ \mathrm{t}]$

$\qquad\qquad\qquad\qquad\qquad\qquad$ > V]]]

$\quad [_{\bar{S}}\ [_{S}\ [_{NP}\ \mathrm{S}]\ [_{VP}\ [_{NP}\ \mathrm{O}]$

We saw earlier that the LCL requires that conjuncts be composed of like categories. This holds in (110a) and (110b), where the structure of the conjuncts is parallel. In (110c) and (110d), though, the conjuncts may not be grouped into like categories, and hence the LCL is violated.

Interestingly, sentences such as (110c) and (110d) are in fact ungrammatical, as may be seen in the paradigm in (111):

(111) a. Kuṭṭi ammayeyum acchan aanayeyum n̲uḷḷi
child mother-and father elephant-and pinched

b. Ammaye kuṭṭiyum aanaye acchanum n̲uḷḷi
mother child-and elephant father-and pinched

c. *Kuṭṭi ammayeyum aanaye acchanum n̲uḷḷi
child mother-and elephant father-and pinched

d. *Ammaye kuṭṭiyum acchan aanayeyum n̲uḷḷi
mother child-and father elephant-and pinched

'The child pinched mother and father (pinched) the elephant'

In (111a) and (111b), the order of subject and object in each conjunct is the same, whereas in (111c) and (111d) it is different. The sentences in (111c) and (111d), then, are just those which the LCL disallows. Only in (111a) and (111b) do the conjuncts form like categories, and hence only these sentences are grammatical.

This effect may also be seen with PP's, as in (112). (Malayalam has postpositions.)

(112) a. Kuṭṭi waṭi koṇṭə aanayeyum amma ulaḱḱa koṇṭə
child stick with elephant-and mother pounding-stick with
acchaneyum aṭiccu
father-and beat
(S PP O-um S PP O-um V)

b. Waṭi koṇṭə annaye kuṭṭiyum ulaḱḱa koṇṭə acchane ammayum aṭiccu
(PP O S-um PP O S-um V)

c. Aanaye kuṭṭi waṭi koṇṭum acchane amma ulaḱḱa koṇṭum aṭiccu
(O S PP-um O S PP-um V)

d. *Kuṭṭi waṭi koṇṭə aanayeyum ulaḱḱa koṇṭə acchane ammayum aṭiccu
(S PP O-um PP O S-um V)

e. *Aanaye kuṭṭi waṭi koṇṭum amma ulaḱḱa koṇṭə acchaneyum aṭiccu
(O S PP-um S PP O-um V)

'The child beat the elephant with a stick and mother (beat) father with a pounding stick'

Here again, the ungrammatical examples, (112d) and (112e), are those which violate the LCL, whereas the grammatical ones, (112a)–(112c), satisfy it.

All of this is just what we should expect, given the coordinate structures I am assuming. As we saw in 2.3.3, the LCL is a consequence of union of phrase markers, and its effects are thus unavoidable in these structures. If coordination were not represented as a union of phrase markers, then we would not expect LCL effects. Surprisingly, perhaps, this prediction is not hypothetical in Malayalam, in that the language exhibits a type of coordination which does not seem to arise from a union of phrase markers. This construction consists of a sequence of two sentences, both of which contain the same verb. An example is given in (113):[26]

(113) Amma kuṭṭiye eṭuṯṯi. Acchan puuccayeyum eṭuṯṯi
mother child took father cat-and took
'The mother took the child. And the father took the cat'

As (114) shows, the verbs in this construction must be the same:

(114) *Amma kuṭṭiye eṭuṯṯi. Acchan puuccayeyum ṉuḷḷi
mother child took father cat-and pinched
'The mother took the child. And the father pinched the cat'

This construction is different from what we expect with union of phrase markers, since the verb *eṭuṯṯi* 'took' is present twice. This is not what occurs in our previous examples, (111) and (112), and is not what the linearization of a union of phrase markers should produce (see section 2.2). (113) must then have some different source. If this is the case, then we should not necessarily expect to observe LCL effects in this construction, and in fact we do not, as evidenced in (115):

(115) a. Amma kuṭṭiye eṭuṯṯi. Puuccaye acchanum eṭuṯṯi
mother child took cat father-and took
b. Kuṭṭiye amma eṭuṯṯi. Acchan puuccayeyum eṭuṯṯi
child mother took father cat-and took
'The mother took the child. And the father took the cat.'

In (115a), the order is SOV *and* OSV, and in (115b) it is OSV *and* SOV. These sentences are grammatical and the same in meaning as (113), which is SOV *and* SOV.

This lack of any strong contrasts among the sentences in (113) and (115) may be compared with the robust contrasts evident in (111) and (112). In the latter case, the two conjuncts must be structurally parallel, as required by the LCL. In the former case, no structural parallelism is necessary. Since these sentences are not represented as a union of phrase markers, no LCL effects result, and it follows that the relative order of the subject and object may be different in each conjunct.

Archangeli's facts are thus easily explained by the LCL. This in turn provides rather striking evidence in favor of the LCL and its derivation from union of phrase markers.

2.4 Interpretation in LF

2.4.1 θ-theory

In this section I address the question of how coordinate structures of the type we have been assuming are interpreted in LF. As stated earlier, coordinate structures consist of two or more sentences co-existing in the same phrase marker. These sentences, like any others, must be syntactically well-formed, i.e. they must satisfy the various conditions on syntactic representations which are imposed by the grammar.[27] Here I will be primarily concerned with the way in which the θ-criterion affects coordination.

Notice that coordinate structures might be thought to violate the θ-criterion, at least in a superficial sense. Consider (116), for example:

(116) John and Mary eat doughnuts

Here there appears to be one θ-position, the subject of *eat doughnuts*, which is occupied by two arguments, *John* and *Mary*, leading to a straightforward violation of the θ-criterion.

There are apparent violations going in the other direction as well, in which one argument receives more than one θ-role, as in (117):

(117) John drinks coffee and eats doughnuts

Here *John* seems to receive a θ-role from both *drinks coffee* and *eats doughnuts*.

In an approach using union of phrase markers, however, in which the θ-criterion applies independently to each of the component sentences, the above examples are not a problem. Consider, for example, the terminal strings in the phrase marker for (116), given in (118):

(118) John eats doughnuts
Mary eats doughnuts

The θ-criterion is clearly satisfied in each of these sentences; there is only one argument in each subject position. (117) works in essentially the same way, as seen in (119):

(119) John drinks coffee
John eats doughnuts

Again, each sentence satisfies the θ-criterion independently.

If this is correct, then we should expect that coordinate structures in which the component sentences do not satisfy the θ-criterion would be ungrammatical. An example of this type is given in (120):

(120) John drinks coffee
$[_{NP}$ e] eats doughnuts

The θ-criterion is violated here, because no argument is in the subject position of *eats doughnuts*, a θ-position. The linearized version of the structure containing those terminal strings is given in (121):

(121) *John and [$_{NP}$ e] eat doughnuts

This is ungrammatical, as predicted by the above analysis of the θ-criterion.[28]

A similar example is given in (122):

(122) John eats doughnuts
John seems that Mary is intelligent

In this case there is an argument in both subject positions, but the second one is not θ-marked. Thus the second sentence gives us a violation of the θ-criterion. As expected, then, the linearization is ungrammatical:

(123) *John eats doughnuts and seems that Mary is intelligent

Thus it appears that our assumption that the θ-criterion applies to each of the component sentences in coordinate structures yields the correct results.

2.4.2 Traditional problems

It is now possible to return to some of the empirical problems with the traditional transformational analyses of coordination. Recall that under one set of assumptions, sentence (3), repeated here as (124), presents difficulties for the derived conjunction analysis:

(124) John and Bill met in the park

(124) is derived from (125) in this approach:

(125) John met in the park and Bill met in the park

(125) is semantically deviant, however, in that here *meet* requires a plural subject. If we assume that underlying structures such as (125) are input to semantic interpretation, then we incorrectly predict that (124) should also be deviant.

Let us now examine this problem from a somewhat different point of view. In the approach to coordination developed here, (124) derives from the union of the phrase markers for the sentences in (126):

(126) John met in the park
Bill met in the park

(126) is syntactically well-formed. In particular, the θ-criterion is satisfied

in each component sentence, and hence the sentence as a whole is grammatical.

Under current standard assumptions, the selectional restriction which states that *meet* requires a plural subject is not syntactic. This can be seen in examples such as (127), in which the subject is grammatically singular, but where the requirement on *meet* is satisfied nonetheless:

(127) The couple met in the park

What is required for semantic well-formedness is for *meet* to be predicated of something which refers to more than one individual, as it is here in (127). This requirement is satisfied as well in (124)/(126). There we see that *meet* is predicated of two NP's, one from each component sentence. The conjunction of these is inherently plural, in that it refers to the two individuals John and Bill. With *or*, of course, the sentence is deviant, since the reference of the subject is not plural:

(128) John or Bill met in the park

(128) is grammatically well-formed, but violates a selectional rule.

Thus, under the above assumptions about the nature of the selectional restriction on *meet* we can account for the well-formedness of (124). The literature contains many similar examples, such as those in (129), for instance, taken from Jackendoff (1977: 190–4):

(129) a. John whistled and Mary hummed at equal volumes
b. The same man got drunk and was arrested by the cops
c. The boy and the girl with mutual interests ...

None of these is problematic in the approach assumed here.

As we saw in section 2.1, the phrasal conjunction analysis also runs into a serious empirical problem with sentences like (6), repeated here as (130), which conjoins an active VP with a passive VP:

(130) John hunted tigers and was killed by snakes

This should be impossible with phrasal conjunction if, as is standardly assumed, Passive is a transformational operation. One approach that one might take in order to save the phrasal conjunction analysis is to drop the assumption that Passive is a transformation and base-generate the two VP's as they appear on the surface (this is the position taken by Gazdar

1981, for example). I will take no stand on this issue here, since in fact it will be immaterial to our analysis. Even if Passive is transformational, we can still generate (130) through union of phrase markers, i.e. through the union of the sentences in (131):

(131) John hunted tigers
John was killed by snakes

Each of these sentences satisfies the θ-criterion; thus the structure as a whole satisfies it.

We see then that some of the most problematic cases in the traditional transformational accounts of coordination need no special provision or stipulation if the union of phrase markers approach is adopted. This is a fortunate result, considering the dead-end that the above problems represented for the traditional analyses. The fact that we have been able to solve these problems gives us some indication that the approach we have taken here is justified.

2.4.3 Binding theory

Another aspect of LF-interpretation that deserves some discussion here is the operation of the binding theory in coordinate structures. We shall see that given the model of coordination developed so far, the standard formulation of the binding theory predicts the correct distribution of anaphors and pronominals.

Let us begin with Principle A of the binding theory, which states that anaphors must be bound (i.e. c-commanded by a coindexed element) within their governing category. In a sentence such as (132), for instance, the anaphor *himself* is c-commanded by *John*:

(132) John$_i$ saw Mary and himself$_i$ in the picture

This binding occurs within the governing category, as seen in (133):

(133)
Mary
[$_S$ John$_i$ saw < > in the picture]
himself$_i$

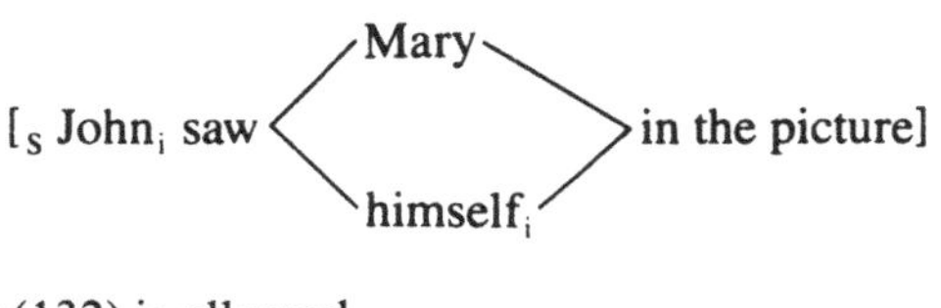

Hence (132) is allowed.

Consider now a somewhat more complex case, in which there is more than one governing category in the sentence. This situation arises with the union of the phrase markers for the sentences in (134), for example:

(134) John saw himself
Mary saw herself

The sentence resulting from (134) is given in (135), and the corresponding structure is partially indicated in (136):

(135) John and Mary saw himself and herself (respectively)

(136) 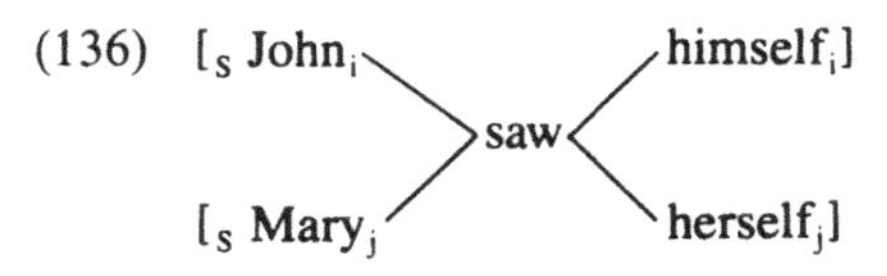

Here *John* c-commands *himself* and *Mary* c-commands *herself*; Principle A is thus satisfied. As we would expect, the same binding relations are possible when (136) receives the alternate linearization known as Gapping, to be discussed in section 2.6:

(137) John saw himself and Mary herself

This follows from our assumption that structural relations such as c-command are determined by the pre-linearization structure.

When *himself* and *herself* in (136) are interchanged, as in (138), the facts are somewhat different:

(138) 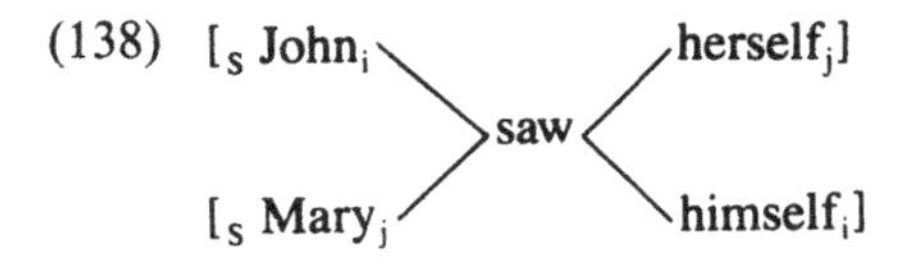

In this case the S-node above *John* does not contain the anaphor *himself*. There is thus no c-command (or binding) relation in the pair *John–himself*. The same of course holds true of the pair *Mary–herself*. The sentences corresponding to (138), then, are ungrammatical, as shown in (139) and (140):

(139) *John and Mary saw herself and himself (respectively)
(140) *John saw herself and Mary himself

These, then, represent violations of Principle A, in that neither *himself* nor *herself* is bound in its governing category.

We saw earlier that NP's conjoined with *and* act like plural NP's. For example, the subject position of a verb like *meet* may be filled with either a plural NP (including NP's such as *the couple*) or conjoined NP's, but not with a singular NP:

(141) a. The boys met in the park
b. The couple met in the park
c. John and Mary met in the park
d. *John met in the park

This is true despite the fact that each of the conjuncts in (141c) is singular. Conjoined NP's also act like plurals with respect to anaphora. Reflexive anaphors which take plural antecedents, such as *themselves*, may also take conjoined NP's as antecedents, as shown in (142):

(142) a. The boys saw themselves (in the mirror)
b. The couple saw themselves
c. John and Mary saw themselves
d. *John saw themselves

Here again in (142c) we see that although each of the conjuncts is singular, when conjoined they are equivalent to a plural NP.[29]

As we would expect, then, anaphors requiring singular antecedents are not allowed in this context, as shown in (143):

(143) *John and Mary saw herself

This is ungrammatical in the same way that the sentences in (144) are:

(144) a. *The girls saw herself
b. *The couple saw herself

In each of these cases in (143) and (144), the subject is plural in reference and thus cannot serve as an antecedent to the singular anaphor *herself*, even though the group referred to does contain a suitable antecedent – *Mary* in (143), one of the girls in (144a), and one member of the couple in (144b).

The analysis just given of the ungrammaticality of (143) might seem at first to be contradicted by the grammaticality of (135), where the singular anaphors *himself* and *herself* are preceded in the string by *John and Mary*. We said with (143) that *John and Mary* acts as a plural NP and thus is not able to be an antecedent of *himself* or *herself*. What makes (135) different is that there *himself* is c-commanded only by *John* and *herself* is c-commanded only by *Mary*. This contrasts with the situation in (143) where *herself* is c-commanded by both *John* and *Mary*. Thus it is only in (143) that the anaphor is c-commanded by the obligatorily plural conjunction of *John* and *Mary*. In (135) each anaphor is c-commanded by a singular NP.

This distinction between singular and plural antecedents can perhaps be illustrated more clearly by examining a sentence such as that in (145):

(145) John and Mary saw himself and a cow

In a *respectively*-reading of (145), the component sentences are as in (146):

(146) John saw himself
Mary saw a cow

In this structure, *himself* is c-commanded by *John*, not by *Mary*, and thus the sentence is well-formed. This situation changes, though, if we take the component sentences to be as in (147):

(147) John saw himself
John saw a cow
Mary saw himself
Mary saw a cow

Now, *himself* is c-commanded by both *John* and *Mary*, and the requirement that *himself* take a singular antecedent is violated. We thus correctly predict this reading of (145) to be disallowed.

We may contrast (145) with the sentence in (148):

(148) John and Mary saw themselves and a cow

In this case the *respectively*-reading is ungrammatical, while the other reading is fine. This is because in the *respectively*-reading structure, *themselves* is c-commanded only by *John*. Since *themselves* requires a plural antecedent, the structure is ill-formed. With the other reading, *themselves* is c-commanded by both *John* and *Mary*, and the requirement on *themselves* is thus met.

We have seen, then, that the operation of Principle A in coordinate structures is neatly accounted for with the model of coordination developed here. The phrase structure configuration produced by the union of two or more phrase markers appears accurately to predict the c-command relations upon which the binding relations are based. In addition, we saw that NP's conjoined with *and* act like plurals with respect to binding theory, just as they do with respect to other areas of the grammar.

We may now turn to Principle B of binding theory, which states that pronouns must be free within their governing category. In an example such as (149), for instance, the pronoun *him* is c-commanded by *John* within its governing category S:

(149)
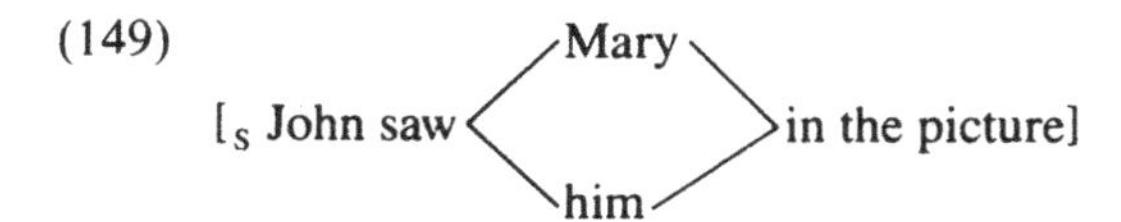

Coreference between *John* and *him* is thus disallowed in sentences such as (150):

(150) John saw Mary and him in the picture

The same holds true in slightly more complex structures as well. Consider the union of the phrase markers underlying the sentences in (151):

(151) John saw him
Mary saw a cow

This results in a structure such as that in (152) and a sentence such as (153):

(152) [$_S$ John — saw — him]
[$_S$ Mary — saw — a cow]

(153) John and Mary saw him and a cow (respectively)

John c-commands *him* in (152) just as it does in (149), so coreference is impossible. This may be seen as well with the alternative Gapping linearization, as in (154):

(154) John saw him and Mary a cow

Here too, coreference is disallowed.

Now let us construct an example in which *John* does not c-command *him*, as in (155):

(155)
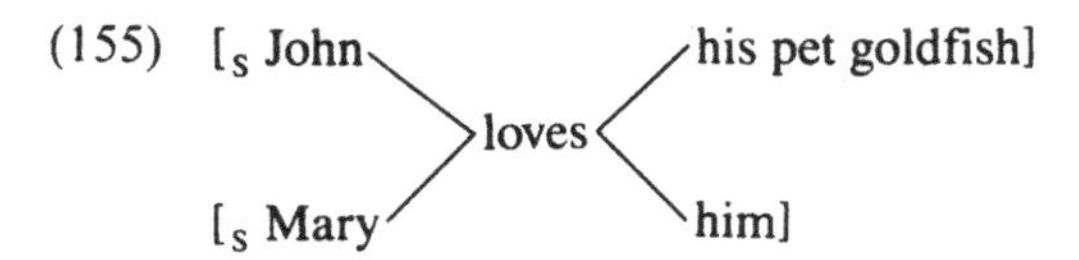

This may be linearized as either (156) or (157):

(156) John and Mary love his pet goldfish and him (respectively)
(157) John loves his pet goldfish and Mary him

In both of these cases, as we would expect, *John* and *him* may be coreferential.

The linearizations given in (156) and (157) assume that the component sentences of the union of phrase markers are ordered so that *John loves his pet goldfish* precedes *Mary loves him.*[30] If we reverse this order, we get the linearizations in (158) and (159):

(158) Mary and John love him and his pet goldfish (respectively)
(159) Mary loves him and John his pet goldfish

Although coreference between *John* and *him* is possible in (158), as it was in (156) and (157), the facts in (159) are somewhat less clear. It appears that coreference is only marginally possible in that linearization. Notice that (159) differs from (156)–(158) in that here *him* precedes *John.* Thus one way to account for the lack of clear coreference in (159) is to say that for some perhaps pragmatic reason, linearizations which order full NP's before coindexed pronouns are highly preferred over those which do not.[31] Because of this, a linearization such as (159) is only fully acceptable when *John* and *him* are not coindexed.

There are many other examples which seem to follow from this generalization about the order of pronouns and their antecedents in coordination. (160) and (161), for example, are presumably alternate linearizations of the same union of phrase markers:

(160) Mary and he love John and his pet goldfish (respectively)
(161) Mary loves John and he his pet goldfish

Coreference is marginal in (160), but possible in (161). This again follows from the assumption that the order *John–he* is preferred over *he–John* when they are coreferential.

It is possible that this restriction on the linearization of pronouns need not be stipulated as something specific to coordination. As Chametzky (1984) points out, the order antecedent–pronoun is "the most unmarked case, that which would be expected, in the absence of structural constraints to the contrary, given the (lack of) lexical content and given/new information status of pronouns." With (160)/(161) for example, the relative order of *John* and *he* is not subject to structural constraints (such as Principle B), so the order *John–he* is the unmarked one. Thus it may be that the linearization facts seen above are simply a reflection of some deeper principle regarding the use of pronouns.

One final point about Principle B concerns sentences such as (162):

(162) John and Mary saw her

Mary and *her* here may not be coreferential. The reason for this is essentially the same as for (143), repeated here as (163):

(163) *John and Mary saw herself

An antecedent of *her* or *herself* must be singular, yet we have seen that NP's conjoined by *and* act like plurals. Thus neither *her* nor *herself* can find an appropriate antecedent in these examples. Coreference is disallowed in (162) in the same way that it is in (164) – cf. (144):

(164) a. The girls saw her
b. The couple saw her

That is, *her* cannot refer to one of the girls or to one member of the couple. Likewise, it cannot refer to one member of *John and Mary* in (162).

Suppose now that we use a pronoun which does take a plural antecedent, as in (165):

(165) John and Mary saw them

The problem noted in (162) is now resolved, but here instead there is a straightforward violation of Principle B. *Them* is bound by *John and Mary* within its governing category, so coreference is disallowed.

This concludes our survey of the distribution of anaphors and pronouns in coordinate structures. We have seen that Principles A and B of the binding theory make correct predictions in this regard.[32] We have had to make two auxiliary assumptions, both of which appear to be independently motivated. First, we said that NP's conjoined with *and* behave like a plural NP. This can be seen from the fact that such NP's satisfy the selectional restrictions of predicates like *meet*. Second, we said that linearizations which place an antecedent to the left of its coindexed pronoun are preferred over those which do the opposite. It was suggested that this might follow from the unmarked character of the order antecedent–pronoun.

2.5 Extraction

In this section we will examine a class of phenomena first discovered by Ross (1967): *wh*-movement within coordinate structures. Our primary concern will be the Coordinate Structure Constraint and the Across-the-Board exceptions to this constraint, the two major generalizations noted by Ross. The facts in this domain are relatively complex, but the relevant facts are directly derivable from the formulation of union of phrase markers we have been using thus far.

2.5.1 Coordinate Structure Constraint

Ross (1967) formulated the Coordinate Structure Constraint (CSC) as in (166):

(166) *The Coordinate Structure Constraint*
In a coordinate structure, no conjunct may be moved, nor may any element contained in a conjunct be moved out of that conjunct.

The first stipulation, that no conjunct may be moved, accounts for the ungrammaticality of sentences like (167):

(167) a. *What did George eat tuna fish and __?
b. *Who did the mailman see __ and his wife?
c. *I know a book which the senator wrote an article and __.

One of the conjuncts has been moved in each of these cases, clearly violating the CSC. Ross pointed out that this first part of the CSC is derivable from the A-over-A condition,[33] assuming that the two conjuncts form a constituent, as in (168):

(168)
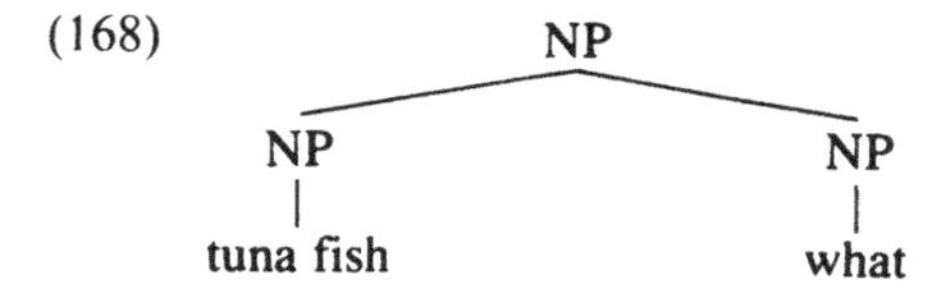

Grosu (1973) and Pesetsky (1982) have argued that including this case in with the rest of the CSC is a false generalization, and they choose to let the A-over-A condition alone bar sentences like (167). However, we shall see that in our system these sentences will be ruled out independently of the A-over-A condition.

The second part of the CSC forbids movement out of a conjunct. This can be seen in (169):

(169) a. *What did Mary cook the pie and Jane eat __?
b. *Who does Tom like __ and Larry hate primates?
c. *This is the man who it was raining and Bill shot __

Again, these examples straightforwardly violate the CSC.

An explanation for these facts may be found, I will show, in the system we have developed thus far. Consider the component sentences of the structure underlying (169a):

(170) a. What did Mary cook the pie?
b. What did Jane eat t?

Recall that each of these must be syntactically well-formed. (170b) is grammatical; the *wh*-phrase *what* receives a θ-role (and Case) by means of its trace. This is not so in (170a): there the *wh*-phrase has no corresponding trace, and, in addition to constituting an instance of vacuous quantification, it receives no θ-role. Since (170a) is ill-formed, it then follows that (169a) is as well. We may thus account for the ungrammaticality of (169a) and the other sentences in (169) and (167).

Notice that one cannot avoid this result by positing a different source for (169a), as in (171):

(171) a. Mary cooked the pie
b. What did Jane eat?

This may have the right meaning, but it cannot be linearized as (169a). A linearization of (171) would have to count *Mary cooked the pie* and *What did Jane eat*? as conjuncts. This is not the case in (169a).

A similar account may be given of the ungrammaticality of sentences like those in (172):

(172) *How loudly is John sick and moaning __?

Here again, one of the component sentences, (173a), is ill-formed:

(173) a. How loudly is John sick?
b. How loudly is John moaning t ?

Sick does not subcategorize for a manner adverb, and thus, by the Projection Principle, there is no trace in (173a). This means that the quantifier phrase *how loudly* has no corresponding variable, and that (173a) hence violates the ban on vacuous quantification. Since (173a) is ungrammatical, so is (172).

Ross noticed that the CSC does not affect the operation of Passive, as seen in the now familiar example shown in (174):[34]

(174) John hunted tigers and __ was killed by snakes

We saw in section 2.4 that this sentence is generable, as in (175):

(175)

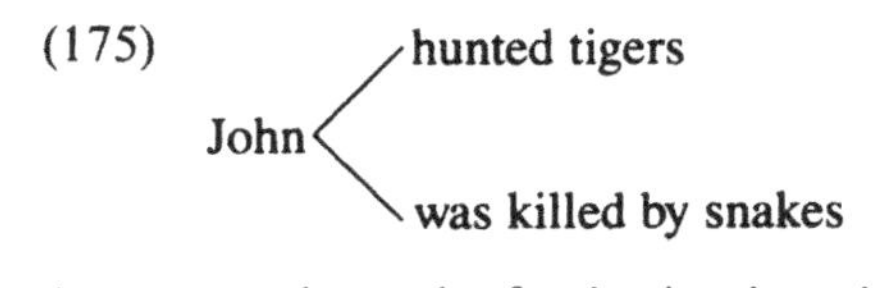

As we saw there, the θ-criterion is satisfied in this case.

We have seen, then, that the CSC effects follow directly from our formulation of the union of phrase markers. This is not the first time that the CSC has been derived from purportedly independent properties of coordination (see, e.g., Schachter 1977; George 1980; Gazdar 1981; Pesetsky 1982; Anderson 1983; Gazdar, Klein, Pullum and Sag 1985; Steedman 1985), but it is nonetheless significant that we have also been able to do it here.

2.5.2 Across-the-Board exceptions to the CSC

Despite the impressive generality of the CSC, there is one systematic class of exceptions to it. Consider sentences like the following:

(176) a. Which man __ ran the race and __ won the prize?
b. Which film did the critics hate __ and the audience love __?
c. How loudly is Mary screaming and John moaning?

The CSC prohibits movement out of a conjunct, but in each of these cases there has been movement out of both conjuncts. While one might expect that this movement, what Ross calls "Across-the-Board" movement, would be an extreme violation of the CSC and consequently ungrammatical, this is not the case. In order to handle the grammaticality of sentences like (176), Ross adds the following condition to the CSC:

(177) unless the same element is moved out of all the conjuncts

I will show here that just as we do not need to stipulate the CSC, we similarly do not need to stipulate this exception to it. Both fall out from the union of phrase markers.

Let us consider the source of the sentences in (176). The component sentences involved are as in (178):

(178) a. Which man t ran the race?
Which man t won the prize?
b. Which film did the critics hate t ?
Which film did the audience love t ?
c. How loudly is Mary screaming t?
How loudly is John moaning t?

Unlike real CSC violations, such as (170), here both component sentences are well-formed, since in each case the *wh*-phrase is coindexed with a trace and thus quantifies non-vacuously.

Thus, the grammaticality of sentences like (176) is unproblematic, given the union of phrase markers approach. The Across-the-Board exceptions to the CSC turn out to be completely regular, rather than exceptional.

2.5.3 Extraction in Palauan

The analysis given above for English applies equally well to the Austronesian language Palauan, in which extraction phenomena appear, superficially at least, to be quite different.

As discussed in Georgopoulos (1983, 1985), Palauan obeys the CSC:

(179) *[a delak [a uleker er ngak [el kmo ngngera [a sensei a milskak
mother asked P me COMP what teacher gave
a buk] me [a Toki a ulterur er ngak]]]]
book and sold P me

'My mother asked me what the teacher gave me a book and Toki sold __ me'

In both English and Palauan, the sentence 'My mother asked me what the teacher gave me a book" is ungrammatical, and hence the sentence in (179) is ungrammatical. Neither language permits vacuous quantification.

Sentences in which both component sentences are grammatical are themselves grammatical:

(180) [a delak a uleker [el kmo ngngera [lulterur __ a Toki el me
mother asked COMP what sold come
er ngak] me [a Droteo ulterur __ el mo er a Toiu]]]
P me and sold go P

'My mother asked what Toki sold __ to me and Droteo sold __ to Toiu'

This, of course, is an instance of Across-the-Board extraction, in that there is a gap in each conjunct.

One interesting fact about Palauan is that it makes use of two extraction strategies. When extraction is from the object of a preposition a resumptive pronoun is used. A gap is left when the extraction is from other positions. This leads to a very clear prediction in the present system. A coordinate structure in which one component sentence obligatorily contains a gap and the other obligatorily contains a resumptive pronoun should be grammatical. This prediction is confirmed, as seen in (181):

(181) a. [akmedengelii a bilas$_i$ [el lebilʔerar ___$_i$ a Cisco] me
I know boat COMP bought and
[a Ioseb a milngesbereber er ngii$_i$]]
painted P it

'I know which boat Cisco bought ___ and Joseph painted (it)'

b. [ngngerang$_i$ [mirruul er ngii$_i$ a Sie] e [a ʔoʔodal a
what made P it her-sister
meʔerar ___$_i$]]
bought

'What did Sie make (it) and her sister buy ___?'

Each component sentence in these examples is grammatical, hence the sentences as a whole are grammatical, despite the fact that a single quantifier binds both a gap and a resumptive pronoun.[35] Our explanation of the CSC thus extends beyond the original set of data which the CSC was designed to account for.[36]

2.5.4 Across-the-Board asymmetries

The description of Across-the-Board movement becomes somewhat more complicated upon closer inspection. Williams (1978) discovered an important asymmetry in the possibility of *wh*-movement out of conjuncts, which can be seen in the set of sentences in (182):

(182) a. This is the man who John saw ___ and Mary kissed ___
b. This is the man who ___ saw John and ___ kissed Mary
c. *This is the man who John saw ___ and ___ kissed Mary
d. *?This is the man who ___ kissed Mary and John saw ___

e. This is the man who John saw ___ and Mary thinks ___ is handsome
f. *?This is the man who ___ saw John and Mary thinks ___ is handsome

When movement is out of structurally parallel positions, as in (182a) and (182b), the result is grammatical. Otherwise, extraction is only possible out of non-matrix subject positions. Thus (182e) is allowed, but (182c, d and f), where movement out of one conjunct is from matrix subject position, are not.

This might seem surprising, given what we have seen so far, because all of the sentences in (182) would appear to be well-formed. In each component sentence, the *wh*-phrase is coindexed with a trace which receives Case and a θ-role, just as in the previous Across-the-Board examples we have seen.

The sentences in (182) are differentiated, however, by Principle C of binding theory.[37] Consider the formulation of this in Chomsky (1982), given here as (183):

(183) An R-expression must be A-free in the domain of the operator that $\bar{A}$-binds it.

This will apply to the structures underlying (182) in (184):

(184)

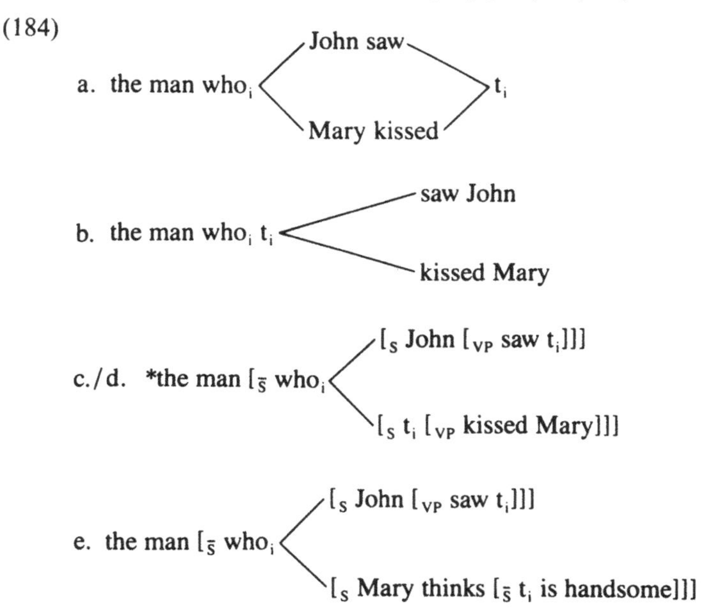

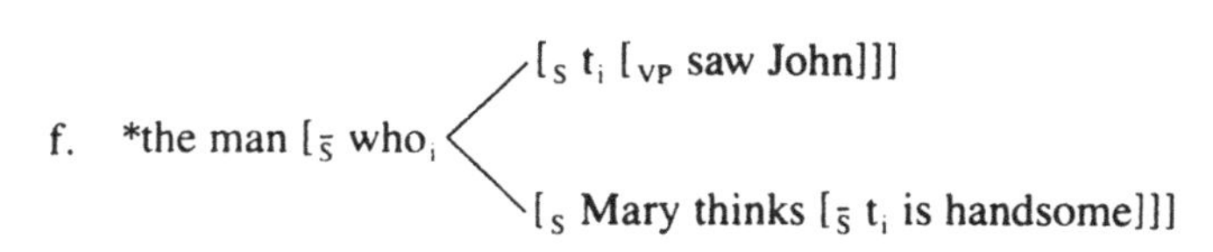

The traces in (184), being variables, are R-expressions, and hence by Principle C they may not be bound by anything in an A-position which is in the domain of the *wh*-phrase operator. Let us see what predictions this makes here. In (184a) and (184b), the traces are not bound by anything within the domain of *who*, thus satisfying Principle C. In (184c/d) (linear order is irrelevant) the trace in the lower conjunct c-commands the trace in the upper conjunct, since the first maximal projection above the former ($\bar{S}$) dominates the latter. The trace object of *saw* is thus bound by the trace in the subject position of *kissed*, which is an A-position in the domain of *who*. Structure (184c/d) consequently violates Principle C. In (184e), neither trace c-commands the other, since in neither instance does the first dominating maximal projection (VP and $\bar{S}$) dominate the other trace. Principle C is thus satisfied here. In (184f), however, the first maximal projection above the trace in the upper conjunct ($\bar{S}$) does dominate the other trace. Since one trace is thus bound by the other within the domain of the operator, a Principle C violation results.

We see, then, that Principle C makes exactly the right predictions here. The grammatical sentences in (182a, b and e) satisfy this principle, while the ungrammatical ones in (182c, d and f) violate it.

This account applies in exactly the same way to such sentences as (185):

(185) This is the man who John saw __ and thinks __ is handsome

The underlying structure is given in (186):

(186) the man who_i John < $[_{VP}$ saw $t_i]$ / $[_{VP}$ thinks $[_{\bar{S}}$ t_i is handsome$]]$

Here again, neither trace c-commands the other, and Principle C is satisfied.[38]

We are also able to rule out sentences like those in (187), discussed in Williams (1978, 1981a).

(187) a. *Who does John like __ and __?
b. *Who does John like __ and friends of __?

The relevant structures are as in (188):

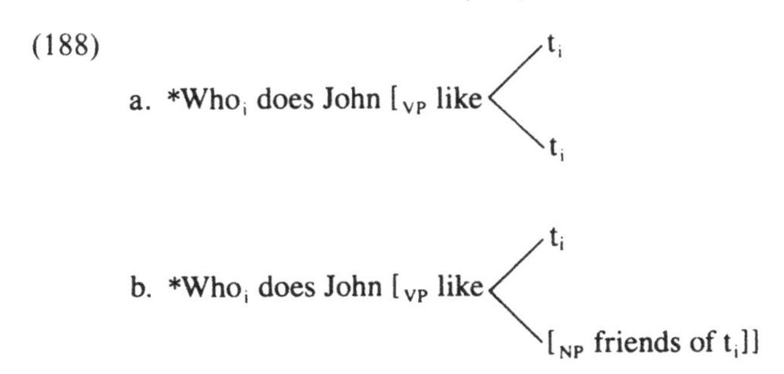

In (188a) there is mutual c-command between the two traces. In (188b) the trace in the upper conjunct c-commands the other trace. In both structures, then, Principle C is violated, yielding the correct predictions in (187).

Notice that sentences like (189) are not excluded:

(189) Who does John like pictures of __ and books about __?

The structure is given in (190):

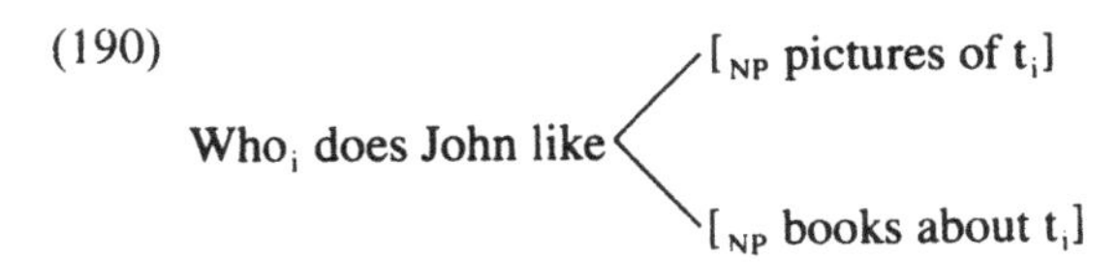

Here neither trace c-commands the other, and Principle C is satisfied.

Thus we see that the asymmetries in the possibility of *wh*-movement out of coordinate structures are the result of the interaction of an independently needed principle of binding theory with the structures which I am assuming to be needed for coordination. The descriptively complex array of data which we have seen in this section is thus derived without stipulation.

2.5.5 ATB asymmetries and GLBC, PCC, ECP

The sentences in (182) above have been the object of considerable attention in recent work. At least three studies have attempted to derive these facts from independently motivated principles of grammar, much as we did in the previous subsection. Gazdar (1981) used his Generalized Left Branch Condition (GLBC), Pesetsky (1982) used his Path Containment Condition (PCC), and in earlier work (Goodall 1983) I used the Empty

Category Principle (ECP).[39] In what follows I will show that these principles cannot be what is responsible for the apparent constraints on Across-the-Board movement.

The three principles mentioned, the GLBC, the PCC and the ECP, are alike in that under certain conditions they disallow gaps in subject position. *That*-t effects such as (191), for instance, are ruled out by all three principles:

(191) *Who do you think that __ has arrived?

The details of how (191) is excluded are not of direct concern to us here. The important point for our purposes is that these very same principles, when combined with some non-trivial assumptions about the nature of coordination, rule out the ungrammatical sentences in (182).

One problem with this is that *that*-t effects are typically quite strong: (191), for example, is completely unacceptable for almost all speakers of standard English. With the Across-the-Board sentences in (182), however, there is a great deal more variation. (182d), for instance, is acceptable to some speakers. Even the worst case, (182c), improves somewhat with some lexical items, as in (192) (see Anderson 1983 for discussion):

(192) This is the dress which Mary bought __ and __ cost $6,000

It thus appears unlikely that it is the same principle which rules out both *that*-t effects such as (191) and the Across-the-Board cases in (182), as is claimed by the analyses under discussion.

A second argument against these analyses concerns *that*-t effects in null subject languages. As is well known, sentences like (191) are fully acceptable in null subject languages like Spanish, as seen in (193):

(193) ¿Quién crees que ha llegado?
'Who do you think that has arrived?'

Following the analysis of Rizzi (1982), this is due to the fact that Spanish shows free subject inversion, as in (194):

(194) a. Juan ha llegado
b. Ha llegado Juan
'John has arrived'

If *wh*-extraction occurs from out of the postverbal NP position, then the violation of the GLBC/PCC/ECP can be avoided, thus allowing for the grammaticality of (193).[40] The same analysis should apply to Across-the-Board movement as well. In each case in (182) where extraction out of matrix subject position results in ungrammaticality, we should be able to extract the *wh*-phrase from the postverbal position, and thus avoid a violation of the GLBC/PCC/ECP. This would predict that the Spanish equivalents of (182c, d, and f) would be grammatical. This prediction is not confirmed, however. The Spanish sentence (195), for example, is unacceptable for most speakers, as is its English counterpart (182c):[41]

(195) *Este es el hombre que Juan vio __ y __ besó a María
'This is the man who John saw and kissed Mary'

Again, this result is difficult to explain in an account where *that*-t effects and Across-the-Board asymmetries are ruled out by the same principle. The parametric variation which gives rise to the contrast between (191) and (193) should produce a similar contrast between (182c) and (195).

One further piece of evidence against these accounts concerns the grammatical sentences (182a, b and e). In the above analyses, these are all grammatical in the same way; they all involve Across-the-Board extraction from non-matrix subject positions. In some languages, though, there is a sharp difference between the (e) and the (a/b) sentences. In both Dutch and French, for example, the equivalents of (182a and b) are grammatical, but (182e) has a status similar to (182c, d and f):

(196) *Ik ken de man die hij aardig vindt en wij hopen dat zal winnen
'I know a man who he likes and we hope will win'
(from Neijt 1979)

(197) *Quel film aimes-tu et crois-tu qui sera primé?
'Which film do you like and do you think will be banned?'

In the analyses that we have been examining, this difference is rather mysterious. (182a, b and e) all receive a uniform treatment, and it is not at all clear why languages which are otherwise quite similar to English should distinguish among them.

We have seen evidence, then, that the source of the asymmetries in (182) does not reside in the GLBC, PCC, or ECP. This in itself, of course, does not render these principles invalid, although it does remove some of the motivation for them.

It is important to note that in the union of phrase markers analysis developed in this chapter, the shortcomings of the analyses we have just seen do not arise. Since Principle C is what is responsible for the asymmetries in (182), we do not expect any correlation, either in English or in null subject languages, between Across-the-Board movement and *that*-t effects. We similarly do not expect any necessary correlation between the grammaticality of (182a/b) and (182e). In both the (a) and (b) sentences there is only one trace, whereas in (182e) there are two. This calls to mind the Bijection Principle of Koopman and Sportiche (1982), given here in (198):

(198) Operators and variables require a one-to-one correspondence

In a language which is particularly sensitive to the Bijection Principle, a sentence like (182e) should be worse than the (a) or (b) versions. Thus Dutch and French may be languages of this type. Whether or not the Bijection Principle is what is ultimately responsible for the difference between Dutch/French and English, we have seen that at least there are grounds for making a distinction between (182e) and (182a/b) in our analysis, since the two kinds of sentences are not structurally identical.

2.5.6 Some remaining problems with ATB asymmetries

The preceding analysis succeeds in accounting for the standard facts concerning asymmetries in Across-the-Board extraction. There are some facts which are rarely mentioned in the literature, however, to which neither this nor the other analyses I have discussed here provide a very satisfactory explanation. I will briefly review these data in what follows below.

It was noted in (182c and d) that sentences in which the extraction sites are linearly adjacent (aside from the conjunction) are worse than sentences in which they are non-adjacent. The relevant facts are repeated here in (199):

(199) a. *This is the man who John saw __ and __ kissed Mary
b. *?This is the man who __ kissed Mary and John saw __

For some speakers, the contrast between (199a) and (199b) is quite strong. The analysis I have presented here does not predict any difference between these two, since both violate Principle C. The linear order of the conjuncts should be irrelevant.

Carol Anderson (1983) suggests a possible explanation for the contrast in (199). Observe that the sentence in (199a) is ambiguous between the two structures given in (200):

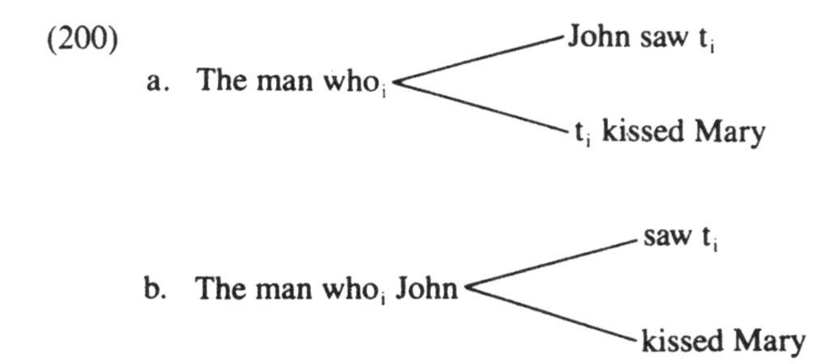

(200a) is the Across-the-Board structure we have been considering up to this point. (200b), whose linearization is identical to that of (200a), is a clear violation of the CSC. Since CSC violations seem to be stronger than ATB violations of Principle C, we then expect sentences such as (199a), which may be parsed as CSC violations, to be less acceptable than sentences such as (199b), which do not have a structure in which they violate the CSC.

This story is supported by the fact that sentences with adjacent gaps which may not be construed as CSC violations are noticeably more acceptable. This is seen in (201) – data from Anderson (1983) and personal communication:

(201) a. That's the candidate who the unions endorsed __ and __ was the overwhelming favorite of the Democrats
b. We went to see a movie which the critics praised __ but __ was too violent for my taste
c. Nancy Reagan was wearing a gown that Galanos designed __ and __ cost over $5,000

The CSC violation reading for each of these sentences is independently either grammatically ill-formed or pragmatically implausible. The relevant structures are given in (202):

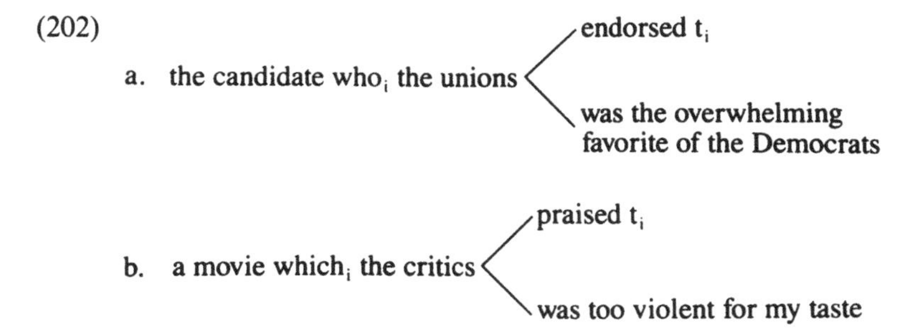

In (202a) and (202b), the verb of the lower conjunct does not agree with its subject, and in (202c) the subject–predicate relation is not very felicitous. Assuming that the structures in (202) are excluded for the above reasons, then the sentences in (201) do not have a reading available to them in which the CSC is violated. We then expect that the acceptability of (201) should be on a par with that of (199b), and this in fact appears to be the case.

What we must say, then, is that a sentence such as (199a), in which one reading is a Principle C violation and the other is a CSC violation, is less acceptable than sentences such as (201), in which one reading is a Principle C violation and the other violates both the CSC and some other principle. Admittedly, this is somewhat odd as an explanation, but I know of no other way to distinguish the two cases.

Another mystery concerns the extraction of embedded subjects and objects. We saw in (182) that the extraction of one matrix subject and one matrix object leads to ungrammaticality, but that the extraction of a matrix object and an embedded subject is allowed. Our analysis utilizing Principle C correctly accounted for these facts. This analysis (and all others of which I am aware) also predicts that extraction of an embedded subject and an embedded object should be grammatical, since in such a configuration neither trace would c-command the other. The data do not bear this prediction out, however:

(203) a. This is the kind of movie which Tom thinks __ pleases Americans and Bill thinks __ frightens Canadians
a′. That is the man who I think __ likes Mary but they think __ kissed Jane
b. This is the kind of movie which Tom thinks Americans like __ and Bill thinks Canadians hate __
b′. That is the man who I think Mary likes __ but they think Jane kissed __
c. ?This is the kind of movie which Tom thinks Americans like __ and Bill thinks __ frightens Canadians
c′. ?That is the man who I think Mary likes __ but they think __ kissed Jane

In the (a) sentences of (203) there is extraction out of two subject positions, and in the (b) sentences it is out of two object positions. In the (c) sentences extraction is out of one subject and one object position. The contrast is not strong, but many speakers find that the (c) sentences are worse than those in (a) and (b). These data thus seem to mimic the data in (182a–d), where a similar (although stronger) contrast obtains within the matrix clause. In the case of (182), we could explain the facts with Principle C, but this is of no help in (203). Whether (203) represents the same phenomenon as (182) or whether it is the result of some more subtle parallelism requirement is a question I will leave open in this study.

2.5.7 Conclusion

In conclusion, we have seen that the Coordinate Structure Constraint, the Across-the-Board violations of it, and the major properties of Across-the-Board asymmetries fall out from the theory of coordination developed in earlier sections.

One interesting difference between this analysis and others is that here there is no necessary equivalence between gaps and empty categories. A given sentence may appear to have many gaps on the surface which all correspond to a single trace in the S-structure representation. We thus make a distinction between Across-the-Board gaps and parasitic gaps, where there presumably is a one-to-one correspondence between surface gaps and empty categories. Such a distinction seems desirable, not only because of differences in their distribution, but also because of the fact that parasitic gaps are somewhat uncommon among languages, whereas Across-the-Board gaps appear to be universal.[42]

2.6 Gapping

We now return to the construction called Gapping, exemplified in (204), repeated from (36):

(204) Mary eats apples and John oranges

It was mentioned in section 2.2 that Gapping seems to violate the general linearization procedure for coordinate structures. If we linearize the union of the phrase markers for the sentences in (205), which is equivalent to (37):

(205) Mary eats apples
John eats oranges

we may derive the sentence in (206), but not the Gapping sentence (204).

(206) Mary and John eat apples and oranges (respectively)

Given the analysis of coordination developed so far, there is no source for (204), i.e. there is no account for Gapping.

Two options are now available to us. We may either modify our analysis so that Gapping is allowed or we may conclude that Gapping is due to some independent process unrelated to the union of phrase markers. There is some evidence that the first of these options is correct. If Gapping were in fact an independent process, then we might expect, as we saw with truncation (section 2.2), that it would be found with more than just coordinating conjunctions like *and*, *or*, or *but*.[43] This is not the case, however. Sentences like (207), from Jackendoff (1971), are ungrammatical, even though the intended meaning is clear:

(207) a. *Sam played tuba whenever Max sax
b. *McTavish plays bagpipes despite the fact that McCawley the contrafagotto d'amore

This follows from our general claim that union of phrase markers is only possible with coordinating conjunctions.

In addition, Gapping seems to observe the parallelism constraint on coordination (LCL) which we discussed in section 2.3. Sag (1976) notes examples such as (208):[44]

(208) a. *Alan went to New York and it seems that Betsy to Boston
b. *Sam hates reptiles and Sandy to talk to Oh
c. *Beth ate yogurt and Norma at midnight

In our terms, the tree diagrams for these sentences would be as in (209):

(209)
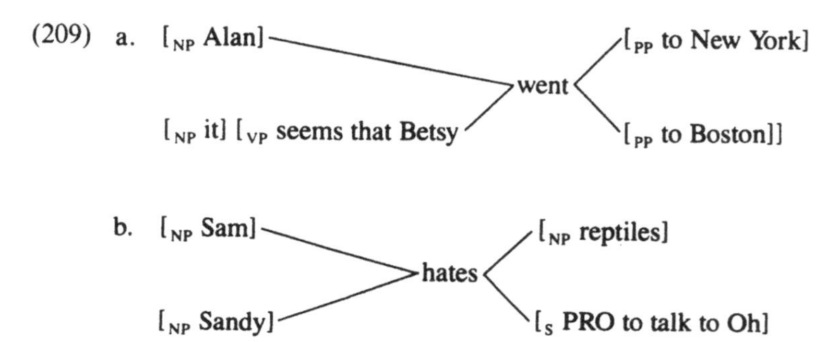

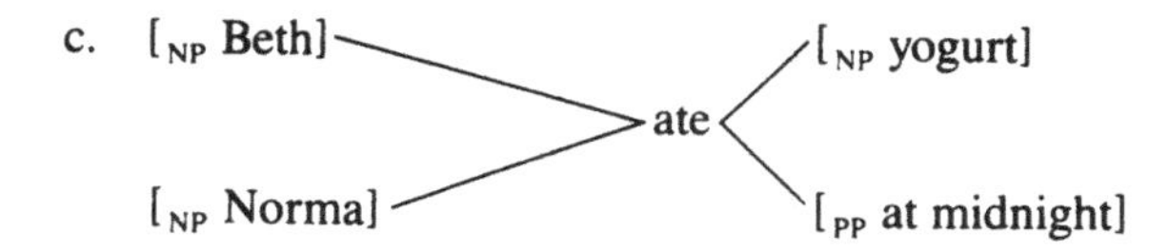

It was seen in section 2.3 that non-parallel structures such as these are ruled out without stipulation through union of phrase markers.[45] This suggests that (209) is the correct structure for (208).

I thus conclude that it is some special property of union of phrase markers which allows Gapping, since this allows us to explain the ungrammaticality of (207) and (208). If this is correct, we are faced with some unusual descriptive problems (assuming that we will be able to generate the Gapping pattern at all), many of which were noted in Jackendoff (1971), the article which initiated the study of restrictions on Gapping.

Some of Jackendoff's observations are as follows. The two component sentences may not contain unlike adverbs:

(210) *Simon quickly dropped the gold and Jack suddenly the diamonds

Unlike auxiliaries are also disallowed:

(211) *Tom will smoke the grass and Reuben might the hash

There are restrictions on what the gaps may contain; (212), for instance, in which the gap contains a verb and an object NP, is ruled out:

(212) *I want Bob to shave himself and Mary to wash himself

The material to the right of the gap is limited generally to one constituent:[46]

(213) *Millie will send the President an obscene telegram, and Paul the Queen a pregnant duck

These examples do not constitute a complete inventory of the peculiarities of Gapping. They suffice, though, to give an idea of the kind of data which must be accounted for. Notice that these restrictions are particular to Gapping; other forms of coordination appear relatively free. For instance, the sentences produced by allowing linearization as it is now formulated to apply to the structures underlying (210)–(213) are awkward, but not ungrammatical:

(210′) Simon quickly and Jack suddenly dropped the gold and the diamonds (respectively)

(211′) Tom will and Reuben might smoke the grass and the hash (respectively)

(212′) Mary and I want Bob to wash himself and to shave himself (respectively)

(213′) Millie and Paul will send the President an obscene telegram and the Queen a pregnant duck (respectively)

Our account of the restrictions on Gapping will thus focus on linearization. (210′)–(213′) show that there is nothing ill-formed about the S-structure representations of (210)–(213).

The subsequent discussion will consist of two parts. First, I will propose an addition to the linearization procedure which will enable us to generate gapped sentences. Second, I will show that this addition carries with it an account of the major restrictions on Gapping. Although there have been several valuable studies on these restrictions,[47] there has been little in the way of a formal explanation of them. For this reason, the significance of the analysis I am about to present extends beyond its empirical coverage.

2.6.1 Linking

We begin with the problem of generating the basic Gapping pattern, as in (204). Recall that this violates our general linearization procedure. Linearization, we saw, may impose an order on pairs of elements which are otherwise unordered, but it does not reorder elements in the phrase marker. In the S-structure of (204), given here as (214), *John* precedes *eats*:

(214)

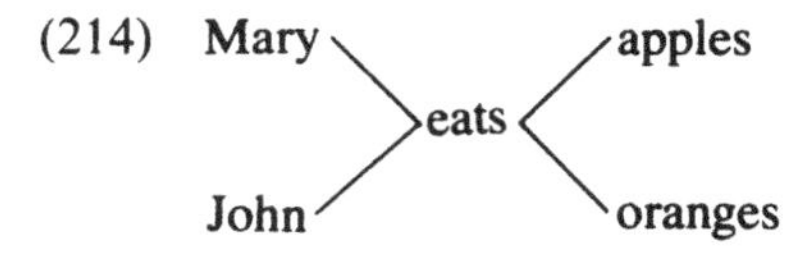

In the surface structure (204), this order is not preserved. It is preserved, of course, in the "normal" linearization of (214), as seen in (206).

Mary and *apples* here are acting as if they were a single conjunct, in that they seem to be treated by linearization as a unit. *John* and *oranges* are placed after *apples*, just as they could be if the S-structure were as in (215):

(215)

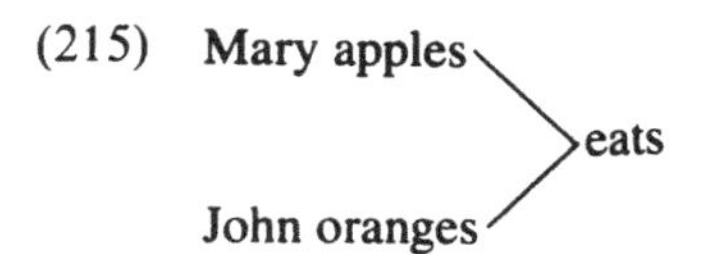

Let us account for this by saying that in a configuration such as (214), *Mary* and *apples* may be "linked" so that they will be treated as a unit by linearization (i.e. linearization treats *Mary* ... *apples* and *John* ... *oranges* as the pair to be ordered; *Mary* ... *apples* then precedes *John* ... *oranges*). A more precise formulation of this process is given in (216):

(216) In the union of the phrase markers for the sentences xyz and vyw, link x and z.

When x and z are linked, linearization must operate as in (217), rather than as in (218), as it would otherwise.[48]

(217)
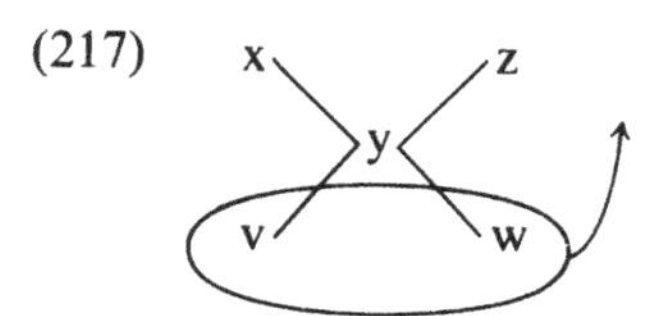

(218)
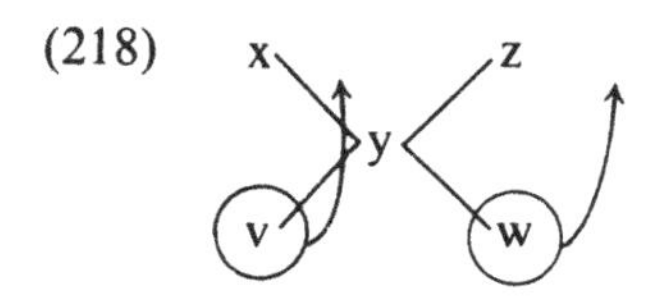

Notice that y in (217) appears to "remain in place." This is because linking requires only that v ... w follow x ... z.

Rule (216), like other rules of grammar, affects a pair of elements. We should expect it to observe other general properties of linguistic rules as well. Specifically, the pair of elements affected should be constituents, and the distance between them should be restricted. If (216) is necessary for the generation of Gapping sentences, then we should see the effects of these properties. To the extent that Gapping displays such effects, we will have evidence for the existence of something like (216). In the rest of this section, I will show that these effects are observable. Let us begin with the requirement that x and y in (216) be constituents. Consider again examples (210), (211), and (213), shown here in (219).

(219) a.
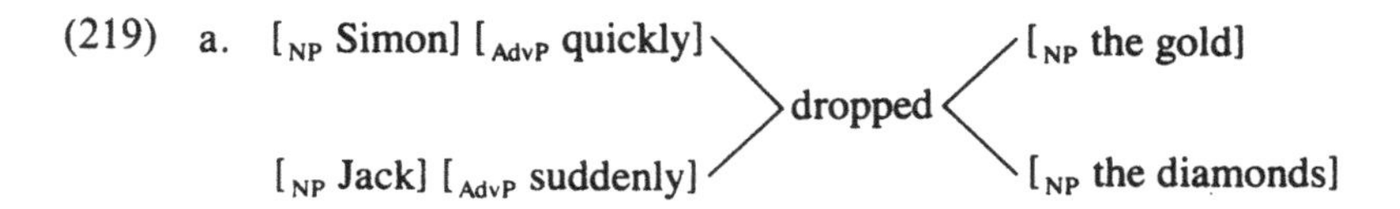

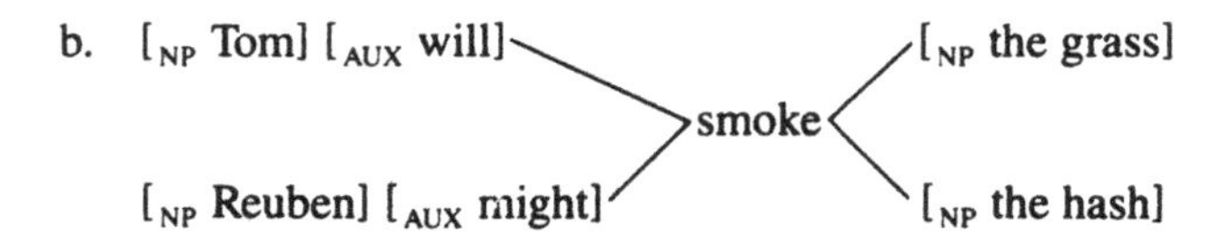

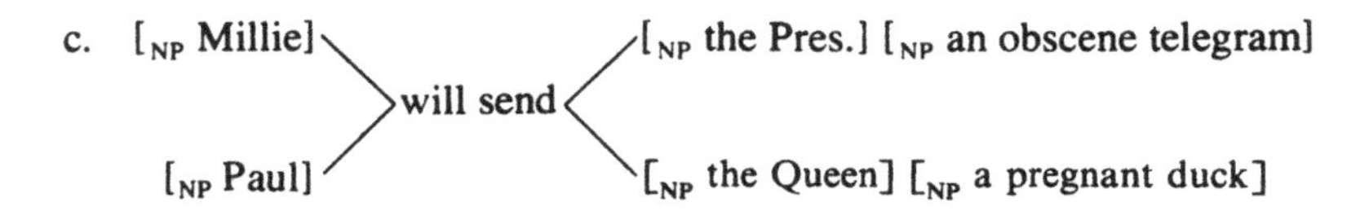

Each of these is well-formed as an S-structure, but in order to derive Gapping surface structures from them, we need to apply rule (216). If (216) only links constituents, then it will not be able to apply, since in each case one of the remnants (i.e. x or z) is not a constituent. Structures (210), (211), and (213) are thus correctly ruled out. The structures in (219) may still be linearized, though, as we saw in (210′), (211′), and (213′). In these cases, we do not need to apply (216) and thus there is no requirement of constituenthood.

Exactly the same results obtain with what Jackendoff (1971) calls "$\overline{\text{N}}$-Gapping," a construction exemplified in (220).

(220) Bill's story about Sue and Max's about Kathy both amazed me

Suppose that (216) applies not just to clauses, as in the standard cases of Gapping, but also to NP's, as in (220). We may then account for the ungrammaticality of sentences like those in (221) (also from Jackendoff 1971):

(221) a. *Bill's funny story about Sue and Max's boring about Kathy both amazed me
b. ?*Ormandy's recording of Ives' 1st on Columbia and Von Karajan's of Mozart's 40th on Angel can be recommended none too highly

I take the structure of the subject NP's in (221) to be as in (222):

(222)
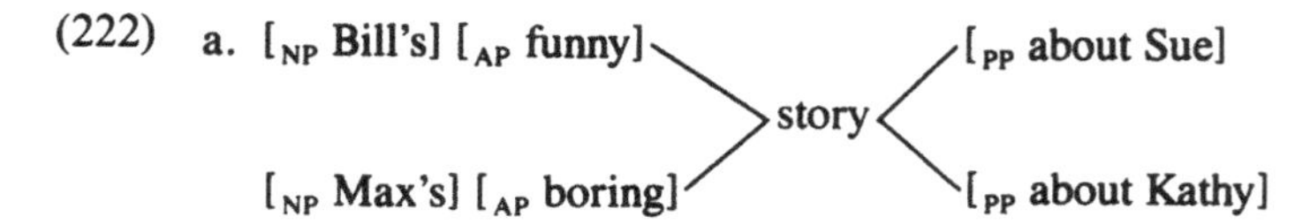

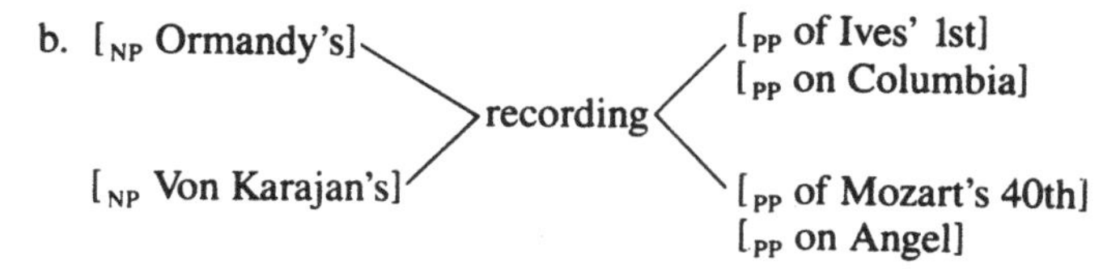

These are ruled out in the same way as (219). The left remnant in (222a) and the right remnant in (222b) contain more than one constituent and (216) is thus not able to apply. In (220), on the other hand, rule (216) is able to apply, and consequently the sentence is allowed.

The linking rule in (216), which was forced on us by our procedure of linearization, thus explains some previously mysterious facts about the remnants in Gapping structures. The requirement that the remnants be constituents was formulated previously in Sag (1976), but here this follows from the nature of rule (216).

We have seen that Gapping may occur within a clause or within an NP. It appears, though, that when (216) applies to one of these domains, it does not affect material outside of the domain. Take, for example, an $\bar{N}$-Gapping sentence like (223):

(223) Ted's wine from New York startled our friends from France and Bill's from California pleased them

This will have a structure as in (224):

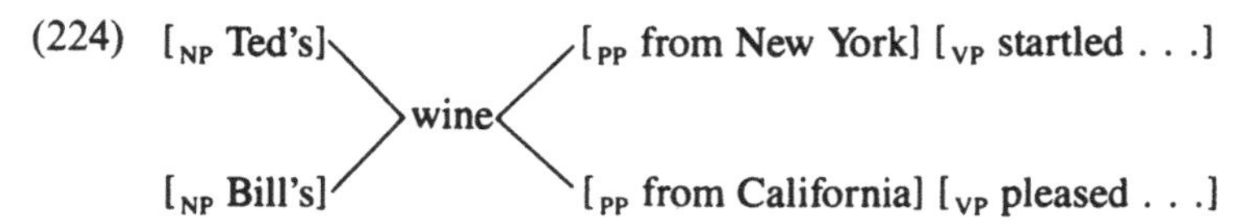

At first it might appear that (216) is not able to generate sentences like this, since the right-side remnants do not form a constituent. But suppose that (216) applies only within NP in this case. *Ted's* will be linked with *from New York*, and the VP will not be linked at all. The usual process of linearization now takes place, and (223) results.[49] Thus, just in this case, where there are remnants outside of the domain of application of (216), will we be able to get what Sag (1976) calls "multiple remnants," as in (223); (216) still rules out cases like (221).

Ordinary clausal Gapping seems to work in essentially the same way, although here it is somewhat less clear how to characterize precisely the domain of application. Nodes dominated by VP (i.e. subcategorized complements of the verb) fall within this domain, whereas non-subcategorized adverbials and PP's which are outside of VP do not. Under this formulation, (225) is parallel to (223).[50]

(225) The French drink wine at 6:00 and the Germans beer at 8:00

Rule (216) applies and links *the French* and *wine*, ignoring the external PP. Linearization produces (225). Here too, the multiple remnants cases fall out, assuming, as seems necessary if we are to account for both clausal and $\bar{N}$-Gapping, that (216) has a variable domain of application.

We should now predict that there will be yet another form of Gapping, in which the domain of application of (216) is the entire clause, including elements outside of VP. No multiple remnants should be allowed here, because there is nothing outside of the domain of application, which is maximal in this case. Compare in this regard (226) and (227):[51]

(226) John spoke with the dean on Wednesday in the garden and Bill with the chancellor on Thursday at school

(227) ??John spoke with the dean on Wednesday in the garden and Bill on Thursday at school

In (226), *John* and *with the dean*, which is within VP, are linked, and we proceed as before. The other remnants are allowed because they are outside the domain of application of (216). In (227), there is nothing for *John* to link to within VP, so the domain of (216) must be the entire clause. The remnants *on Wednesday in the garden* do not form a constituent, however, and (216) is thus not able to apply. When there is only one remnant, as in (228), (216) may apply and the sentence is consequently grammatical:

(228) John spoke with the dean on Wednesday and Bill on Thursday

The situation is perhaps even clearer in the following examples:

(229) Bill went for a walk at 5:00 and Jane at 6:00

(230) ??Bill went for a walk at 5:00 on Tuesday and Jane at 6:00 on Thursday

Only in (229) is rule (216) able to pick out two constituents. (230) may be contrasted with the grammatical (231):

(231) Bill ate a steak at 5:00 on Tuesday and Jane a hot dog at 6:00 on Thursday

In (231), as in (226), rule (216) may apply within the subcategorized arguments of the verb, yielding a grammatical sentence.[52]

Thus our linking rule (216) is able to account both for the constituenthood of Gapping remnants and for multiple remnants. It is important to note that these results have followed not from stipulation, but from the independently needed rule (216), together with reasonable assumptions about its application. This is a significant advance over previous treatments, where these facts have been accounted for in a relatively unprincipled fashion. Indeed, it has always been mysterious in traditional analyses of Gapping (where the gap is brought about by deletion) why it is that the remnants must be constituents, while no such property holds of the gap. This is just the opposite of what one would expect, since it is the gap in these analyses which is operated on and which one thus might expect to be a constituent. The remnants are simply part of the environment in the structural description of the rule. In our analysis, on the other hand, it is the remnants themselves which are operated on and which thus are constituents.

We now turn to evidence for a locality condition on (216), i.e. a requirement that linking should not apply over an unbounded distance. As mentioned earlier, this too is a general property of linguistic rules affecting pairs of elements, thus, evidence that there is such a condition on Gapping will be evidence in favor of (216).

Notice that it is not clear *a priori* what principle should constrain the distance between x and z in (216). Subjacency, for example, is generally assumed to restrict movement, something which does not occur in (216).[53] Similarly, binding theory affects the distance between antecedents and anaphors, yet in (216) there are no such notions. Here I will assume that linking is constrained by Koster's (1978) general Locality Principle, and I will show that this gives us a good approximation, at least, of the facts of Gapping.

Consider the following part of the Locality Principle:

(232) No rule involves α_{i+1}, γ (where α c-commands γ) in:
$\ldots, \alpha_{i+1}, \ldots, \alpha_i, \ldots, \gamma, \ldots$ (i $\geqq$ 1)
unless α_{i+1} is more prominent that α_i.

The subscripts indicate relative distance of the α's from γ. Prominence is defined on a hierarchy of grammatical relations, in which subject is more prominent than indirect object, which in turn is more prominent than direct object. Now suppose that this principle is relevant to the linking rule (216). Clearly x and z in (216) are equivalent to α_{i+1} and γ here, respectively. Let us take the case where α_{i+1} is a subject. (216) will only be able to apply, then, when there is no subject between the two elements to be linked, because in that case α_{i+1} would not be more prominent than α_i. I assume that a subject coreferent with α_{i+1} is not of concern here, but that only a subject referentially distinct from α_{i+1} will block application of the rule.[54] Thus application of (216) is blocked by the Locality Principle when y contains a subject distinct from x.

That this prediction turns out to be true can be seen in the contrast between (233) and (234):

(233) John promised Bill to shave himself and Mary to wash herself
(234) *John persuaded Bill to shave himself and Mary to wash himself

These have the structures shown in (233′) and (234′):

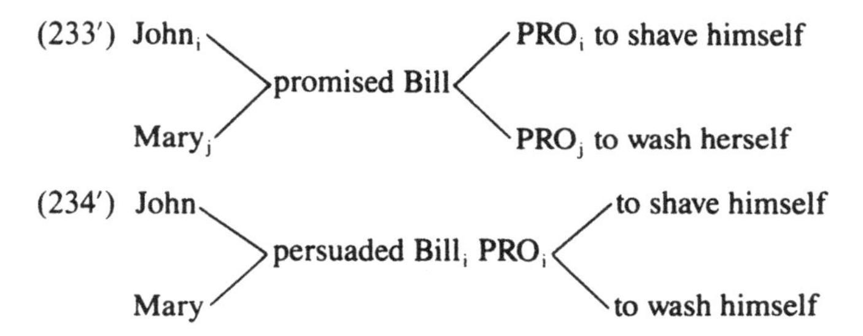

Our linking rule (216) may not apply in (234) because of the presence of an intervening subject (PRO$_i$), a situation which does not arise in (233).

The same effect may be seen with $\overline{\text{N}}$-Gapping. Consider sentences (235) and (236) and their structures in (235′) and (236′):

(235) Your boss's promise to you to raise salaries and the government's to stop inflation are both insincere
(236) *Your boss's pressure on you to work harder and the government's to pay your taxes are both hard to live with

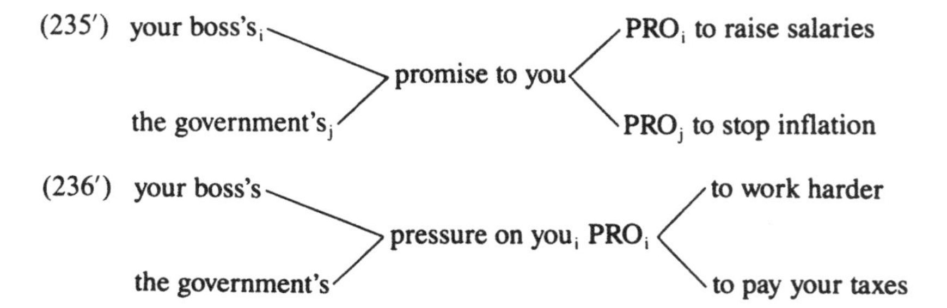

Here again the two sentences are distinguished by the absence, in (235), and the presence, in (236), of an intervening subject. Thus the Locality Principle seems to make the correct predictions about the applicability of rule (216).[55] This provides further evidence that (216) is what is responsible for Gapping.

The effect of the above analysis is quite similar to that of a condition on Gapping proposed in Kuno (1976), given here in (237):

(237) *The Tendency for Subject–Predicate Interpretation*
When Gapping leaves an NP and VP behind, the two constituents are readily interpreted as constituting a sentential pattern, with the NP representing the subject of the VP.

In (234) and (236) the remnants of Gapping are not interpreted as subject–predicate, and they are hence ungrammatical by (237).[56] For these simple cases, then, the Locality Principle and (237) make the same predictions. They should differ, though, in cases where the remnants do form a subject–predicate relation but where there is nonetheless an intervening subject. (238) is such a case:

(238) *The Senator persuaded the lobbyist to ask him to vote for the measure and the congressman to vote against it

Although the length of this example makes it difficult to get clear judgements, I believe that it is ungrammatical. Compare it with the equally lengthy, but more acceptable, (239):

(239) The Senator decided to promise the lobbyist to vote for the measure and the congressman to vote against it

The structures for these sentences are given in (238′) and (239′):

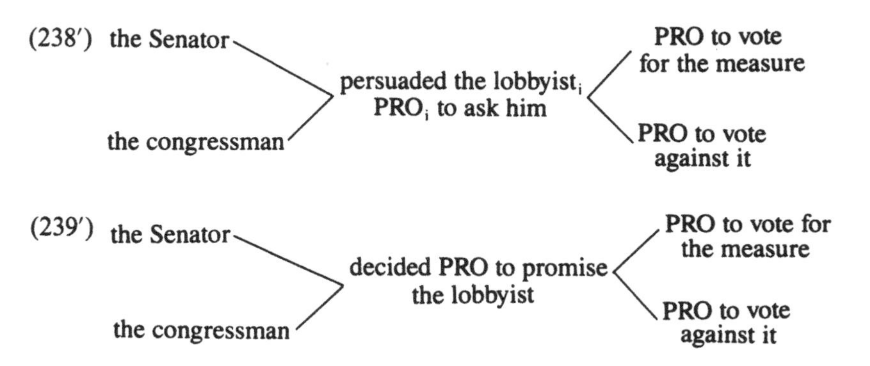

Only in (238) is there a distinct intervening subject. In both sentences, though, the remnants are interpreted as subject and predicate. Thus to the extent that the contrast between (238) and (239) is reliable, we have evidence in favor of the Locality Principle over the Tendency for Subject–Predicate Interpretation.[57]

We have seen, then, that it is necessary to add the special rule (216) to our linearization procedure in order to generate Gapping sentences. Evidence that this formulation is correct has come from the fact that Gapping exhibits certain properties which follow directly from reasonable assumptions about the operation of (216).

As with every other analysis, there are a number of things about Gapping which are not explained here. Sag (1976) notes, for instance, that the second remnant cannot be as in (240):

(240) *On Tuesday, Sam must have seemed happy and on Wednesday, must have seemed sad

It also appears that the first remnant cannot be a sentential subject:[58]

(241) *That Harry is a fool bothers Dick and that Bill is a fool Sam

A further problem relates to the possibility of getting two gaps rather than one (as in all our previous examples):

(242) Jack begged Elsie to get married and Wilfred Phoebe

It is tempting to attribute the second gap to truncation, as in (243), which we saw in section 2.2 (this is essentially the proposal of Stillings 1975):

(243) Jack begged Elsie to get married and Wilfred begged Phoebe

As Sag (1976) points out, though, this seems unlikely, since the second gap in these cases appears to be dependent on the first:

(244) Betsy believed Peter to be sexy, and
a. Alan Barbara
b. *Alan believed Barbara

One interesting fact about these cases is that we only get two gaps when the sentence would be ungrammatical with only one. Compare, then, (242) and (244a) with (245):

(245) a. *Jack begged Elsie to get married and Wilfred Phoebe to elope
b. *Betsy believed Peter to be sexy and Alan Barbara to be neurotic

The sentences in (245) are out, presumably, because of the constituenthood requirement.[59]

I leave these, and the many other problems which undoubtedly remain, to future research. This initial treatment of Gapping within the union of phrase markers approach to coordination has been very fruitful. We have been able to produce, arguably for the first time, a principled explanation for the number of remnants in Gapping and for the distance between them.

2.6.2 A language without linking?

Given the analysis of Gapping proposed above, one might expect to find a language which does not have rule (216) and which thus does not exhibit Gapping. Since (216) is an addition to the procedure of linearization, we could easily imagine a coherent system without it. It has been claimed in the literature (see Sjoblom 1980 and references cited there) that Chinese is a language without Gapping, and in our system it is tempting to attribute this to the absence of (216). Li (1985) convincingly demonstrates, however, that the lack of Gapping in Chinese is only apparent. For some reason, Gapping remnants in Chinese may not be bare nouns. This then rules out the Chinese equivalents of the most common Gapping examples in English:[60]

(246) *Laowang chile pingguo, Laoli juzi
'Laowang ate apples, and Laoli oranges'

Compare (246) with (247), where the NP's contain specifiers:

(247) Laowang chile sange pingguo, Laoli wuge juzi
'Laowang ate three apples, and Laoli five oranges'

I have no explanation for this contrast, but let us take (247) as evidence that Chinese does have the rule (216). As with English, we now predict that Chinese will exhibit effects of (216) in Gapping sentences. Li does not provide examples relevant to the Locality Principle as discussed above, but there are data showing that the constituenthood requirement holds in Chinese just as it does in English. Observe (248)–(250):

(248) *Xiaozhang hui chiguang wode dangao, Laowang hui nide pingguo-pai
'Xiaozhang can eat my cake, and Laowang can your apple pie'

(249) *Laowang zixide tiaoxuanle yijian yifu, Laoli turande yishuang xiezi
'Laowang carefully chose a dress, and Laoli suddenly a pair of shoes'

(250) *Qishui, Zhangsan maile liangping, guozhi, Lisi sanping
soda bought 2-bottles juice 3-bottles
'Zhangsan bought two bottles of soda, and Lisi three bottles of juice'

(248) and (249) are parallel to examples we saw earlier in English. In (250) two clauses with topics are cojoined. In each case, one of the elements which needs to be linked by (216) is not a constituent, thus preventing the application of this rule. This provides additional evidence in favor of (216). I leave the possibility open, then, of having a language with union of phrase markers but without (216).

2.6.3 Forward and backward Gapping

Ross (1970) distinguishes between forward Gapping, as in (251), and backward Gapping, as in (252).

(251) John eats apples and Mary oranges
(252) *John apples and Mary eats oranges

In English, of course, only forward Gapping is possible. Recall from our discussion of (217), repeated here as (253), that the forward Gapping order is forced by linearization together with the linking rule (216):

(253)

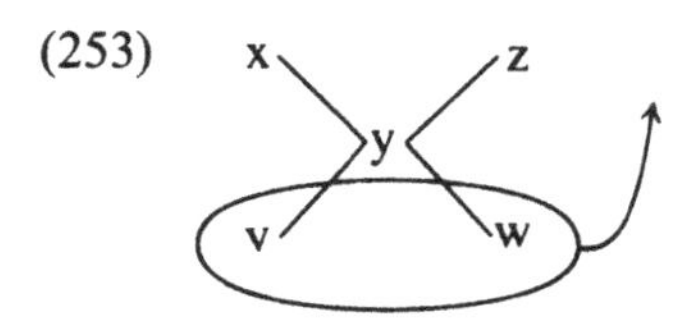

(216) links x and z. After linearization, x ... z precedes v ... w. Linearization does not directly affect y, since it is already ordered. This derives a string like (251), while excluding (252). The fact that the impossibility of backward Gapping falls out from linearization appears to be a positive result, since it is has been reported (see Sjoblom 1980) that no verb-medial language has backward Gapping.

Backward Gapping should also be disallowed in verb-initial languages, as may be seen in (254):

(254)

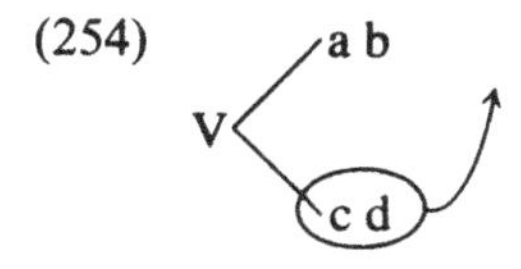

Again, the verb is not affected by linearization, so it remains in initial position. It is impossible to get a backward Gapping order like ab *and* Vcd. This also seems desirable, since there is no attested verb-initial language with backward Gapping.

The situation should be just the opposite with verb-final languages:

(255)

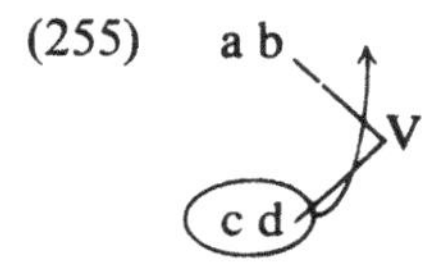

Here again the verb remains in place; the other elements are linearized to the left of it. The result will then be backward Gapping, and forward Gapping should be excluded. Although Sjoblom (1980) reports some exceptions (e.g. Basque), this prediction is correct for most verb-final languages, including the extensively studied ones such as Japanese.

We have seen, then, that linearization makes strong predictions about the kind of Gapping which a given word order will correlate with. These predictions seem to be correct, for the most part. "For the most part" is probably the best we can hope to do in this kind of exercise, since there are many variables which we (and others who have written on this topic) are leaving uncontroled. We are ignoring, for instance, difficult questions of word order in languages where the position of V is not fixed, as well as the question of the unity of Gapping phenomena. It is conceivable that a language would have a construction which looks like Gapping but which does not derive from the union of phrase markers. There would, of course, be no reason to expect that this construction would fall into one of the patterns predicted by linearization. In any event, the predictions made by union of phrase markers and linearization in this regard are clear and testable. The initial results are encouraging.

2.6.4 Gapping without linking

In the previous section we saw how simple cases of Gapping are derived in three types of languages. One interesting fact about this analysis is that only with verb-medial languages is the linking rule (216) necessary. In the other two cases linearization alone suffices to derive the Gapping patterns. We predict, then, that the unusual properties which we have seen to be associated with Gapping in English, and which I have claimed are the result of linking, will not be found with Gapping in verb-initial and verb-final languages.

There is some indication that this prediction is correct. Recall that one of the properties forced on us by linking is that only two Gapping remnants are allowed (in the general case). This was evidenced in examples like (210), repeated here as (256):

(256) *Simon quickly dropped the gold and Jack suddenly the diamonds

In a language where Gapping does not depend on linking, this restriction should not be found. Hankamer (1971) claims that in Japanese and Korean, two verb-final languages, sentences like (256) are grammatical, as may be seen in the Korean example below:

(257)	Nayka	kamcalul	ppalli,	Chelswuka	papul	chenchenhi,	mekessta
	I	potatoes	quickly	Chelswu	rice	slowly	ate

'I ate potatoes quickly and Chelswu rice slowly'

Although further work clearly needs to be done, this makes it appear that the constituenthood requirement on remnants is not valid in Japanese and Korean. If correct, this provides additional evidence for rule (216).

2.7 Subject–verb agreement

At this point we have examined in some detail the process which linearizes a union of phrase markers. We have seen that this process has two components: the general linearization principle given in section 2.2 and the special linking rule for Gapping given in section 2.6. In this section I will examine how linearization interacts with subject–verb agreement in English.

Let us begin by outlining a rudimentary analysis of English agreement. Following standard assumptions, I will say that there is a node AGR within INFL, as in (258):

(258)

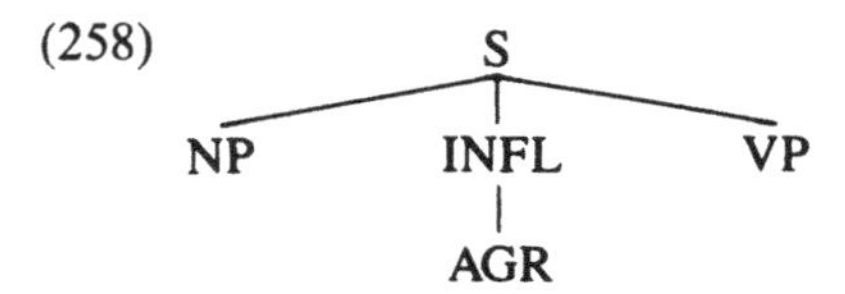

In tensed clauses, the person and number features on NP are copied onto AGR. In PF, AGR "hops" onto the verb, yielding the appropriate morphological form.

Our main concern here will be the question of the level of grammar at which the person/number features are copied onto AGR. Notice that for English it is clear that this does not occur at D-structure. Consider, for example, the sentences in (259):

(259) a. It seems that the girls have arrived
b. The girls seem to have arrived

Here we see that the verb *seem* agrees with the subject NP that is present at S-structure. If the feature copying onto AGR were to take place at D-structure, then there would be no agreement between *the girls* and *seem* in (259b). We thus conclude that the copying of the features takes place at some point "after" D-structure, i.e. at S-structure or PF.

For standard sentences without coordination, it will not make any difference whether we choose to do feature copying at S-structure or PF, since the subject–verb configuration is the same at both levels. For most sentences with coordination as well, the choice between the two levels is without consequence. Consider the union of the phrase markers for the sentences in (260), for example:

(260) John eats apples
Mary eats apples

Suppose that the conjunction for this union is *and*. At S-structure the subject of the verb *eat* is *John* and *Mary*, which, as discussed in section 2.4, is interpreted as plural. Thus if feature copying occurs at this level, then *eat* will be marked plural. Now suppose, on the other hand, that feature copying takes place at PF, after (260) has been linearized as (261):

(261) John and Mary eat apples

Here again the subject NP is the plural *John and Mary*, so *eat* is marked as plural. Thus for (260) we obtain the result that *eat* is plural regardless of whether feature copying takes place at S-structure or PF.

There are two cases, however, in which linearization does affect the subject–verb configuration, and where therefore the choice of level for feature copying is crucial. We shall see that in both of these cases, feature copying must occur at PF. The first case concerns certain kinds of *respectively* sentences, such as that produced by the union of the phrase markers for the sentences in (262):

(262) John plays the tuba
Mary sings songs

At S-structure, both *play* and *sing* have singular subjects. In one possible linearization of (262), though, this changes – as seen in (263):

(263) John and Mary play the tuba and sing songs (respectively)

Here the subject position of *play* and *sing* is occupied by *John and Mary*, which is plural. The fact that (263), in which the verbs show plural agreement, is grammatical suggests that feature copying occurs after linearization. The ungrammaticality of (264) supports this.

(264) *John and Mary plays the tuba and sings songs (respectively)

If feature copying took place at S-structure, then (264) would be grammatical.

The second case which provides evidence for feature copying at PF concerns Gapping linearizations. Consider the union of the phrase markers for the sentences in (265):

(265) John eats apples at home
Mary eats apples at work

Here the plural *John and Mary* is in the subject position of the verb *eat*. When this is given a Gapping linearization, however, only *John* is in the subject position – as seen in (266):

(266) John eats apples at home and Mary at work

If, as we have claimed, agreement features are copied after linearization at PF, then we correctly predict that *eat* will be marked singular, as in (266), and not plural, as in (267):

(267) *John eat apples at home and Mary at work

Here again, feature copying at S-structure would give us the wrong results.

Notice that the agreement facts are different if we linearize (265) as in (268), with a *respectively* reading:

(268) John and Mary eat apples at home and at work (respectively)

In this case, *John and Mary* is in the subject position and the verb consequently shows plural agreement.

We have now seen two kinds of evidence that the copying of person/number features onto AGR occurs at PF. In (263) verbs which have singular subjects at S-structure end up with a plural subject at PF. In (266) a verb with a plural subject at S-structure has a singular one at PF. In both of these cases, subject–verb agreement follows the PF configuration.

This analysis of agreement commits us to the view that the value for the feature "number" on the subject of the verb may be different from one syntactic level to the next. More specifically, the value for this feature on a given verb's subject may not be the same in PF as it is in S-structure or LF. Interestingly, there is some independent evidence that this is correct, in that an NP may have one value for the purposes of subject–verb agreement, assumed here to occur in PF, and another for the purposes of LF. For example, consider the selectional restriction on verbs such as *meet* and *disperse* (discussed in section 2.4) which requires the subject to be plural. I have assumed that this is a function of the LF side of the grammar. Some NP's, such as *that couple* and *the crowd*, qualify as plurals for this selectional restriction, but nevertheless are singular for subject–verb agreement. This may be seen in (269):

(269) a. That couple meets in the park every Sunday
b. The crowd is dispersing at this very moment

In these examples the two NP's appear to be simultaneously plural for one rule and singular for another. In our terms, they are plural in LF and singular in PF.

We can also construct examples of the opposite type, where an NP is plural in PF but not so in LF. In section 2.4 we saw that anaphors like *each other* require a plural antecedent. Let us assume that this requirement is stated in LF. Consider in this regard the sentence in (270):

(270) *Every Sunday, John and Mary see each other and kiss each other (respectively)

Following the analysis of section 2.4, (270) violates the above requirement because each instance of *each other* has only a singular antecedent (i.e. *John* and *Mary*). Thus for the purposes of LF, there is no plural NP *John and Mary*; there are only the two singular NP's *John* and *Mary*. In PF, on the other hand, *John and Mary* does constitute a plural NP. This can be seen in the fact that the agreement on the verbs *see* and *kiss* is plural, a phenomenon that we observed earlier in (263). Even though (270) is ungrammatical as it is, it becomes considerably worse if we make the verbs singular (i.e. *sees* and *kisses*); thus here again we see that what counts as being plural in one level of the grammar is not necessarily plural in another.[61]

In conclusion, the agreement facts discussed here follow immediately if we assume that the feature copying which underlies agreement occurs at PF. This means that in some circumstances a verb will have a plural subject at one level of grammar and a singular subject at another. There is evidence independent of the phenomena at issue here, as we have seen, that such circumstances do arise.

2.8 Right Node Raising

The phenomenon known as Right Node Raising (RNR), exemplified in (271), exhibits some unusual properties:

(271) Mary kissed and Jane hit that tall man in the black suit

Principal among these is the fact that the "right node" must generally be a constituent (see Abbott 1976 for discussion). This may be seen in (272), for example:

(272) *Mary kissed and Jane hit that tall man in the black suit at 8:00

This is unexpected, if (272) derives from a structure like that in (273):

(273) 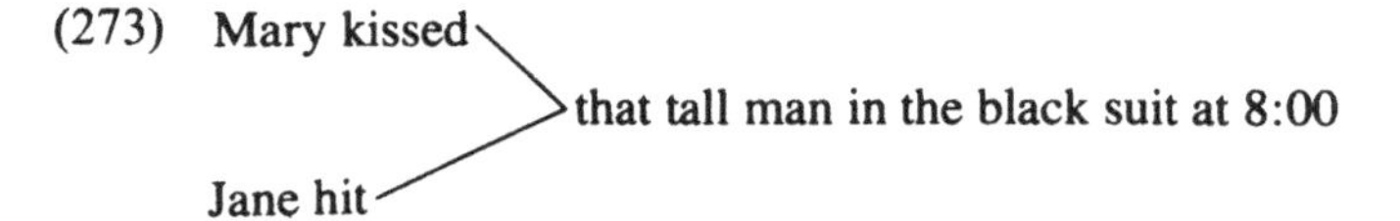

Given (273) as input, linearization should produce (272).

I have no explanation as to why (272) is impossible. I note, however, that RNR appears to be a phenomenon distinct from union of phrase markers. First, RNR may occur with both coordinating and non-coordinating conjunctions:

(274) John throws out and Mary eats, anything that happens to be in the refrigerator

(275) John throws out, whereas Mary eats, anything that happens to be in the refrigerator

Union of phrase markers occurs only with coordinating conjunctions.
Second, RNR does not obey the LCL:

(276) John throws out, and I read in the paper yesterday that Mary eats, anything that happens to be in the refrigerator

As we saw in section 2.3, the LCL is a necessary property of true coordination.

RNR, unlike Gapping, thus seems to be different in important ways from the type of coordination we have examined in this chapter.[62]

2.9 Summary

The central claim of this chapter has been that phrase markers in coordination consist of phrase markers for two or more sentences. Some pairs of strings in the set thus do not satisfy *dominates* or *precedes*. When coupled with reasonable assumptions about the nature of the rest of the grammar, this derives many of the major properties of coordination. The surface patterns of coordination follow from the fact that the output of the syntax must be linearized. The Law of the Coordination of Likes follows from the fact that a node from one component sentence may dominate elements from another. The Coordinate Structure Constraint, the Across-the-Board exceptions to it, and Across-the-Board asymmetries follow from the θ-criterion and Principle C of binding theory. Gapping requires an additional statement about linearization, but this is compensated for by the fact that many otherwise unexplained aspects of this construction may be derived from this one statement. All of this indicates that the phrase structure representation we have assigned to coordination is correct. This in turn argues for the existence in phrase markers of the type of parallel structures discussed in chapter 1.

3 *Romance causatives*

3.1 Prelude

In the previous chapter we saw how a coordinate sentence may be represented as a phrase marker with more than one string of terminal elements. The sentence in (1), for example, is represented as in (2):

(1) John sailed his boat and rode his bike

(2) {S, NP sailed his boat, John VP, John V his boat, John sailed NP, John sailed his boat, S, NP rode his bike, John VP, John V his bike, John rode NP, John rode his bike}

The phrase marker in (2) contains two distinct terminal strings: *John sailed his boat* and *John rode his bike*. In standard formulations of phrase structure, co-existing terminal strings such as these are disallowed. It was seen in chapter 2, however, that many important properties of coordination argue for the existence of multiple terminal strings in a single phrase marker.

Assuming this to be true, it now makes sense to ask whether it is also possible to have phrase markers with more than one structural analysis, that is, more than one set of non-terminal nodes. To a certain extent, this situation exists in phrase markers such as (2), where, corresponding to the two terminal strings, there are the two VP's which dominate *sailed his boat* and *rode his bike*. However, one can also imagine phrase markers which contain only a single terminal string but which nonetheless have more than one set of non-terminals.

Consider for example the union of the phrase markers for trees (3) and (4), given in (5):

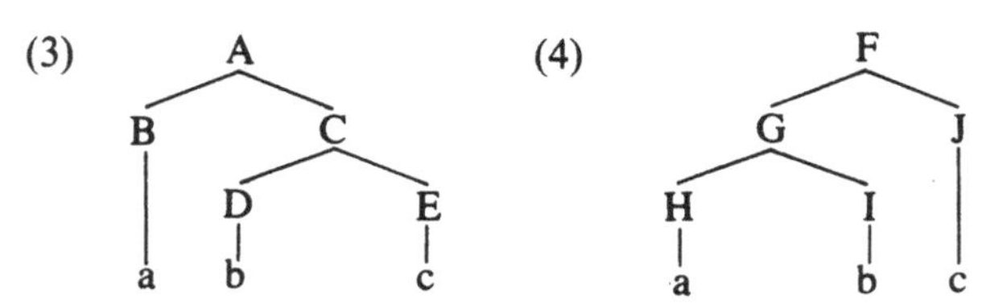

(5) {A, Bbc, aC, aDc, abE, abc, F, Gc, Hbc, aIc, abJ, abc}

Trees (3) and (4) have the same terminal string, but different structures. When they are combined in (5), however, the structures appear somewhat less different. Strings such as aDc and aIc, for instance, are equivalent if we assume category-identity between D and I (as we must, given that they dominate the same lexical item). D and I are in the same terminal environment (a__c) and dominate the same terminal elements; hence it follows that they are non-distinct. Eliminating all such redundancy from (5), we get a set such as (6):

(6) {A, Bbc, aC, aDc, abE, abc, Gc}

Here the only strings which do not satisfy *dominates* or *precedes* are aC and Gc.

I hypothesized in chapter 1 that phrase markers such as (6) should be allowed to exist by our theory of phrase structure. What this means is that the constituent C exists in parallel with the constituent G. Now although this geometric configuration may be allowed, this is no guarantee that it will in fact arise, since it is difficult to imagine a case where such a structure would be grammatically well-formed. For example, consider the phrase marker (7), configurationally equivalent to (6).

(7) {S, NP likes Mary, John VP, John V Mary, John likes NP, John likes Mary, G Mary}

Ignoring for the moment the last string in this set (G *Mary*), the tree associated with (7) is as in (8):

(8)
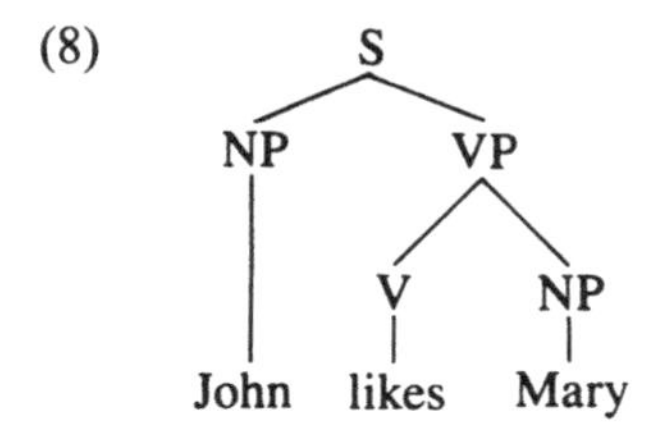

When we add G *Mary* back in, *John* and *likes* then form a constituent G, as in (9):

(9)
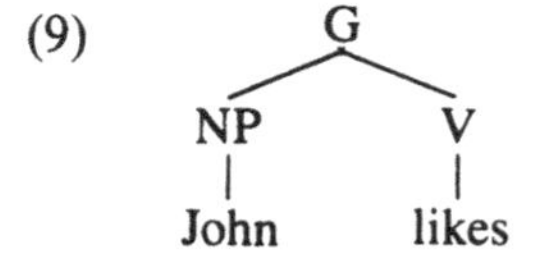

As in (6), in (7) we thus have two simultaneous analyses: one where *John* and *likes* are a constituent G, and one where *likes* and *Mary* are a constituent VP. It is clear that the analysis with VP is well-formed, but what about the constituent G? By $\bar{X}$-theory, G must be a projection of one of its daughters. Since NP is maximal, G then can only be a projection of V, let us say VP. If G is VP, then in that analysis, *John* is the object of *likes*. In the other analysis, *Mary* is the object of *likes*. Let us assume, uncontroversially, that NP-complements are only allowed when they are subcategorized for. The verb *likes* subcategorizes for one NP, and thus cannot take both *John* and *Mary* as complements, as (7) requires. Similarly, in the analysis of (7) where *John* and *likes* form a VP, *Mary* is the subject of S, while in the analysis where *likes* and *Mary* form a VP, *John* is. This also leads to deviance, since there are two NP's which receive a subject θ-role.

Thus the fact that we in principle allow structures like (7) as properly constructed phrase markers does not mean that these will be allowed by the subsystems of grammar which I am assuming. In fact, it is conceivable that all such structures would be ruled out independently, thus making moot the question of whether to allow them as possible phrase markers. I shall argue below, though, that there are phrase markers containing, as in (7), one terminal string and parallel non-terminals which do meet all other conditions of grammar and which thus are allowed to surface.

Allowing sets like (7) does not mean that any sort of structure with multiple analyses of a single string is possible. Recall from our discussion of parallel structures in chapter 1 that I use this term to refer only to pairs of nodes which do not satisfy precedence or dominance. This is the case in (7) with the monostrings G *Mary* and *John* VP, with the result that there is one analysis with the node G and one with the node VP. However, one can easily imagine simultaneous structures in which there are no such nodes. Consider again the tree in (3), repeated here as (10):

(10)

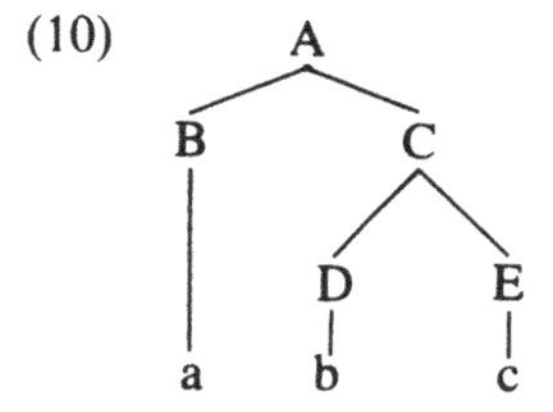

Suppose that the string abc were to have another analysis in which nodes D and E were immediate daughters of A, as in (11):

(11)

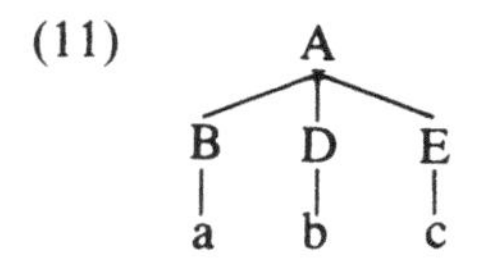

If we combine these structures, we get a set as in (12):

(12) {A, Bbc, aC, aDc, abE, abc, A, Bbc, aDc, abE, abc}

Eliminating the redundancy in (12) gives us (13):

(13) {A, Bbc, aC, aDc, abE, abc}

In (13), each pair of strings satisfies either *precedes* or *dominates*. Notice, then, that (13) is exactly the phrase marker for the structure in (10), and that it is impossible to construct a single phrase marker in our terms in which structures (10) and (11) co-exist in parallel planes.

This contrasts with the phrase marker in (6), where one analysis is as in (10), and the other is as in (14):

(14)

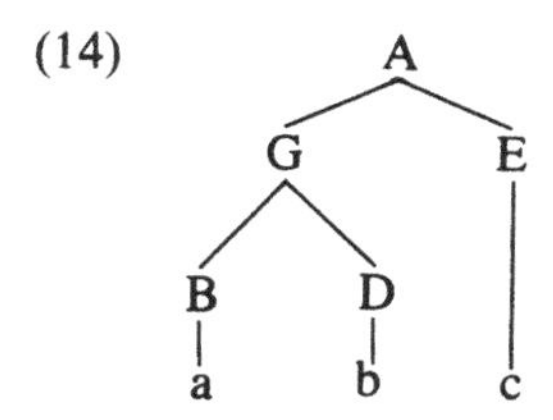

(10) does not contain node G, and (14) does not contain node C, since it is just these two nodes which neither dominate nor precede one another and hence define the two structures available in (6). In (13), on the other hand, all pairs of nodes satisfy dominance and precedence and hence there is only a single structure. This constraint on possible simultaneous structures is an important one, and one to which we will return later.

We have seen, then, that phrase markers which contain a single terminal string with multiple structural analyses are, first, generally ruled out independently by the grammar and, second, much more constrained than one might imagine. This means that only a small number of the conceivably possible simultaneous analyses will in fact be expressible as phrase markers in the system used here, and that out of this limited class, most, if not all, will be grammatically ill-formed.

In this chapter and the next I show that phrase markers such as (6) do exist in natural language; that is, that certain constructions call for simultaneous structural analyses of a single terminal string. Evidence for this position comes primarily from the causative construction in several Romance languages. I shall also argue that the limited class of possible simultaneous analyses permitted here is sufficient for the characterization of natural language phenomena. This last point, of course, cannot actually be demonstrated, but merely suggested.

3.2 Introduction

The rest of this chapter concentrates on the causative construction in Romance. This is a traditional area of inquiry in syntactic research, and there has been extensive discussion of it in a variety of frameworks (see, e.g., Aissen 1974; Bordelois 1974; Kayne 1975; Rouveret and Vergnaud 1980; Gibson and Raposo 1982). What I will argue here is that many of the basic facts of Romance causatives may be accounted for quite elegantly if we assume for them a structure of the type discussed in the previous section. Before we begin a presentation of the proposed analysis, it will be useful to review some of the major properties of this construction. My focus throughout will be on French and, to a lesser extent, Spanish, with occasional attention to Italian.[1]

The most problematic descriptive area in Romance causatives concerns the complement clause embedded under the verb *faire* 'to cause'. This clause may be either tensed or infinitival, as shown in (15) and (16), respectively:

(15) Marie a fait que l'enfant mange la tarte
'Mary made the child eat the cake'

(16) Marie a fait manger la tarte à l'enfant
'Mary made the child eat the cake'

The tensed complement of *faire* in (15), behaves just like the tensed complement of other verbs, but the infinitival complement in (16) exhibits a number of properties which are peculiar to this construction. It is these properties which will be our main descriptive challenge.

Consider first the problem of the order of the major elements in the embedded clause in (16). We see that the verb (*manger*) appears first, followed by the direct object (*la tarte*) and then the subject (*l'enfant*). This is strikingly different from the canonical order in, for example, (15).

Another peculiar property of this construction concerns the case-marking of the NP's in the complement clause. When this clause is transitive, as in (16), the subject is marked with *à*, much as one would expect from an indirect object, as in (17), for example:

(17) Jean a donné le livre *à l'enfant*
'John gave the book to the child'

In fact, when the subject NP is cliticized it shows up as a dative clitic, as seen in (18):

(18) Marie *lui* a fait manger la tarte
'Mary made him eat the cake'

When the complement clause under *faire* is intransitive, as in (19), the subject NP receives no special (overt) marking:

(19) Marie a fait rire *l'enfant*
'Mary made the child laugh'

When this NP is cliticized, however, it shows up as an accusative clitic, as seen in (20):

(20) Marie *l'*a fait rire
'Mary made him laugh'

In summary, the subject NP appears to act like an indirect object complement when the verb is transitive and like a direct object complement when the verb is intransitive.[2]

Another possibility for the embedded subject is that it may be absent altogether or appear in a *by*-phrase, as seen in (21):

(21) Marie a fait manger la tarte (par l'enfant)
'Mary had the cake eaten (by the child)'

This is reminiscent of the situation with underlying subjects in passive sentences, which similarly may be absent or in a *by*-phrase:

(22) La tarte a été mangée (par l'enfant)
'The cake was eaten (by the child)'

Kayne (1975) points out several other parallels between the "*faire-par*" construction in (21) and Passive. For example, idiomatic expressions which are non-passivizable are also not acceptable in *faire-par*. An instance of this phenomenon is given in (23):

(23) a. Sa famille a cassé la croûte
'His family had a snack'
b. *La croûte a été cassée par sa famille
'A snack was had by his family'
c. *Il a fait casser la croûte par sa famille
'He made a snack be had by his family'

When the subject is expressed outside of a *by*-phrase, as in our original example (16), these idioms are possible:

(24) Il a fait casser la croûte à sa famille
'He made his family have a snack'

All of this suggests that there is a real similarity between the status of the subject in (21) and in (22).

The final problem in the description of Romance causatives which we will consider here is the placement of clitic pronouns. At an informal descriptive level, we can say that clitics in French appear attached to the verb of which they are a complement. Thus (25a) is possible, but (25b) is not:

(25) a. Jean veut que l'enfant *la* mange
b. *Jean *la* veut que l'enfant mange
'John wants the child to eat it'

With the infinitival complement of *faire*, however, the situation seems to be much more complex. When the direct object alone is cliticized, for example, it may appear only on the matrix verb *faire*, as seen in (26):

(26) a. *Marie a fait *le* manger à l'enfant
b. Marie *l'*a fait manger à l'enfant
'Mary made the child eat it'

This is just the opposite of what the paradigm in (25) would lead us to expect, since in (26) the clitic attaches to a verb of which it does not appear to be a complement. It is not possible to state simply that the accusative clitic never attaches to the embedded verb, though, because under certain circumstances it may, at least marginally, as in (27):

(27) Marie l'a fait *le* manger
'Mary made him eat it'

The subject of the embedded clause may be cliticized onto *faire*, but never onto the embedded verb:

(28) a. Marie *lui* a fait manger la tarte
b. *Marie a fait *lui* manger la tarte
'Mary made him eat the cake'

When the embedded verb takes a dative complement, however, it does not cliticize very well onto either verb, even though its morphological form is the same as the cliticized subject's in (28). This is seen in (29):

(29) a. *Jean *lui* a fait écrire Marie
b. ?*Jean a fait *lui* écrire Marie
'John made Mary write to him'

Interestingly, the status of the embedded subject affects the possibilities for the cliticization of other arguments. When the subject is expressed in a *by*-phrase, the facts are somewhat different than above. The accusative clitic, for example, may under no circumstances appear on the embedded verb (compare (27)):

(30) a. Marie *l*'a fait manger par l'enfant
b. *Marie a fait *le* manger par l'enfant
'Mary had it eaten by the child'

Dative complements may appear on either verb (compare (29)):

(31) a. Jean *lui* a fait écrire par Marie
b. Jean a fait *lui* écrire par Marie
'John had it written to him by Mary'

Neither these facts nor those in (26)–(29) accord with the general picture on clitics in (25).

The above description of the unusual properties associated with *faire* applies as well (optionally) to *laisser* 'to let,' and to perception verbs such as *voir* 'to see,' *entendre* 'to hear,' etc. This can be seen in sentences such as those in (32).

(32) a. Marie a laissé manger la tarte à l'enfant
'Mary let the child eat the cake'
b. Marie a vu manger l'enfant
'Mary saw the child eat'
c. Marie a entendu rire l'enfant
'Mary heard the child laugh'

Our discussion will mostly center on *faire*, but the analysis may be understood to affect these other verbs too.

The questions which we must answer in our account of the infinitival complement in Romance causatives may now be summarized as follows:

(33) a. Why is the word order VOS?
b. Why does the subject receive the surface case-marking of an object?
c. Why does cliticization depart from the normal pattern?

As always, we shall not be content with merely stipulative answers to these questions; our goal, rather, is to provide some understanding as to why the facts pattern as they do and not otherwise. With this in mind, I shall argue that answers to the questions in (33) fall out naturally if we assume the phrase structure configuration for Romance causatives which will be described in the next section.

3.3 Parallel structures

3.3.1 *Faire* and subcategorization

In earlier treatments of Romance causatives (e.g. Kayne 1975) the array of data which was briefly described in section 3.2 was the result of a fairly complex system of rules, many of which were specific to the construction. I take a somewhat different approach here, in that the peculiarities of the causative construction will result from the phrase structure representation that causatives are associated with, rather than from any specific rule. General principles of grammar, in conjunction with the posited structure, will predict the range of data that we in fact find.

Let us return to our original causative sentence (16), repeated here as (34):

(34) Marie a fait manger la tarte à l'enfant
'Mary made the child eat the cake'

I propose here that sentences such as this contain two simultaneous structures, given in (35):[3]

(35) a.

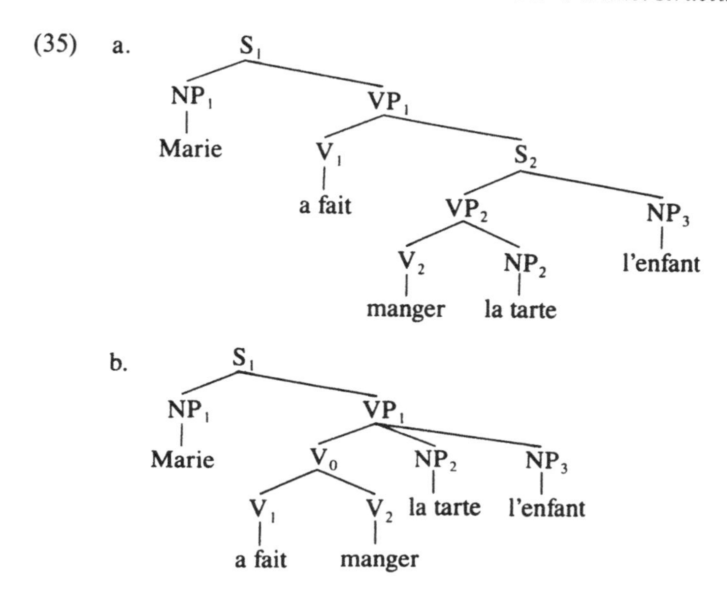

The actual phrase marker is given in (36):

(36) $\{S_1$, NP_1 a fait manger la tarte l'enfant, Marie VP_1, Marie V_1 manger la tarte l'enfant, Marie a fait S_2, Marie a fait VP_2 l'enfant, Marie a fait V_2 la tarte l'enfant, Marie a fait manger NP_2 l'enfant, Marie a fait manger la tarte NP_3, Marie V_0 la tarte l'enfant, Marie a fait manger la tarte l'enfant$\}$

In (36), neither *precedes* nor *dominates* obtains between the pairs *Marie* V_0 *la tarte l'enfant – Marie a fait* S_2 and *Marie* V_0 *la tarte l'enfant – Marie a fait* VP_2 *l'enfant*. This then is a phrase marker of the type discussed in section 3.1, where the node V_0 conflicts with nodes S_2 and VP_2. The terminal string *Marie a fait manger la tarte l'enfant* thus contains two conflicting analyses: one with V_0 and one with S_2 and VP_2. The other nodes are common to both analyses. (36) falls within the limited range of simultaneous analyses possible in this system.

In section 3.1 I claimed that even when we consider only the restricted class of parallel structures which are expressible as phrase markers, most of these are ill-formed on independent grounds. It is thus a claim of some interest to say that (36) is well-formed. In the rest of this chapter I show that structures like (36) do give rise to well-formed outputs, and that these outputs correspond to what is actually found with Romance causatives.

First let us consider the question of how (36) arises. I assume, following Zubizarreta (1982), that when *faire* subcategorizes for an infinitival $\bar{S}$ complement, it at the same time must join with another verb to form a complex verbal unit. In other words, *faire* must satisfy two subcategorization frames: $+\_\bar{S}$ and $+\_V$. Thus *faire* will require a structure like (36), since only there will both subcategorization frames be satisfied. Notice that this is all that need be said; the specifics of the structure follow from what is allowable as a set of simultaneous analyses. The fact that when V_1 and V_2 form a constituent, that constituent (V_0) governs NP_2 and NP_3, for example, follows from the fact that V_0 neither precedes nor dominates S_2 or VP_2, thus defining a separate analysis for the terminal string. Since V_0 is then not in the same analysis as S_2 and VP_2, V_0 may directly govern NP_2 and NP_3.

Another consequence of the double subcategorization of *faire* is that V_2 must be adjacent to *faire* even in the analysis where *faire* takes an $\bar{S}$ complement. The only way both subcategorization frames will be satisfied is if V_2 is in initial position within S. Following the tradition in transformational studies of this construction, we might assume that this result is effected by a rule which fronts some projection of V. This type of analysis is not really possible here, however. Since *faire* is lexically specified to take both $\bar{S}$ and V, then given the Projection Principle, this requirement must be met at all syntactic levels. If VP is fronted transformationally, then by definition it is not fronted at D-structure, thus leaving the lexical requirement of *faire* unmet at this level and thus violating the Projection Principle.

This fronting analysis is unnecessary, however, as Manzini (1983) has shown. We may assume instead that here VP is ordered before NP within the clause. This of course is just the reverse of the normal NP–VP order. Pesetsky (1982) has argued, though, that this canonical NP–VP order is a reflex of the fact that Case-assignment requires adjacency, rather than the result of a phrase structure rule. He assumes an articulated structure of S as in (37):

(37)

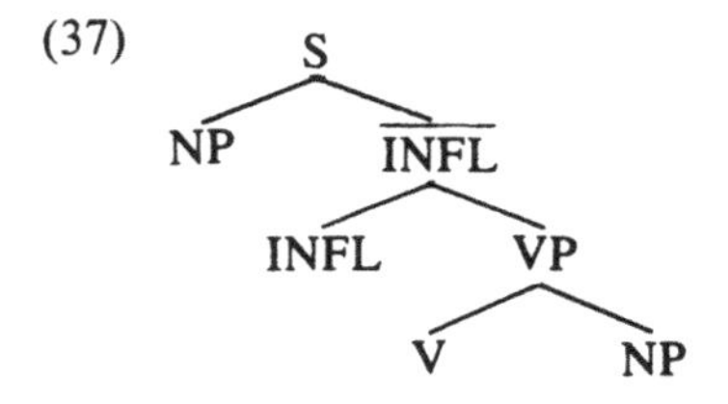

It is Case theory, rather than $\bar{X}$-theory, which determines whether NP must appear to the left or right of $\overline{\text{INFL}}$, that is, whether the structure of S is as in (37) or (38):

(38)

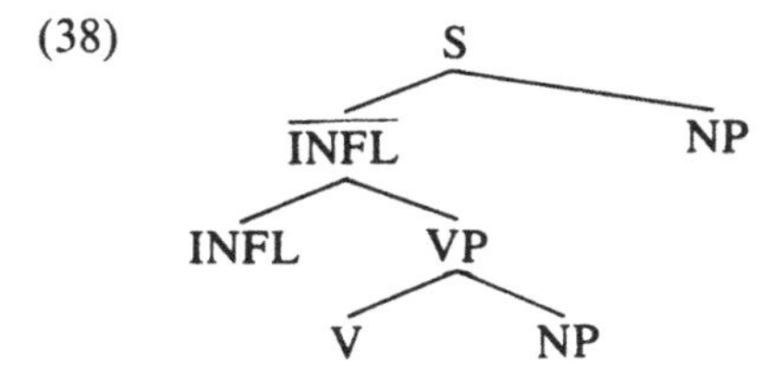

In a finite clause the subject NP receives Case from INFL. Since Case is assigned under adjacency, the subject will not receive Case in (38), where INFL and NP are not adjacent. It thus follows that (37) is the only possible structure for finite clauses.

In an infinitival clause with lexical subject NP's, the subject receives Case from outside of S (from a verb such as *believe*, for example). If the subject is to the left of $\overline{\text{INFL}}$, it will be adjacent to the Case-assigner; if it is to the right, it will not be. Thus again structure (37) is forced by Case theory.

One can imagine other ways of implementing this idea without necessarily invoking $\overline{\text{INFL}}$. Even with the traditional tripartite structure in (39):

(39)

one might be able to argue that INFL can only assign Case leftward, or that for morphological reasons it must appear to the left of VP. In any event, I will assume here that Pesetsky's basic point, that the position of NP within S is determined by Case theory, is correct. $\bar{X}$-theory, under this view, leaves the position of NP unspecified.

It follows, then, that VP may appear clause-initially, as in (35a), in order simultaneously to satisfy the lexical requirement that *faire* take both $\bar{S}$ and V. Nothing in $\bar{X}$-theory will prevent this. Case theory could conceivably prevent such a configuration, though, since we have yet to see how the subject will receive Case. Addressing this question will require some discussion of Case-assignment in general and of the Case-assigning properties of complex verbs such as V_0 in particular. This is the subject of the following subsection.

3.3.2 Case-assignment

I claimed above in (36) that the two verbs from the matrix and embedded clauses form a constituent, V_0, which is itself a "complex verb." The main empirical content of this notion "complex verb" is that V_0 may take on the Case-assigning properties of one (and only one) of its daughters, V_1 or V_2. This means that V_0 will potentially be able to assign Case to the NP's that it governs (namely, NP_2 and NP_3). This means in addition that NP_2 will potentially be able to receive Case from either V_0 or V_2, since it is governed by both. NP_3, on the other hand, may only receive Case from V_0, that being the only verb which governs it. Notice that I am assuming here that *faire* is not an Exceptional Case Marking verb, that is, that it is not able to assign Case to the embedded subject NP_3. This is a reasonable assumption, given that NP_3 never appears adjacent to *faire*:[4]

(40) *Marie a fait l'enfant manger la tarte

Faire is able to assign Case indirectly to NP_3, however, by means of V_0. V_0 may take on the Case-assigning properties of *faire*, and then assign Case to NP_3, in a manner to be made clear below.

Given the centrality of Case to the present analysis, it will be useful to look now in some detail at the theory of Case that I am assuming. This theory is standard in all important respects, but some aspects of the theory which are normally not particularly interesting become critical in the context of the structure of (36). I will now go through these aspects individually.

First, I assume that the assignment of Case by a verb is, like all rules, optional.[5] In simple examples, of course, this will not make any difference. If the verb optionally does not assign Case to an NP complement, that NP will not pass the Case Filter and the structure will be ruled out. Case-assignment thus gives the appearance of being forced in such instances. In (36), this assumption has some important consequences. Both V_2 and V_0 govern and may assign Case to NP_2. If Case-assignment is optional, then one of these verbs may withhold its Case while the other assigns it. As always, if neither verb assigns Case, then the structure will be ruled out by the Case Filter.

A closely related assumption is that NP's may not be Case-marked more than once. Again, in simple examples the effect of this is not readily visible, since a given NP is generally governed by only one potential Case-assigner. This is not true in (36), however, where NP_2, as mentioned, is governed by both V_2 and V_0. If our view here is correct, then NP_2 may receive Case from either V_2 or V_0, but not both, since in the latter instance NP_2 would end up being doubly Case-marked.

A third interacting assumption is that when a verb assigns Case, the entire Case array must be assigned. This obviously only affects verbs with more than one Case. Take the verb *donner*, for example, which we may assume assigns both accusative (ACC) and dative (DAT) Case (cf. *Marie a donné la tarte à l'enfant*). The claim is that *donner* may assign either no Case or both accusative and dative, but not just one of them. This will also affect verbs which optionally assign a second Case, such as *faire*, which may optionally assign dative in addition to accusative (cf. *Marie a fait quelquechose* (*à quelqu'un*)). This requirement means that a verb like *faire* will never be able to assign dative Case without also assigning accusative, since it would then be assigning only part of its obligatory Case array. It may of course assign accusative without dative. This assumption also, while innocent enough in the simple cases, has important consequences in (36). Suppose that V_0 takes on the Case array of *faire* (i.e. __ACC (DAT)). V_0 may then assign no Case, assign Case only to NP_2 (ACC), or assign Case to both NP_2 and NP_3 (ACC and DAT, respectively). The one possibility which is excluded is for V_0 to assign Case only to NP_3 (DAT). Note that it would otherwise be possible to do this while still satisfying the Case Filter, since NP_2 may receive Case from V_2. Under the above assumptions, though, this way of satisfying the Case Filter is not allowed.

Finally, we need to specify the structural configuration under which Case is assigned, and here again I will simply follow standard assumptions. A verb may assign Case only to NP's which it governs. Accusative Case may be assigned only to an NP adjacent to the verb, while dative Case may be assigned to a non-adjacent NP. Accusative Case carries no special morphological marking, but dative Case requires the preposition *à*, through which Case is transmitted from the verb to the NP. The Case array which a given verb has is part of that verb's lexical specification. Causative verbs, i.e. *faire*, *laisser*, and the perception verbs, are specified to contribute the Case array __ACC (DAT) to the complex verb. With *faire* and *laisser*, at least, this is the same as the Case array needed for simple clauses.

3.3.3 Summary

In summary, our proposal thus far is that *faire* subcategorizes for an $\bar{S}$ complement and a verb simultaneously, giving rise to the structure in (36), with two possible analyses. In one of these analyses there is a complex verb which may inherit the Case-assigning properties of its constituents. This verb may then assign Case to the NP's which it governs (i.e. the NP's of the embedded clause). The interaction of the two potential Case-assigners, the complex verb and the verb of the embedded clause, with the NP's of the embedded clause is constrained by general properties of Case theory.

3.4 The distribution of lexical NP's

3.4.1 Transitive and intransitive clauses

At this point we are able to return to the empirical problem of Romance causatives reviewed in section 3.2. We shall see how the analysis just presented in section 3.3 is able to account for these facts in an extremely simple way. In this section we deal primarily with the problem of the distribution of lexical NP's in the embedded clause. The distribution of clitics will be discussed in section 3.5.

To begin, let us consider the case where the clause embedded under *faire* is transitive. As discussed earlier, this has the structure in (36). Tree diagrams for the two analyses are repeated here as (41):

(41)

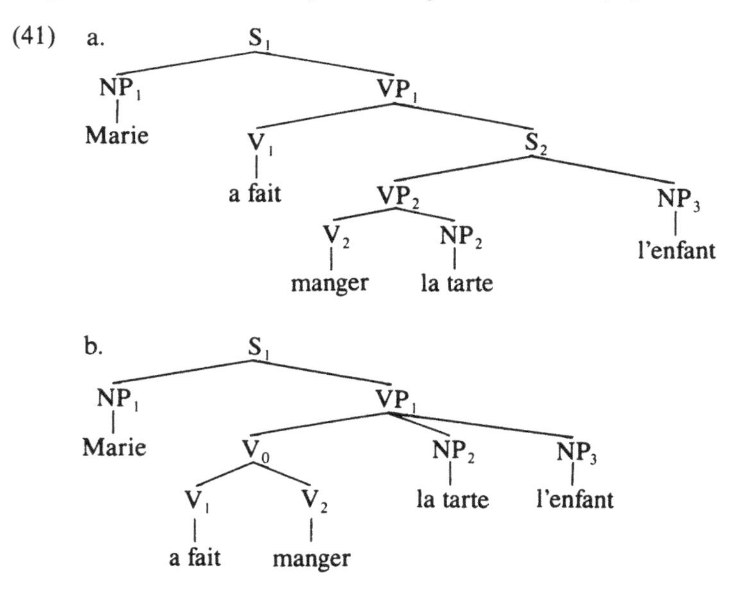

In (41a) VP is to the left of NP in the embedded clause. This order is only possible if either the subject NP does not need Case (e.g. if it is PRO) or if it receives Case from something other than INFL. We know that the subject does need Case here, since it is lexical, so it follows that it receives Case from something other than INFL (which in any event is not able to assign Case here, being infinitival). NP_3 is not governed by either V_1 or V_2, and hence may not receive Case from either of those verbs, but it is governed by V_0 in (41b). Suppose that V_0 takes on the Case array of *manger*, presumably __ACC. V_0 would then be able to give Case to NP_2, but not to NP_3. Suppose, on the other hand, that it is *faire* which passes its Case array to V_0. As mentioned earlier, I take the Case array of *faire* to be __ACC (DAT). V_0 may then assign ACC to NP_2 and DAT to NP_3. We then expect NP_3 to be marked with dative *à*, as in fact it is:

(42) Marie a fait manger la tarte à l'enfant
'Mary made the child eat the cake'

Notice that under the assumption discussed in section 3.3 that NP's may not be doubly Case-marked, we must say here that *manger* does not assign its Case, since if it did, NP_2 would receive Case both from *manger* and V_0. V_0 is forced to assign its Case, because that is the only way in which NP_3 can pass the Case Filter.

Now let us consider the case where the clause embedded under *faire* is intransitive. In our terms this would have a structure as in (43).

(43)

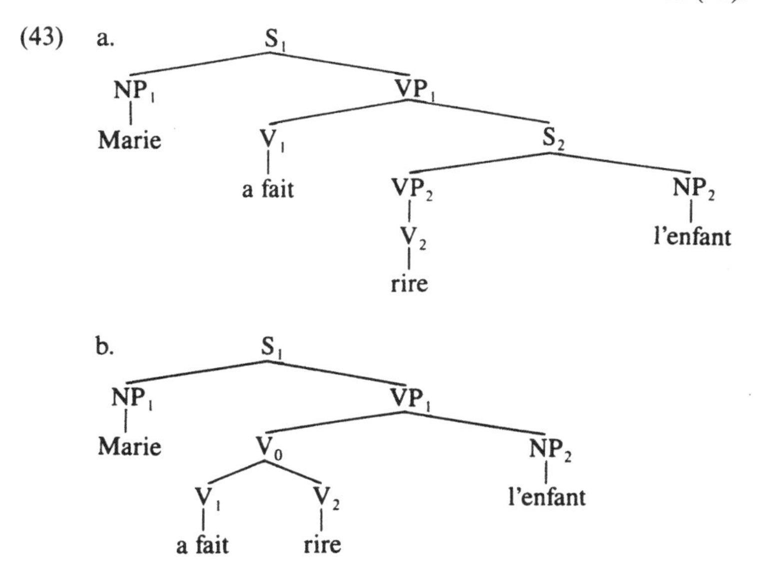

The story here is straightforward. NP_2 cannot receive Case from either V_1 or V_2, but it can from V_0. V_2 in fact has no Case to assign, so V_0 must receive its Case array from V_1. V_0 may then assign ACC to NP_2. The resulting surface structure is then as we would expect:

(44) Marie a fait rire l'enfant
'Mary made the child laugh'

The fact that the subject of the embedded clause is marked dative when the verb is transitive and accusative when the verb is intransitive thus falls out here without stipulation.

There is a class of apparently intransitive verbs which allow the subject to be marked either dative or accusative (see Kayne 1975: 210, fn. 9; Gibson and Raposo 1982: 59). This may be seen in (45) with *écrire*:

(45) a. Marie a fait écrire l'enfant
b. Marie a fait écrire à l'enfant
'Mary made the child write'

(45a) may be accounted for in the same way as (44). It is the sentence in (45b) which seems mysterious. It appears that the complex verb is assigning DAT to *l'enfant* without assigning ACC to anything else, counter to the general pattern of Case-assignment discussed above. Manzini (1983), though, claims that the verbs which pattern as in (45) generally are transitive verbs which here are used intransitively. Let us assume, then, that verbs like *écrire* (and *téléphoner* 'to phone,' *parler* 'to speak,' *répondre* 'to answer') contain an implicit object which may receive Case.[6] V_0 then assigns ACC to this implicit object and DAT to the subject of the embedded clause, *l'enfant*. (45b) is assimilated in this way to the general transitive pattern in (42). In (45a) the implicit object is either not present or does not receive Case, thus allowing *l'enfant* to be marked ACC.

This solution to the problem of (45b) is reminiscent of Kuroda's (1965) solution to an apparently similar problem in Japanese, where the subject of an intransitive clause in the causative construction is Case-marked as if it were the subject of a transitive clause (i.e. with *ni*). Kuroda's rule of "Intransitivization" has the same effect as our "implicit object." In both instances, sentences such as (45b) contain, at some level, a direct object.

3.4.2 PP complements

We may now turn our attention to verbs embedded under *faire* which take PP complements. An example of this may be seen in the structure in (46):[7]

(46) a.

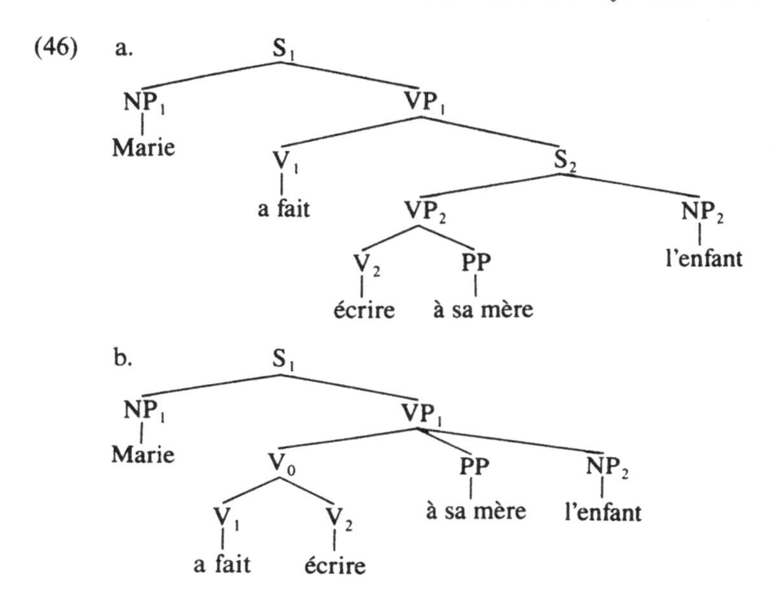

As usual, (46) is the only structure which satisfies the subcategorization frame of *faire*. Let us see how Case is assigned here. As in all of our previous examples, NP_2 cannot get Case from either V_1 or V_2. The only remaining source of Case, then, is V_0. Since *écrire* assigns no Case here (it is being used intransitively), V_0 must get its Case array from *faire*. Thus the Case array of V_0 is __ACC (DAT). Now V_0 must somehow get Case to NP_2. NP_2 is not adjacent to V_0, so it may not receive ACC. The only Case which it is structurally able to receive is DAT. Under the theory of Case assumed here, though, V_0 may not assign DAT without also assigning ACC, given its Case array. There is nothing in (46) to which ACC may be assigned, thus DAT may not be assigned either. Consequently, there is no Case which V_0 may assign to NP_2. This exhausts the possibilities for Case-marking NP_2. Structure (46) thus has no way of satisfying the Case Filter, and we should predict that it would give rise to no well-formed output. This prediction seems to be correct:[8]

(47) a. *Marie a fait écrire à sa mère l'enfant
b. *Marie a fait écrire à sa mère à l'enfant
'Mary made the child write to his mother'

(47) shows that (46) is ungrammatical both when NP_2 is marked ACC (as in (47a)) and when it is marked DAT (as in (47b)). This result follows from the analysis proposed earlier.

From what we have seen so far, it would appear that for Case reasons the infinitival complement of *faire* is simply unable to take a PP complement. This is not true, however, as may be seen in (48), noted in Kayne 1975: 203:

(48) Marie a fait écrire l'enfant à sa mère
'Mary made the child write to his mother'

L'enfant in (48) is adjacent to the verb, and as a result, apparently, is able to receive accusative Case. I will assume that (48) is an instance of PP Extraposition (see, e.g., Gueron 1980), in which PP appears to the right of NP_2 in (46). NP_2 may then receive Case and the sentence is allowed.[9]

3.4.3 PP complements in Spanish

It will be illuminating at this point to compare what we have seen in French with comparable constructions in Spanish. Strozer (1976) and Zubizarreta (1982) point out that verbs in Spanish generally may assign either ACC or DAT to animate direct objects. An example of this is given in (49) (=Zubizarreta's (88)).[10]

(49) a. Pedro lo sirvió
'Peter served him(ACC)'
b. Pedro le sirvió
'Peter served him(DAT)'

Verbs in French do not appear to have this property, however, as may be seen in (50):

(50) a. Pierre l'a servi
'Peter served him(ACC)'
b. *Pierre lui a servi
'Peter served him(DAT)'

I take this to mean that whereas the canonical Case array for transitive verbs in French is __ACC, in Spanish it may be either __ACC or __DAT. This will hold as well for the Spanish causative verb *hacer*, which can assign either __DAT or __ACC (DAT), unlike French *faire*, which assigns only __ACC (DAT).

This difference between French and Spanish, which will need to be stated completely independently of the causative construction, should give rise to a similar difference between French and Spanish with regard to structures like (46), if what we have said so far is correct. Recall that (46) is ungrammatical in French because NP_2 receives no Case. ACC may not be assigned without adjacency and DAT may not be assigned unless ACC is assigned. We have just seen, however, that this last statement is not true for Spanish. DAT in that language may be assigned independently of ACC. Thus V_0 in the Spanish equivalent of (46) should be able to assign DAT to NP_2 and the resulting sentence should be grammatical. As Jaeggli (1981) has pointed out, sentences like (47b) are in fact good in Spanish:[11]

(51) María hizo escribir a su mamá al niño
'Mary made the child write to his mother'

This argues in favor of the analysis of PP complements presented here.

3.4.4 Passive

We have seen so far that Case theory is able to predict the distribution of overt lexical NP's in the causative construction. We might ask now how this system interacts with a morphological process such as Passive, which is known to affect the possibilities of Case-assignment.

I assume here, uncontroversially, that passive morphology absorbs the accusative Case of the verb to which it is attached. I will assume in addition that passive morphology on either constituent of V_0 is sufficient to absorb Case from V_0 as a whole. That is, V_0 will not be able to assign accusative Case if either V_1 or V_2 is marked with passive morphology.

Consider, then, a structure like (52):[12]

(52)

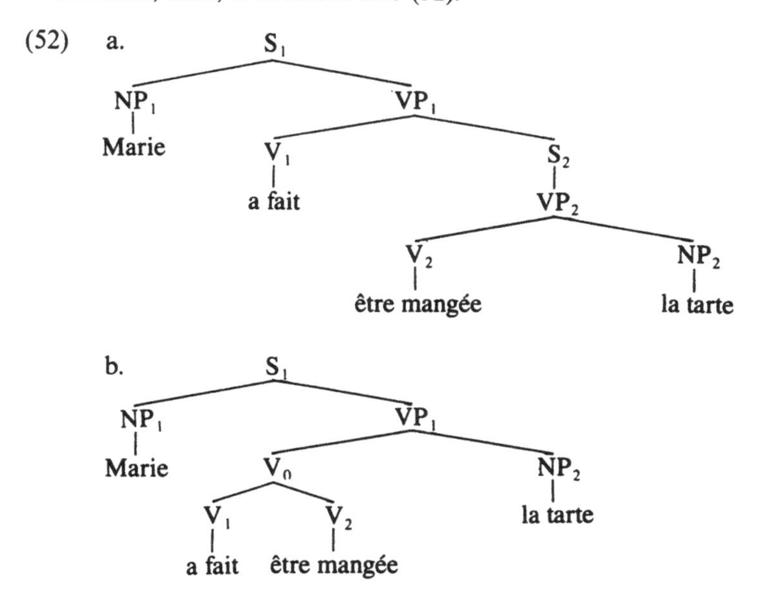

The passive morphology on V_2 prevents V_0 from assigning Case. NP_2 thus does not receive Case, and there is no empty Case-marked position to which it may move. The sentence should be out, as in fact it is, as (53) shows (noted in Kayne 1975: 251):

(53) *Marie a fait être mangée la tarte
'Mary made be eaten the cake'

Notice that the passive morphology on V_2 does not affect the status of NP_1, which remains a θ-position. The θ-criterion thus prevents movement from NP_2 to NP_1, as in (54):

(54) *La tarte a fait être mangée
'The cake made be eaten'

Now let us consider passive morphology on V_1. The relevant D-structure is given in (55):[13]

(55) a.

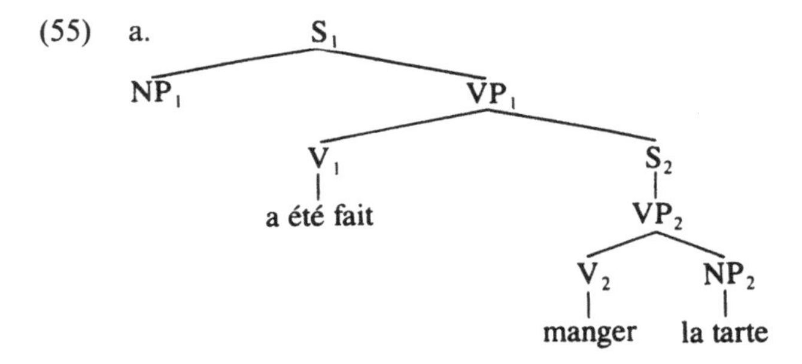

b.

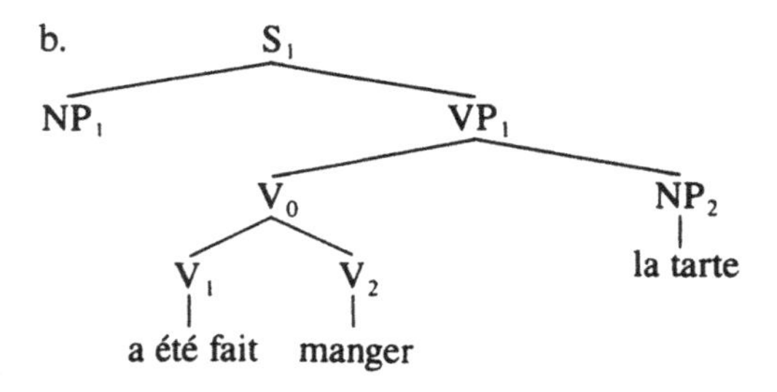

Here, as in (52), passive morphology prevents V_0 from assigning Case to NP_2. Unlike (52), however, in (53) *la tarte* may move to NP_1, where it may receive Case. The S-structure is then as in (56):

(56) a.

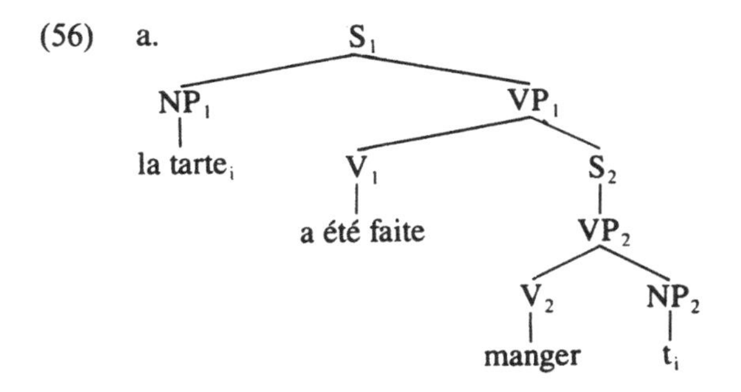

b.

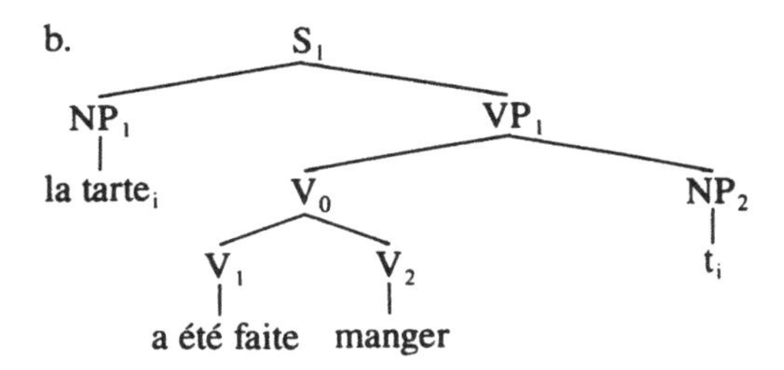

The question now is whether the relation between *la tarte* and its trace is well-formed, that is, whether t_i, as an anaphor, is bound in its governing category. According to the structure in (56a), it is not. The governing category for t_i is S_2, and t_i is not bound within S_2.[14] According to the structure in (56b), on the other hand, t_i is bound within its governing category, the governing category here being S_1.

We now run into an interesting question with regard to the operation of binding theory on parallel structures such as (56). We have seen that for a given element the governing category may be different in each structure. Is it sufficient, then, for an anaphor to be bound in one of these governing categories, or must it be bound in both? Given the theory elaborated so far, there is no reason to prefer one answer to this question over the other. It is not surprising, then, that there is cross-linguistic variation in the grammaticality of (56). If t_i must be bound in both governing categories, then (56) should be bad, since t_i is not bound when the governing category is S_2. This seems to be the situation in French and Spanish, as seen in (57a) and (57b). respectively:[15]

(57) a. *La tarte a été faite manger
b. *El pastel fue hecho comer
'The cake was made eat'

If, on the other hand, t_i need only be bound in one of its governing categories, then (56) should be good, since t_i is bound when the governing category is S_1. Italian appears to work like this, as seen in (58) (from Burzio 1981):

(58) Quei brani furono fatti leggere
'Those passages were made read'

Thus the fact that the present theory is indeterminate with respect to the grammaticality of (56) seems to be a good result. A language may arbitrarily choose one option or another for the operation of binding theory in simultaneous analyses. As we have seen in (57) and (58), the two available options are attested.[16]

The claim that the binding theory functions in Italian as described above receives further support from lexical anaphors, as in (59) (from Zubizarreta 1985):

(59) $Piero_i$ ha fatto rasare se $stesso_i$ a Maria
'$Peter_i$ made Mary shave $himself_i$'

Here, the anaphor *se stesso* is bound within the governing category S_1, although not within S_2. As expected, the result is grammatical.[17]

In summary, the effects of passive morphology on both the upper and lower verbs are predictable if we assume that this morphology absorbs Case and that Case is what principally determines the distribution of lexical NP's in the causative construction.

3.4.5 *Faire-par*

The one remaining major sentence type with *faire* which we have not yet accounted for is exemplified in (21), repeated here as (60):

(60) Marie a fait manger la tarte (par l'enfant)
'Mary had the cake eaten (by the child)'

What differentiates (60) from the other sentences we have examined is that in (60) the subject of the embedded clause is either non-overt or expressed in a *by*-phrase. It is the purpose of this section to explain how this is possible.

One potential analysis of (60) which will not work in the present system is to claim that there is an empty category, perhaps PRO, in the position of embedded subject. This would give (60) a structure as in (61) in our terms:

(61)

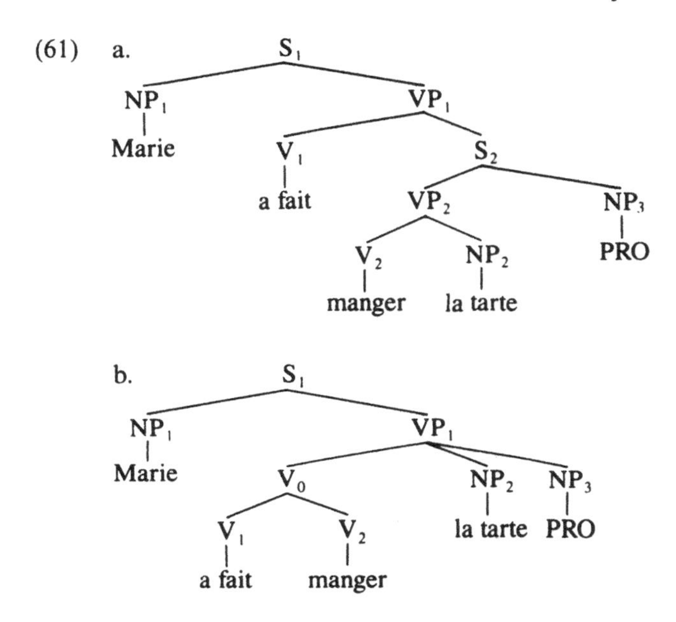

(61) is ill-formed, however. NP_3 is governed by V_0, in violation of the requirement that PRO be ungoverned. No other empty category in NP_3 would work either. If NP_3 were an anaphor (i.e. trace), it would not be bound, in violation of Principle A of the binding theory. If NP_3 were a variable, it would again not be bound, in violation of the general prohibition of free variables. Thus (61) is not well-formed with any empty category for NP_3.

The analysis which I wish to propose instead is one essentially along the lines of Zubizarreta (1985), in which *faire* may delete the subject θ-role of V_2, i.e. the verb with which it joins to form a complex verb.[18] It is not surprising that *faire* is able to do this. First, *faire* subcategorizes for V_2 and thus might reasonably be expected to be able to specify its properties. Second, we have seen that no θ-marked empty subject is allowed to exist in the complement clause of *faire*. The only way to permit a non-overt subject, then, will be if the subject is not θ-marked.

Notice that if V_2 assigns no θ-role to its subject, then NP_3 will not be θ-marked, will not be Case-marked, and will not be properly governed. This means, essentially, that no known type of empty category may appear in this position. Let us assume, then, that NP_3 does not dominate anything, and that it hence does not block formation of the complex verb V_0.[19] Instead of (61), then, we have (62):

(62) a.

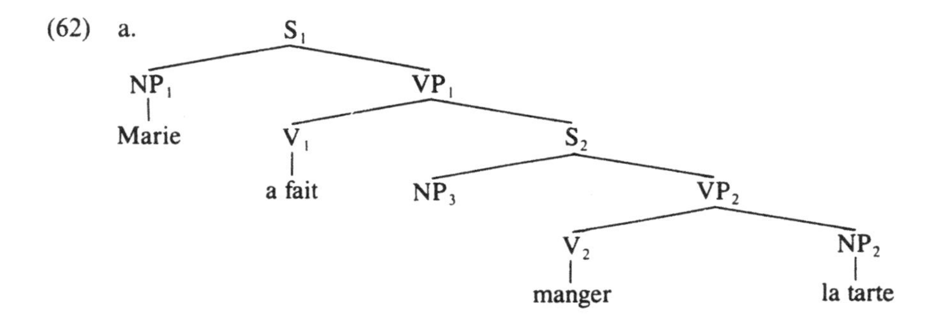

b.

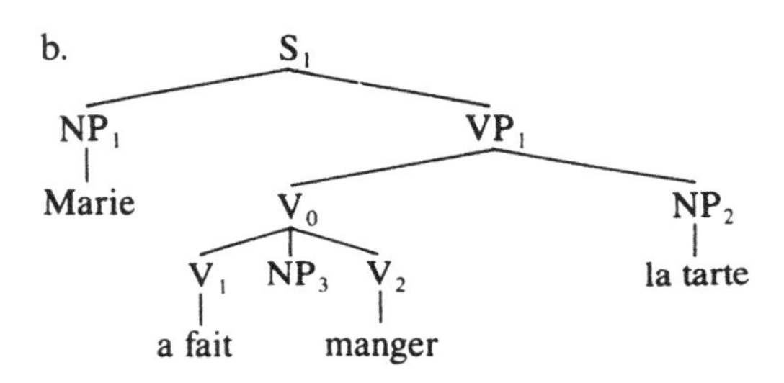

Thus, if V_2 assigns no subject θ-role, a well-formed output is possible.[20] If V_2 does assign a θ-role, on the other hand, then no output is possible unless the subject is overt.

The deletion of the subject θ-role mentioned above is exactly the same process as that triggered by passive morphology. As in the passive construction, then, here the subject may appear in a *by*-phrase, as seen in (60). In addition, those idioms which for whatever reason require the subject θ-role to be assigned will be as ungrammatical with *faire-par* as they are with Passive.[21] An example of this is given in (63), repeated from (23):

(63) a. Sa famille a cassé la croûte
'His family had a snack'
b. *La croûte a été cassée par sa famille
'A snack was had by his family'
c. *Il a fait casser la croûte par sa famille
'He made a snack be had by his family'

In (63b) and (63c), the subject θ-role of *casser* has been deleted, and thus the idiomatic reading is disallowed. As we would expect, then, idioms like these are able to be embedded under *faire* if the θ-role is not deleted. This is seen in (64), repeated from (24):

(64) Il a fait casser la croûte à sa famille
'He made his family have a snack'

A further similarity between *faire-par* and Passive will be considered in section 3.5.5.

We have seen, then, that the basic properties of *faire-par* follow from the assumption that *faire* may optionally trigger deletion of the subject θ-role of V_2. It is interesting that this solution is allowed, even expected, under the present system, whereas one involving an empty category in the subject position of V_2 is not. The former solution, but not the latter, predicts the existence of the *par*-phrase and the non-existence of idioms as in (63c). The fact that only this analysis is allowed here is, of course, a positive result.

3.4.6 Summary

This concludes our discussion of the distribution of lexical NP's in Romance causatives. We have been able to account for a fairly complex range of data in a straightforward and plausible way.

We may now answer the first two of the questions posed in (33) above. First, the word order of the complement of *faire* is VOS because only in that way may *faire* subcategorize for both a clause and a verb. Second, the subject of the complement clause is Case-marked as an object because it receives its Case from the complex verb (of which *faire* is a part) which governs it. This is the only way for the subject to get Case. An answer to the third question, concerning the distribution of clitics, is provided in the following section.

3.5 The distribution of clitic pronouns

3.5.1 A theory of clitics

I now turn to what traditionally has been the most problematic area in the description of Romance causatives: the positioning of clitics. As mentioned in section 3.2, there are two main problems we must face. One is that clitics often appear attached to *faire* rather than to the verb of which they seem to be a complement. This runs counter to the general pattern of clitics in French. The other problem is that there seem to be some peculiar restrictions on when a clitic may appear on the lower verb, as exemplified in the contrast between (65a) and (65b) (repeated from (26a) and (27), respectively):

(65) a. *Marie a fait *le* manger à l'enfant
'Mary made the child eat it'
b. Marie l'a fait *le* manger
'Mary made him eat it'

Thus even if we are able to account for the appearance of clitics on *faire*, we are still left with the problem of determining which clitics may appear on which verb.

I argue in this section that solutions to these problems follow straightforwardly from the analysis of causatives developed above, given an adequate theory of clitics. The theory of clitics which I adopt here is essentially that of Borer (1983) and Jaeggli (1981). The crucial aspects of this theory may be stated quite simply: clitics receive Case from the verb to which they are attached and this verb governs an empty category in an object position with which the clitic is associated. Consider, for example, a sentence like (66):

(66) Marie *l*'a mangé[e]
'Mary ate it'

The clitic *le* receives accusative Case from the verb *manger*. The NP object which *manger* subcategorizes for thus does not receive Case, and consequently may not be lexically filled. Although this position does not itself receive Case, it is associated with a Case-bearing element, namely, the clitic. We may think of this association between the clitic and the empty NP as being a chain, but all that is necessary for this analysis is that the two be associated in some way. The precise nature of this association and of the position occupied by the clitic is an interesting question (see Sportiche 1983 for recent discussion), but it need not be solved in advance of the analysis to be presented here.

I claimed in section 3.4 that Case plays a crucial role in determining the distribution of lexical NP's. In the theory of clitics just described, similarly, it is the assignment of Case which allows a clitic to appear on a verb. Since the properties of Case-assignment in the causative construction have already been worked out in some detail, the distribution of clitics should now trivially follow. This is indeed the case, as we shall presently see. In fact, clitics will provide a stronger confirmation of our analysis than was possible with lexical NP's, since clitics show overtly which verb is assigning Case.

3.5.2 Transitive clauses

Let us begin with transitive clauses embedded under *faire*. In this case, there are two arguments which are potentially cliticizable (the subject and object of the lower verb) and two verbs which potentially take clitics (the complex verb, V_0, and the embedded verb, V_2). These two verbs may take clitics by virtue of the fact that they assign Case.[22] We can now discuss the interaction of the two verbs with the two arguments.

Consider first the subject argument. This may only cliticize onto V_0 because that is the only verb which governs the subject position. We thus do not find the subject cliticized onto V_2:

(67) a. *Marie a fait *lui* manger la tarte
b. *Marie a fait *le* manger la tarte
'Mary made him eat the cake'

If the subject is cliticized on V_0, however, V_0 may then assign ACC to *la tarte* and DAT to the clitic, yielding (68):

(68) Marie *lui* a fait manger *la tarte*
'Mary made him eat the cake'

Case-assignment here works in essentially the same way as in the non-cliticized version in (69), repeated from (42):

(69) Marie a fait manger *la tarte à l'enfant*
'Mary made the child eat the cake'

In (69) as well, the complex verb assigns both ACC and DAT.

Now consider the object argument. Unlike the subject, it is governed by the lower verb and thus should be able to cliticize onto it. Suppose that this happens, as in (70):[23]

(70) *Marie a fait *le* manger *à l'enfant*
'Mary made the child eat it'

Manger assigns ACC to *le*. Now we have the familiar problem of getting Case to the subject, but here there is no solution. *L'enfant* is not in the right position to receive ACC, and V_0 may not assign DAT without also assigning ACC. Since V_0 is the only potential Case-assigner for the subject, *l'enfant* is thus left without Case. Hence we derive the ungrammaticality of (70).

If *le* is attached to V_0, though, the problem of assigning Case to *l'enfant* will be solved. The complex verb may now assign ACC to *le* and DAT to *l'enfant*, in accord with its Case array. As predicted, then, the result is grammatical:[24]

(71) Marie *l*'a fait manger *à l'enfant*
'Marie made the child eat it'

The placement of *le* here shows that it is the complex verb which is assigning accusative Case.

In the examples we have seen so far, the only allowable position for clitics has been on the complex verb. This has not been the result of a stipulation about the placement of clitics, but rather it has followed from principles of Case-assignment. The subject may cliticize only onto the complex verb because that is the only verb from which it may get Case. The object may cliticize onto the lower verb, but if it does, then the subject will not get Case. This situation is exactly parallel to (69), where the only allowable output, I have claimed, is when both arguments receive Case from V_0. The behavior of clitics shows this overtly.

There is one way in which clitics and overt NP's differ, however. I stated in section 3.5.1 that the verb assigns Case directly to the clitic. By implication, the position of the empty category associated with the clitic should not matter for purposes of Case-assignment, as long as it is governed by the verb. Specifically, a verb should be able to assign accusative Case to a clitic even if the empty category associated with that clitic is not adjacent to the verb. This can be tested with the downstairs subject. Suppose that the object is cliticized onto *manger*, as in (70). We have seen already that V_0 may not assign DAT to the subject here. ACC may not be assigned either, because *l'enfant* is not adjacent to the verb. If the subject is a clitic, however, adjacency should not matter, and ACC should be available. This is seen in (72):[25]

(72) Marie *l*'a fait *le* manger
'Mary made him eat it'

The first clitic, attached to V_0, is the subject and the second, attached to V_2, is the object. (72) appears to be acceptable to some speakers and marginal for others. This result is not surprising in the present framework.

With those speakers for whom the adjacency requirement on Case-assignment applies even to the empty categories associated with clitics, even though Case may not be directly assigned to that empty category, (72) will be bad. With those for whom this does not hold, (72) will be good. (73) has a similar status:

(73) Marie *l'*a fait manger *la tarte*
'Mary made him eat the cake'

The NP *la tarte* receives Case from *manger* and the clitic *le* receives Case from V_0. Unlike the other examples we have seen, then, (72) and (73) do not follow the Case-assignment pattern of sentences with lexical NP's, such as (69), but this difference follows from an independently motivated distinction in the way that clitics and lexical NP's receive Case.

(72) is the first example we have seen where both arguments are cliticized. We predict that this should also be possible when V_0 assigns ACC and DAT. This is seen in (74) (noted in Kayne 1975: 269):

(74) Marie *le lui* a fait manger
'Mary made him eat it'

The accusative clitic *le* is associated with an empty category which is adjacent to V_0, so (74) does not have the marginal status of (72) and (73). As expected, (74) contains one accusative and one dative clitic, reflecting the Case array of the complex verb. Clitic patterns such as (75) are hence disallowed:

(75) *Marie *les l'*a fait manger
'Mary made them eat it'

since V_0 is unable to assign ACC-ACC.[26]

3.5.3 Intransitive clauses

Cliticization with embedded intransitive verbs also follows straightforwardly from our analysis. Recall that in sentences like (76), repeated from (44):

(76) Marie a fait rire *l'enfant*
'Mary made the child laugh'

the subject of the complement clause, *l'enfant*, is governed by and receives accusative Case from the complex verb. It, of course, is not governed by the embedded verb, *rire*. As expected then, the clitic may appear on the complex verb, but not on *rire*:

(77) a. Marie *l'*a fait rire
b. *Marie a fait *le* rire
'Mary made him laugh'

Here again, the placement of clitics mirrors exactly the assignment of Case within the complement.

3.5.4 PP complements

In section 3.4.2 we saw that a PP complement of the embedded verb in effect prevents Case from being assigned to the subject. ACC may not be assigned because the subject is not adjacent to the verb, and DAT in French may not be assigned without previously assigning ACC. Unless the PP is extraposed, there is no well-formed output within the grammatical system presented here.

This situation does not change when the PP complement is cliticized.[27] The empty category associated with this clitic will still be adjacent to the verb, thus preventing the subject from receiving Case. Consider (78) for example (noted in Kayne 1975: 283).

(78) a. *Marie *lui* a fait écrire *l'enfant*
b. *?Marie a fait *lui* écrire *l'enfant*
'Mary made the child write to him'

In both (78a) and (78b) the empty category complement of *écrire* intervenes between the complex verb and *l'enfant*, thus blocking Case-assignment. (78b) seems to be somewhat better than (78a), but both are unacceptable.

In our terms, then, the source of the ungrammaticality of (78) is the Case Filter, which rules (78) out by virtue of the fact that the embedded subject does not receive Case. The clitic *lui* by itself, on the other hand, is well-formed. It may receive Case from either *écrire* or the complex verb, and hence may appear on either one. We predict, then, that in sentences where the embedded subject does not need Case, cliticization of the PP complement should be freely allowed.

There are two constructions in which this situation arises. One is *faire-par*, discussed in section 3.4.5, where the embedded verb assigns no subject θ-role and thus need not assign Case to the subject position. *Lui* should be able to cliticize freely, and this seems to be true, essentially, as seen in (79):[28]

(79) a. Marie *lui* a fait écrire (par l'enfant)
b. Marie a fait *lui* écrire (par l'enfant)
'Mary made write to him (by the child)'

(79a) is preferred over (79b), but both seem to be possible. The complex verb does not assign accusative Case to anything here, so it doesn't matter that the empty category associated with *lui* is adjacent to *écrire*.

Another relevant example concerns embedded unaccusative/ergative verbs, which do not assign a θ-role to subject position. This subject position, then, does not require Case. The object is able to receive Case from V_0, as in (80):

(80) Dieu a fait apparaître *la Vierge* aux enfants
'God made the Virgin appear unto the children'

where *la Vierge* receives accusative Case from V_0. Since *la Vierge* is the object of *apparaître*, it is adjacent to it, as required. *La Vierge* is thus able to receive Case regardless of the status of the PP complement. As expected, then, the PP complement may cliticize onto either verb, as seen in (81):

(81) a. Dieu *leur* a fait apparaître *la Vierge*
(from Gibson and Raposo 1982)
b. Dieu a fait *leur* apparaître *la Vierge*
'God made the Virgin appear unto them'

Here, as in (79), but not (78), the Case Filter is satisfied.

Thus the peculiar behavior of these dative clitics is predicted by our analysis. They are allowed only when they do not interfere in assigning Case to the subject NP. This means, loosely speaking, that they are allowed only when there is no lexical subject.

3.5.5 *Faire-par*

In section 3.4.5, we saw that the so-called *faire-par* construction is the result of *faire* optionally deleting the subject θ-role of the embedded verb (i.e. the verb which it subcategorizes for). We saw that in this respect *faire* has the same effect as passive morphology. In this section, I will examine the behavior of clitics in this construction. Since by definition there is no subject argument here, our attention will focus on the object clitic.

Having seen that Passive and *faire* are alike in their ability to delete a subject θ-role, we may now ask whether they are alike in other ways as well. Notably, Passive has the additional property of "absorbing" accusative Case, i.e. preventing the verb from assigning accusative Case. Chomsky (1981: 124) suggests that the co-occurrence in the passive morpheme of these two properties, deleting the subject θ-role and absorbing Case, is not coincidental. He and Burzio (1981) discuss the observation in (82), which appears to be largely correct:

(82) A verb that assigns Case to its object assigns a θ-role to its subject. (=Chomsky's 2.6.39)

Thus there do not appear to be verbs which assign no subject θ-role but which do assign objective Case. What we generally find instead are verbs like *hit*, which assigns a subject θ-role and accusative Case, and passive forms like *was hit*, which assigns no subject θ-role and no accusative Case.

Let us suppose that (82) is true and that there is some reason why these properties are connected. The dual properties of Passive, then, are simply an instance of this generalization. *Faire* should then act in the same way. Aside from deleting the subject θ-role of its sister verb, it should also suppress its accusative Case. Consider, for example, our sentence (83), repeated from (60):

(83) Marie a fait manger *la tarte* (par l'enfant)
'Mary made eat the cake (by the child)'

We must now say that *manger* cannot assign accusative Case, since it has been absorbed by *faire*. As with Passive, though, here also there is a way to give Case to the object NP. In Passive this is done by moving the NP to a Case-marked position, but here this is not necessary (or possible). What happens instead is that *la tarte* is able to receive Case from its other governor, namely V_0. In this way sentences like (83) may satisfy the Case Filter, even though *manger* does not assign Case.

If the above is correct, then we should be able to see the effects of (82) quite clearly with clitics. Since the object is only able to receive Case from the complex verb, and not from the embedded verb, the object clitic should likewise appear only on the complex verb and not on the embedded verb. These are exactly the effects which obtain, as seen in (84) (noted in Rouveret and Vergnaud 1980):

(84) a. Marie *l*'a fait manger
b. *Marie a fait *le* manger
'Mary had it eaten'

(84b) represents just what (82) disallows. *Manger* assigns Case, as evidenced by the clitic *le*, but does not assign a θ-role to the subject. Since we are saying that when *manger* assigns no subject θ-role it also assigns no accusative Case, this state of affairs is ruled out.

The ungrammaticality of (84b), then, falls out very simply from what is plausibly a general constraint on the properties of verbs. To the extent that our analysis of the contrast in (84) works, it provides further evidence for the validity of something like (82).

3.5.6 Reflexive *se*

One clitic which we have not yet discussed, but which may be neatly accounted for with the analysis presented so far, is the reflexive clitic *se*. I will adopt here an analysis like that of Wehrli (1984), in which reflexive *se* has the property of absorbing the object argument.[29] This differs crucially from the other object clitics we have seen, which absorb Case but leave the argument itself intact. Reflexive *se*, unlike these other clitics, thus has no empty category associated with it.

Given this analysis, the interaction of *se* with the causative construction now follows without stipulation. Consider first reflexive *se* attached to the embedded verb. As Wehrli points out, this makes the verb effectively intransitive, since it has no object, either overt or empty. Just as with simple intransitive verbs, then, the subject is adjacent to the (complex) verb and is hence marked accusative. This is seen in (85) (from Wehrli):

(85) Jean a fait *se* laver *Marie*
'John made Mary wash herself'

Notice that *Marie* is adjacent to the complex verb because there is no empty category in the object position of *laver*. With a clitic which does have an empty category, the facts come out quite different. In (86), for example,

(86) *Jean a fait *le* laver (à) *Marie*
'John made Mary wash it'

laver does have an empty object. *Marie* is thus not adjacent to the complex verb and cannot get Case.

Now let us consider reflexive *se* attached to the complex verb. Since the complex verb is not lexical, it does not itself subcategorize for NP arguments. It does govern arguments, though, as we have seen in previous discussion. The effect of attaching *se*, then, will be to prevent the complex verb from governing a direct object (i.e. adjacent) complement. This will, in turn, prevent the lower verb from taking a direct object, since the direct object of the lower verb is also the direct object of the complex verb. Sentences such as (87), in which the complex verb does govern an adjacent NP, are hence disallowed:[30]

(87) *Jean *s*'est fait laver *Marie*
'John made Mary wash him'

The crucial difference, then, between (85) and (87) is that in (85) *laver* is prevented from taking a direct object argument, but the complex verb may, whereas in (87) neither verb may take a direct object. Thus *Marie* is allowed in (85), as the object of V_0, but not in (87), where it cannot be the object of either verb.

If we eliminate the argument *Marie* in (87), though, the sentence should be grammatical; (88) shows that in fact this is true:

(88) Jean *s*'est fait laver (par Marie)
'John had himself washed (by Mary)'

Se here absorbs the object argument of the complex verb and, as a consequence, of *laver*.

As promised, then, the possibilities for the cliticization of *se* fall out from the analysis developed so far.

3.5.7 Clitics in Spanish

It was argued in section 3.4.3 that the Case array of the Spanish causative verb *hacer* may be either __ACC (DAT), as in French, or simply __DAT. This allows the assignment of Case in causatives in Spanish to be slightly more flexible than in French. In a sentence like (89), for example:

(89) María hizo comer el pastel al niño
'Mary made the child eat the cake'

there are two ways for Case to be assigned. First, V_0 may assign ACC and DAT to *el pastel* and *el niño*, respectively, as in French. The second way is for *comer* to assign ACC to *el pastel* and for V_0 to assign DAT to *el niño*, as is allowed by its Case array. Recall that this last possibility is excluded in French. If the lower verb assigns Case to its object, then there is no way for the subject to get Case.

As usual, we can expect the placement of clitics to display these two ways of Case-assignment overtly. This is shown in (90) (noted in Zubizarreta 1982):[31]

(90) a. María *se lo* hizo comer
b. María *le* hizo comer*lo*
'Mary made him eat it'

(90a) is just like the French pattern.[32] The complex verb assigns ACC to the clitic *lo* and DAT to *se.* In (90b) the lower verb *comer* assigns ACC and the complex verb assigns DAT. This may be compared with French (91) (noted in Kayne 1975: 270):

(91) *Marie *lui* a fait *le* manger
'Mary made him eat it'

It is a striking fact that the contrast between (90b) and (91) may be derived from a difference between the two languages in Case-assignment which is needed independently.[33]

Another area where this difference should have an effect is in the cliticization of PP complements. We saw in section 3.4.3 that Spanish allows sentences like (51), repeated here as (92):

(92) María hizo escribir a su mamá al niño
'Mary made the child write to his mother'

The complex verb assigns DAT to the subject, *el niño.* Sentences with a cliticized PP complement, as in (93), should be good in the same way:[34]

(93) a. *María *le* hizo escribir *al niño*
b. María hizo escribir *le al niño*
'Mary made the child write to him'

(93a) is out, presumably because the complex verb must assign DAT twice (to *le* and to *el niño*), in violation of its Case array. In (93b) *escribir* assigns DAT to *le* and V_0 assigns DAT to *el niño.* This is, predictably, impossible in French, as we see in (94) (see also (78b)):[35]

(94) ?*Marie a fait *lui* écrire *à l'enfant*
'Mary made the child write to him'

This contrast also follows from the difference between French and Spanish discussed above.

3.5.8 Conclusion

We have now answered the third and final question posed in section 3.2 concerning the patterning of clitics in Romance causatives. It was seen there that the behavior of these clitics appears to diverge in many perplexing ways from what is typically found elsewhere in non-causative constructions. In this section, however, we have seen that the placement of clitics in Romance causatives does not require any special stipulations; in causatives, as elsewhere, they are an overt manifestation of Case-assignment by the verb. What makes causatives special is that there are two verbs, each of which may assign Case, which govern partially overlapping sets of arguments. The fact that clitics behave as predicted gives evidence for the parallel structures described in section 3.3.[36]

It is worth noting that the present analysis takes an approach which is rather different from previous work in this area. My central claim in this section has been that the distribution of clitics in causatives derives from their being a spell-out of Case. I have made no use of locality conditions which may or may not constrain the relation between a clitic and its associated empty category. In most other work, locality conditions have played a major role in the analysis. In Kayne (1975) and Rouveret and Vergnaud (1980), for instance, it is the Specified Subject Condition (see Chomsky 1973) which accounts for much of the data discussed in this section.

Rouveret and Vergnaud's version of the SSC is given in (95):

(95) No rule can involve X, Y in the structure
...X...[$_\alpha$...Y...]... α = S or NP
where Y is in the domain of the subject of α and X is not in α.

To see how this general approach might work, consider again sentence (78a), given here as (96):

(96) *Marie *lui* a fait écrire l'enfant
'Mary made the child write to him'

Take *lui* to be X in (95) and the empty category to be Y. If there is a rule which relates the two, then this rule will be blocked in (96) because the empty category is in the domain of the subject (*l'enfant*). In a sentence like (97) (=(79a)), on the other hand, the empty category is not in the domain of the subject (there is none), so the two may be related:

(97) Marie *lui* a fait écrire (par l'enfant)
'Mary made write to him (by the child)'

Hence the distinction between (96) and (97). Recall that in our analysis (96) is ruled out because *l'enfant* does not receive Case.

In terms of government–binding theory, the SSC-type analysis claims that the empty category associated with the clitic is an anaphor, and thus subject to Principle A of the binding theory. As mentioned earlier, though, the nature of this clitic–empty category relationship is currently a matter of some controversy, and it is not clear that it should be constrained by Principle A. One interesting aspect of the present analysis, then, is that it demonstrates that it is possible to give an empirically adequate, and arguably insightful, account of clitics (in causatives, at least) without reference to conditions such as the SSC/Principle A.

Another difference between our analysis and previous work is that most earlier approaches assumed a D-structure representation of causatives which was very different from the S-structure representation. That is, D-structure consisted of an ordinary sentential complement structure, while S-structure was "reduced" in some sense. In the analysis developed here, on the other hand, both types of structure co-exist at both levels of representation. We have seen that clitics provide important evidence for this view, if we assume that they are an overt manifestation of Case. Since Case is assigned at S-structure, a sentence in which we see Case being assigned according to both configurations is evidence that they both exist at S-structure (and by implication at D-structure as well). The examples in (98) are of this type:

(98) a. (=81b)) Dieu a fait leur apparaître la Vierge
'God made the Virgin appear unto them'
b. (=(85)) Jean a fait se laver Marie
'John made Mary wash herself'
c. (=(90b)) María le hizo comerlo
'Mary made him eat it'
d. (=(93b)) María hizo escribirle al niño
'Mary made the child write to him'

The clitic on the lower verb in each of these examples (*leur*, *se*, *lo*, and *le*, respectively) shows that this verb assigns Case. At the same time, the other NP in each sentence (*la Vierge*, *Marie*, *le*, and *el niño*, respectively) can only be Case-marked by the complex verb. This has been the principal motivation for saying that the sentential complement structure and the "reduced" structure (with a complex verb) both exist at the same level(s) of representation. Thus the present analysis differs from most previous ones not so much in the nature of the configurations assumed, but rather in the syntactic level at which these configurations are present.

It is interesting to note, then, that the first proposal for these kinds of parallel structures with *faire*, in Zubizarreta (1982), uses the cliticization facts to a very different end. Zubizarreta points out that in the *faire-par* construction clitics may never attach to the lower verb, whereas in other uses of *faire* they may. This may be seen in the contrast between (99) (=(84b)) and (100) (=(72)):

(99) *Marie a fait *le* manger
'Mary had it eaten'
(100) Marie *l*'a fait *le* manger
'Mary made him eat it'

Zubizarreta uses this contrast to argue that in (99) there is a complex verb, while in (100) there is not.[37] In our analysis, on the other hand, both the complex verb and the lower verb may potentially take clitics, given that both may potentially assign Case. *Faire*, however, may optionally suppress the subject θ-role and accusative Case-assigning ability of the lower verb. This is what happens in (99), and hence the lower verb *manger* is unable to take an accusative clitic. Both (99) and (100) contain parallel structures; the difference results from optional properties of *faire*. In our analysis, unlike Zubizarreta's, *faire-par* is not really a separate construction. Apart from the differences noted, *faire-par* receives the same analysis as the standard use of *faire*.

A further difference between this analysis and Zubizarreta's concerns the nature of the parallel structures themselves. In Zubizarreta's system, they are not "parallel" in exactly the same sense that they are here, since for some components, such as Case theory, only the "reduced" structure is visible. This sharply contrasts with the system developed here, where crucially the grammar has access to both structures. Thus we need to say only that *faire* subcategorizes both for a clause and a verb, and no stipulations need to be made about how the grammar will treat the resulting structures (see chapter 5 for more discussion).

3.6 Conclusion

The purpose of this chapter was to argue that Romance causatives provide evidence for two simultaneous structural analyses of a single terminal string. It was seen that by assuming that *faire* takes a clausal complement and forms a complex verb with the verb of that complement, the major properties of Romance causatives follow.[38] We relied quite heavily on Case theory, since I claimed that the complex verb is able to assign Case.

The overall result has been, in addition to the descriptive coverage attained, a much simpler fragment of grammar than those which have previously been proposed. We have been able to avoid invoking, for instance, a rule of VP-preposing or a special constraint on clitic–empty category binding. Many problems remain, no doubt, but the evidence provided so far gives considerable justification for the claim that parallel syntactic structures exist.

4 *Restructuring*

4.1 Introduction

In the last chapter we saw that the French causative verb *faire*, and its equivalent in other Romance languages, forms a complex verb with the verb of the lower clause. Under this assumption we were able to explain the otherwise surprising behavior of the arguments in this lower clause. Rizzi (1982) analyzes a construction in Italian, generally referred to as Restructuring, where quite similar phenomena may be observed.[1]

First, clitic arguments of the embedded clause may appear on the matrix verb, as seen in (1):[2]

(1) Piero *ti* verrà a parlare di parapsicologia
'Peter will come to speak to you about parapsychology'

This fact may be accounted for by stating that *verrà a parlare* is a complex verb which is able to assign Case to the arguments that it governs. Thus the clitic *ti* is able to appear attached to a verb of which it is apparently not a complement.

Second, arguments from the lower clause may move into matrix subject position, as in (2):

(2) Finalmente [le nuove case popolari]$_i$ *si* comincerrano a costruire t_i
'Finally the new council houses will begin to be built'

This normally is only possible with arguments of the verb to which *si* is attached. (2) also may be explained, then, if *comincerrano a costruire* is a complex verb.

Finally, the matrix verb may take an auxiliary which is normally associated with the lower verb. For instance, the verb *volere* normally selects the auxiliary *avere*. The verb *tornare*, on the other hand, selects the auxiliary *essere*. In a sentence like (3), then, *volere* may take *essere* rather than *avere*:

(3) Mario è voluto tornare a casa
'Mario has wanted to return home'

Here again, we might account for this phenomenon by saying that the complex verb may take on the properties (in this case, auxiliary selection) of the lower verb.

Thus there is some initial plausibility for supposing that in Restructuring there is a complex verb just like what was proposed for causatives. Another hypothesis which at first appears to be equally plausible, however, is that Restructuring verbs are actually auxiliaries (like *avere* and *essere*) rather than main verbs. The facts of (1)–(3) would then be easily explained because, under this hypothesis, what we have been referring to as the embedded verb would now be the main verb of a monoclausal sentence. We would then expect arguments of this verb to cliticize onto the auxiliary, as in (1), the object to move into subject position, as in (2), and the main verb to select the aspectual auxiliary, as in (3).

Zubizarreta (1982) has shown, however, that Restructuring verbs do not appear to be auxiliaries. First, Restructuring verbs, unlike auxiliaries, may co-occur without limit, as in (4) (from Zubizarreta's (49)):[3]

(4) Pedro la querría poder volver a empezar a leer
'Peter would want to be able to go back to beginning to read it'

Auxiliaries in Romance and other languages are generally tightly constrained in this regard.

Second, Restructuring verbs do not undergo preposing, as do auxiliaries in Italian. Compare, then, (5) and (6) with (7):

(5) Essendo state le mele mangiate...
'The apple having been eaten...'

(6) Essendosi le mele mangiate...
'The apple having been eaten...'

(7) *Essendosi potute le mele mangiate...
'The apple having been able to be eaten...'

Essendosi potute, with the Restructuring verb *potere*, may not be preposed.

We may thus assume that Restructuring verbs are not auxiliaries, but rather, as we initially supposed, real verbs which subcategorize for another verb, thus forming a complex verb. In this respect they are like causative *faire*. In our analysis of causatives, though, I claimed that *faire* simultaneously subcategorizes for both $\bar{S}$ and V. So far in Restructuring we have seen evidence for V, but not for $\bar{S}$. We should now ask whether Restructuring requires the parallel structures which we saw were necessary for causatives, or whether a simple complex verb analysis will suffice.

In the analysis of causatives, evidence for the existence of simultaneous structures came primarily from Case-assignment. In examples such as (8) Case is assigned from both the embedded verb and the complex verb:

(8) María *le* hizo comer*lo*
'Mary made him eat it'

Since the complex verb only exists when *hacer* subcategorizes for V, and the embedded verb only exists as an independent Case-assigner when *hacer* subcategorizes for $\bar{S}$, (8) shows that these two subcategorization frames must co-exist in the same structure. Only then can different arguments receive Case from different verbs, as occurs in (8).

Such evidence is lacking for Restructuring, however. Notice that (8) is possible only because the Case arrays of the two verbs are different: the complex verb may assign DAT while the embedded verb assigns ACC. We shall see in Restructuring, though, that the Restructuring verb does not contribute a Case array to the complex verb. This immediately entails that the Case array of the complex verb will always be non-distinct from that of the embedded verb. Thus it will be impossible to construct examples such as (8) with a Restructuring verb, given the fact that verbs must assign their entire Case array; (9), for example, is excluded, because here the complex verb assigns only part of its Case array (i.e. DAT, instead of ACC DAT).

(9) **Te* quiero dar*lo*
'I want to give it to you'

For independent reasons, then, we are unable to provide evidence comparable to (8) to show that two analyses exist in the same phrase marker.

There is evidence of a somewhat less direct nature, however. Notice that if the Restructuring verb takes an $\bar{S}$ complement, there is the possibility that an overt complementizer will appear. If, on the other hand, this verb only subcategorizes for V, then we should not expect any complementizers. In fact we do find complementizers with some verbs in this construction, even when it is clear that there is a complex verb:

(10)

a. $\text{Piero } \textit{lo} \left\{ \begin{array}{l} \text{sta } \textit{per} \\ \text{comincia } \textit{a} \\ \text{finisce } \textit{di} \end{array} \right\} \text{leggere}$

$\text{`Peter} \left\{ \begin{array}{l} \text{is going} \\ \text{is beginning} \\ \text{is finishing} \end{array} \right\} \text{to read/reading it'}$

(from Rizzi 1982)

b. $\text{Pedro } \textit{lo} \left\{ \begin{array}{l} \text{tiene } \textit{que} \\ \text{volvió } \textit{a} \\ \text{acaba } \textit{de} \end{array} \right\} \text{leer}$

$\text{`Peter} \left\{ \begin{array}{l} \text{has} \\ \text{began again} \\ \text{just finished} \end{array} \right\} \text{to read/reading it'}$

This is just what we would expect if these verbs subcategorize for both $\bar{S}$ and V. The placement of the clitic reflects the existence of the complex verb; the complementizer reflects the existence of $\bar{S}$.

Another piece of evidence comes from Rizzi (1982), who discusses sentences such as (11):

(11) Su questo punto, non *ti* saprei *che* dire
'On this point, I wouldn't know what to say to you'

The position of the *wh*-phrase *che* suggests that there is a COMP node between the two verbs. (11) is marginal, according to Rizzi, but the fact that it is possible at all is difficult to explain in an analysis where the Restructuring verb does not take an $\bar{S}$ complement and the COMP node should then not be present.[4]

I will assume, then, based on the evidence in (10) and (11), that Restructuring verbs subcategorize both for $\bar{S}$ and for V.[5] This means that Restructuring will be associated with the same kind of parallel structures as in the causative construction.

One problem with this position is that, as Rizzi (1982: 27–9) has pointed out, Restructuring and causatives differ in at least three crucial properties. First, the complex verb in Italian causatives never takes on the auxiliary of the embedded verb. In (12), then, *essere* is not possible, even though this is the auxiliary which *venire* normally selects:

(12) $\text{Mario lo} \left\{ \begin{array}{l} \text{ha} \\ \text{*è} \end{array} \right\} \text{fatto venire}$

'Mario has made him come'

(12) may be compared with (3), where the complex verb selects the auxiliary *essere.*

Second, we have seen that Passive is not permitted with the embedded verb in causatives:

(13) *Gianni ha fatto essere picchiato Piero da Mario
'John has had Peter be beaten by Mario'

With Restructuring, though, this is possible:

(14) Piero gli poteva essere presentato
'Peter was allowed to be introduced to him'

The position of the clitic *gli* here shows that (14) is a Restructuring construction.

Third, the complex verb in causatives does not usually take dative clitics which are associated with PP complements of the embedded verb, as seen in (15):

(15) *?Mario *gli* farà scrivere Piero
'Mario will make Peter write to him'

Such sentences are completely acceptable with Restructuring verbs:

(16) Mario *gli* vuole scrivere
'Mario wants to write to him'

The above differences, and others which we shall see as we proceed, present a substantial challenge to the system we developed in the last chapter. I claimed there that many important properties of causatives derive from the fact that these sentences contain two simultaneous analyses. We have seen evidence in this section that Restructuring sentences also require this type of structure. One might initially expect, then, that the properties which we derived in the case of causatives would show up as well with Restructuring. As we have seen, though, this is only partially true. In the rest of this chapter I will show why it is that Restructuring differs from causatives in certain respects.

4.2 Restructuring and parallel structures

4.2.1 Basic structure

As discussed in the previous section, I will assume that Restructuring verbs simultaneously subcategorize for both $\bar{S}$ and V. This means that a sentence such as (17) will be assigned a structure as in (18).

(17) Juan quiere comer el pan
'John wants to eat the bread'

(18) {S_1, NP_1 quiere comer el pan e, Juan VP_1, Juan V_1 comer el pan e, Juan quiere S_2, Juan quiere VP_2 e, Juan quiere V_2 el pan e, Juan quiere comer NP_2 e, Juan quiere comer el pan NP_3, Juan V_0 el pan e, Juan quiere comer el pan e}.

In (18) we see that there are two pairs of strings which satisfy neither *dominates* nor *precedes*: *Juan quiere S_2 – Juan V_0 el pan e* and *Juan quiere VP_2 e – Juan V_0 el pan e*. Thus, the non-terminal node V_0 bears no relation to either S_2 or VP_2. V_0 does bear relations to other nodes, as displayed in (19a):

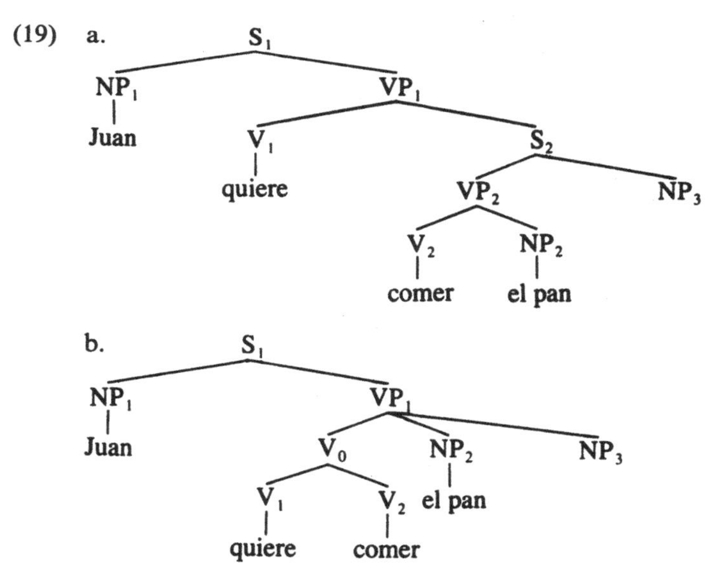

Notice that the subcategorization requirement is met here. *Querer* has an $\bar{S}$ complement in (19a) and a V complement in (19b).

4.2.2 Case-assignment

In our discussion of causatives in Romance we saw that the status of the subject of the embedded clause turned out to be a central concern. This is the only argument which is not Case-marked from within its own clause in the $\bar{S}$ analysis. We saw two ways of overcoming this difficulty. One is to allow the embedded subject to be Case-marked by the complex verb. This is the only verb which may potentially Case-mark it, because it is the only verb which governs it. The complex verb is able to assign Case, because it receives a Case array from the causative verb *faire*. The second way to overcome the problem of the embedded subject is to delete the subject θ-role. I assumed that a subject position which receives no θ-role and no Case (i.e. which is not syntactically "visible" in any relevant sense) may be absorbed in the complex verb. In essence, then, by deleting the subject θ-role we are deleting the subject, in that it no longer plays any significant role in the syntax.

In our treatment of Restructuring, too, our attention will focus necessarily on the status of the embedded subject. One important difference, though, lies in the Case-assigning abilities of the complex verb. I wish to claim that the Restructuring verb itself is unable to contribute a Case array to the complex verb. That is to say, the Case array of the complex verb derives from the Case-assigning abilities of V_2, not V_1. This assumption seems to be necessary in a language such as Italian, where matrix verbs taking infinitival complements do not assign Case. This is shown in (20) (from Burzio 1981: 6.4.3 (49b)), where we see that the matrix Restructuring verb *volere* may not passivize:

(20) *Quel film sara voluto vedere (da tutti)
'That film will be wanted to see (by everyone)'

Following Stowell (1981), only verbs which assign accusative Case may take passive morphology. The fact that *volere* in (20) does not passivize thus implies that in the context of an infinitival complement, *volere* does not assign Case.[6] The complex verb in Restructuring must then receive its Case array from the embedded verb.

4.2.3 Lexical NP's, PRO, and θ-role deletion

Let us now look more specifically at the kinds of embedded subjects which may or may not be permitted in Restructuring. The type of structure which I am proposing, of course, is exactly the same as that assumed for causative sentences such as (21):

(21) Juan hizo comer el pan (a María)
'John made (Mary) eat the bread'

The way Case is assigned, however, is different. Our question here, then, is what types of NP's can appear in the position NP_3 in (19).

It is clear that NP_3 cannot be lexical, because there is no way for it to receive Case. V_0 takes on the Case array of V_2 (__ACC here) and is thus only able to assign Case to NP_2 in (19). In general, since the Case array of V_0 is non-distinct from that of V_2, V_0 will only be able to assign Case to complements of V_2. The embedded subject, then, will never be able to receive Case. Sentences like (22) are thus excluded:

(22) *Juan quiere comer el pan a María
'John wants Mary to eat the bread'

(22) differs from (21), in that in (21) V_0 may assign Case to NP_3.

Since NP_3 is not a Case-marked position in (19), we might expect PRO to be able to appear there. This is not possible, however, because although NP_3 is not Case-marked, it is governed (by V_0). Assuming that PRO must be ungoverned, NP_3 may not be PRO.[7] We saw in chapter 3 that this is true of causatives as well.

We have seen, then, that our system allows neither lexical NP's nor PRO to appear in the position of NP_3. Although we can rule out (22), we are still without an explanation for the grammaticality of (17), where the embedded verb *comer* does not have an overt subject. One possible solution, which we saw was attested in causatives, is for V_1, the Restructuring verb, to delete the subject θ-role of V_2. When NP_3 does not receive a θ-role it does not need Case, nor may it be PRO. I have assumed that it may thus appear to the left of VP and be absorbed into the complex verb.

However, this analysis fails to generate (17). We saw in chapter 3 that when the subject θ-role is deleted, the verb loses its ability to assign accusative Case. *El pan* in (17) would then not be Case-marked. This analysis also fails to allow sentences where V_2 in (19) is ergative (=unaccusative), since these verbs have no subject θ-role to be deleted. Consider first a sentence where the object of the ergative verb is lexical. If the embedded subject position were Case-marked, then the embedded object of the ergative verb, which does not receive Case, could move to this position. We have seen, however, that the subject is not able to receive Case in Restructuring. As a consequence, then, we do not find sentences like (23), where the object is lexical:

(23) *Juan quiere venir a los estudiantes
'John wants the students to come'

This contrasts with causatives, of course, where the embedded object is able to receive Case from the complex verb, as in (24):

(24) Juan hizo venir a los estudiantes
'John made the students come'

Having seen that lexical NP's are disallowed in embedded object position, now let us consider empty NP's. Since the position is θ-marked but not Case-marked, the only possible empty category is PRO. If the object of the embedded ergative is PRO, it must move to an ungoverned position; but none is available, since the object position is governed by V_2 and the subject position by V_0.

Thus, from what we have seen so far, it would appear that no well-formed output should be possible when the embedded verb is ergative. This is clearly wrong, however, since such sentences are allowed when the embedded object is null, as seen in (25):

(25) Juan quiere venir
'John wants to come'

The analysis wherein V_1 deletes the subject θ-role of V_2 has no effect here, there being no subject θ-role, and it thus fails to allow (25). We conclude, on the basis of (25) and (17), that this process of θ-role deletion does not occur in Restructuring.

There are further grounds for thinking that this is correct. First, the obligatory interpretation of (17) is that John wants John to eat the bread, and not, as the θ-role deletion analysis would predict, that John wants some other person to eat the bread (as in (21), for example). Second, these sentences do not allow *by*-phrases, as seen in (26):

(26) *Juan quiere cómer el pan por María
'John wants to eat the bread by Mary'

This runs counter to what we would expect if Restructuring, like causatives and Passive, could delete the subject θ-role of the embedded verb. It is interesting, then, that this analysis is disallowed independently in the case of (25) and (17).

Summarizing what we have seen so far, the fact that V_1 in Restructuring contributes no Case array to the complex verb means that no well-formed output is possible for these sentences with the machinery we developed for causatives. This holds true both when the embedded subject is lexical and when it is null.

4.2.4 θ-role assignment

In essence, then, the problem we have seen with Restructuring is that there is sometimes a mismatch between θ-roles and Case. That is to say, there may be an argument of the embedded infinitival clause which is unable to receive Case. This situation arises whenever the matrix verb assigns a θ-role (either to its subject or object). Consider, for example, the sentence in (27):

(27) Gianni vuole telefonare

Under standard assumptions, both *volere* and *telefonare* assign a θ-role to their subject, thus giving us two NP arguments here. There is only one Case-marked position, however: the subject position of *volere*. Since this position is occupied by *Gianni*, the subject of *volere*, the other NP argument (the subject of *telefonare*) has no way to receive Case. We saw earlier that the subject of the embedded verb may not be PRO. Hence the θ-position of the embedded clause is associated with no Case-marked position, in violation of the Case Filter.

The same situation obtains in cases such as (28), where the matrix verb is ergative, and in (29), where the embedded verb is ergative:

(28) Gianni è andato a telefonare
(29) Gianni vuole venire

Here, as in (27), there are more θ-positions than Case-marked positions. In all three examples, the "extra" θ-position is in the embedded clause. This mismatch between θ-positions and Case-marked positions, of course, does not arise when the matrix verb assigns no θ-role, as in (30):

(30) Gianni deve telefonare

Here there is one θ-position (the subject position of *telefonare*) and one Case-marked position (the subject position of *dovere*). The single NP argument, *Gianni*, is thus able to be both Case-marked and θ-marked.

From what we have seen thus far, then, the lack of a one-to-one correspondence between θ-positions and Case-marked positions in the Restructuring sentences in (27)–(29) should lead to ungrammaticality – contrary to fact. To solve this problem, we will have to look more closely at the relation between the complex verb and θ-role assignment.

In the analysis of causatives in chapter 3, I claimed that the complex verb may take on the Case-assigning abilities of the verbs which it dominates. We may assume that it is also able to assign the θ-roles of these verbs. This assumption in general has no empirical consequences for causatives. Consider a sentence such as (31), for example:

(31) Jean a fait rire Marie
'John made Mary laugh'

V_1 and V_2 here each have one θ-role to assign to their subject. These are passed on to V_0, which assigns one to its subject (*Jean*) and one to its object (*Marie*). Thus these two argument positions are θ-marked both by V_0 and by one of the member verbs of V_0, but they receive the same θ-role from both verbs. We see, then, that the θ-roles assigned by V_0 are equivalent to the set of θ-roles assigned by V_1 and V_2. The only difference is that the external (i.e. subject) θ-role of V_2 is an internal (i.e. complement) θ-role for V_0.

We may assume that the same possibilities exist with the complex verb in Restructuring. Thus in a sentence such as (27), the θ-roles of V_1 and V_2 are passed on to V_0, which assigns one to its subject and one to its object (the subject of *telefonare*). As with causatives, here the θ-roles assigned by V_0 are equivalent to the set of θ-roles assigned by V_1 and V_2. Hence we still incorrectly expect (27) to be ruled out by the θ-criterion, since the subject position of *telefonare* receives a θ-role, but no Case.

However, it is not necessary for the complex verb to assign its θ-roles in this way. As we saw in the analysis of *faire-par* in section 3.4.5, the external θ-role of V_2 may be affected when V_2 appears in a complex verb. Thus V_0 here need not assign the external θ-role of V_2 in exactly the same way that V_2 would in isolation. It could, for example, assign both θ-roles to its subject. The subject position of *volere* in (27), then, would be a θ-position, while the subject position of *telefonare* would not. Notice that this solves the problem described earlier regarding the mismatch between θ-positions and Case. Now there is one θ-position and one Case-marked position, giving us a one-to-one correspondence between θ-positions and arguments. The θ-criterion is thus satisfied, given a formulation of it as follows: each argument is associated with one and only one θ-position and each θ-position is associated with one and only one argument.[8] We can see, then, that by saying that V_0 (in addition to V_1 and V_2) assigns θ-roles and that the assignment of the external θ-role of V_2 may be altered, we are able to attain a well-formed output for Restructuring constructions like (27).

I will assume that the number of θ-positions may be reduced in this way only when this is necessary in order to yield a well-formed structure. In a causative structure like (31), for instance, it is not necessary for the complex verb to assign both θ-roles to one position, since the θ-criterion is satisfied already without this. In (27), on the other hand, a θ-criterion violation can be avoided only by assigning two θ-roles to one position, i.e. by making the number of θ-positions equal to the number of Case-marked positions. Thus the assignment of θ-roles by the complex verb differs from what the simple verbs would do in isolation in (27), but not in (31).

The reassignment of θ-roles by the complex verb is constrained by an important restriction. In Williams (1981b) it is claimed that morphological processes may affect external θ-roles, but not internal θ-roles. For our purposes, this means that when V_1 and V_2 combine to form a complex verb, the assignment of internal θ-roles must not be altered. If V_1 or V_2 assigns an internal θ-role, then V_0 must assign this θ-role to the same position. With external θ-roles of V_1 or V_2, though, V_0 may reassign them to different positions if necessary. As we shall see below, this independently motivated distinction between the behavior of the two types of θ-roles will play an important part in the analysis of Restructuring.

Let us now see in more detail how θ-roles are assigned in Restructuring. Consider first examples (27)–(29), which appeared at first to be violations of the θ-criterion and/or Case Filter. In (27), as we have seen, V_1 and V_2 each have an external θ-role, and V_0 must assign them both to a single position if a θ-criterion violation is to be avoided. Since they are both external θ-roles, V_0 assigns them to its subject position; *Gianni* occupies this position, and thus receives a θ-role and Case. The other NP position (the subject position of *telefonare*) is neither θ-marked nor Case-marked, and thus may be absorbed into the complex verb. (27) satisfies both the θ-criterion and the Case Filter, since the Case-marked argument *Gianni* is associated with a single θ-position.

In (28) also there are two θ-roles: the internal θ-role of *andare* and the external θ-role of *telefonare*. Here again they must be assigned to a single position. V_0 cannot assign them both to the subject position of *telefonare*, since this would alter the assignment of the internal θ-role of *andare*, and this is disallowed. The only possibility, then, is to assign both θ-roles to the object position of *andare*, thus leaving the internal θ-role of *andare* intact and reassigning only the external θ-role of *telefonare*, which now becomes an internal θ-role for V_0. *Gianni* thus occupies the object position of *andare* at D-structure, and moves to the subject position at S-structure, where it receives Case. The subject position of *telefonare* is absorbed into the complex verb. In this example too, then, there is one θ-position, one argument, and one Case-marked position, and the θ-criterion and Case Filter are satisfied.

In (29), V_1 has an external θ-role and V_2 has an internal θ-role. As in the above two examples, V_0 must assign both θ-roles to one position. In this case, they must be assigned to the object position of V_2, since the assignment of internal θ-roles may not be altered, as we have seen. In D-structure, then, *Gianni* appears in this object position. It moves into matrix subject position at S-structure, where it receives Case.

As we saw earlier, there is no mismatch between θ-positions and Case in Restructuring with a matrix raising verb, as in (30). V_1 has Case to assign and V_2 has an external θ-role to assign. Now when the complex verb assigns this single θ-role, it may assign it either to its own subject position or to its object position (i.e. embedded subject position). In the first case, there will be no movement (*Gianni* will be generated in matrix subject position), but in the second case there will. As we shall see in the following section, the position to which this single θ-role is assigned with raising verbs is a matter of lexical idiosyncrasy. Some verbs require that it be assigned to matrix subject position; others require that it be assigned to matrix object (=embedded subject) position.

In summary, I have claimed here that both the complex verb and the individual verbs may assign θ-roles. The complex verb may alter the assignment of the member verbs' θ-roles, however, in such a way that two θ-roles are assigned to a single position. This is necessary in certain structures, because otherwise one of the arguments would not receive Case. By assigning two θ-roles to a single position, we in effect make the number of θ-positions equal to the number of Case-marked positions, thus allowing each argument to receive Case.

The principal difference between Restructuring and the causative construction, then, is that the causative verb determines the Case array of the complex verb, while the Restructuring verb does not. This means that with causatives, but not with Restructuring, an argument of the embedded verb which is not Case-marked by that verb may be Case-marked by the complex verb. Instead of supplying additional Case, the complex verb in Restructuring may reduce the number of arguments by assigning two θ-roles to one position. Thus both causative and Restructuring verbs provide a way of dealing with arguments of the embedded clause which are not Case-marked within that clause.

The mechanics which the two classes of verbs have available to them are essentially the same; only the effects are different. In both constructions the complex verb may optionally assign Case and/or θ-roles. With causatives, it makes no difference whether it is the complex verb which assigns θ-roles or the individual verbs. It does make a difference which verb assigns Case, however, in that some arguments are only able to receive Case from the complex verb. With Restructuring, the situation is just the reverse. Whether or not the complex verb assigns Case is not particularly important, but whether or not it assigns the θ-roles is. Only the complex verb is capable of reassigning θ-roles in such a way as to satisfy the θ-criterion. This difference in the way the two sets of verbs utilize parallel structures is a reflex of the way in which the complex verb receives its Case array. Since the Case array of the causative complex verb is different from that of the embedded verb, no reassignment of θ-roles is necessary. Since the Case array of the Restructuring complex verb is the same as that of the embedded verb, θ-roles may need to be reassigned in order for the θ-criterion and Case Filter to be satisfied.

The system of θ-role assignment described here was necessary to account for basic Restructuring sentence patterns like (27)–(29), while maintaining the analysis of parallel structures used for causatives in chapter 3. In the following sections we shall see that this system makes interesting and correct predictions about some of the more subtle aspects of the behavior of Restructuring verbs.

4.3 Consequences

4.3.1 Auxiliary selection

One of the exceptional properties of Restructuring concerns the selection of auxiliaries in Italian, as was briefly discussed in section 4.1. Here I will show how auxiliary selection works and how this interacts with the analysis of Restructuring just proposed to produce the correct configuration of data.

The analysis of auxiliary selection which I adopt here is that of Perlmutter (1978, 1983) and Burzio (1981). The essential principle is given here in (32) (=Burzio's 2.4.3 (101a)):

(32) The auxiliary will be realized as *essere* when a binding relation exists between the subject and a nominal constituent of the predicate (where an element is a constituent of the predicate if and only if it is either part of the verb morphology or it is governed by the verb).

The auxiliary will be realized as *avere* otherwise. For our purposes, the basic idea is that *essere* will be selected in a clause when there is a binding relation between the subject and an NP governed by the verb. A "binding relation" exists only "between elements which do not have independent thematic roles" (Burzio 1981: 150). Thus the relation between an NP and its trace will trigger the selection of *essere*, as in (33) (*intervenire* is ergative):

(33) Maria$_i$ *è* intervenuta t$_i$
'Mary has intervened' (Burzio's 5.4.2 (69a))

Maria here is not in a θ-position. The relation between an NP and a reflexive or between an NP and PRO, however, will not cause *essere* to be selected. In these cases the two elements do have independent thematic roles. This may be seen in (34) and (35):

(34) Maria$_i$ *ha* accusato se stessa$_i$
'Mary has accused herself' (Burzio's 5.4.2 (70a))

(35) [Alcuni studenti]$_i$ *avevano* sperato di PRO$_i$ uscire in fretta
'A few students had hoped to get out soon'
(Burzio's 5.4.2 (72))

Here the auxiliary *avere* is selected.

The implications for auxiliary selection in Restructuring are now clear. When the NP in matrix subject position receives its θ-role from an NP position governed by the verb, i.e. when there is movement into subject position, the auxiliary selected will be *essere*.

Let us consider those cases first. In a sentence like (29), for example, the complex verb assigns both θ-roles to the object of *venire*. The matrix subject position consequently receives no θ-role. As would be expected, then, sentences of this type show up with the auxiliary *essere*, as seen in (36):

(36) Gianni$_i$ *è* voluto venire t$_i$
'John has wanted to come'

The verb *volere* 'to want' normally assigns an external θ-role, but here the complex verb assigns it to the object of *venire*. *Gianni* thus appears in matrix subject position as a result of movement.

When the matrix verb normally assigns no external θ-role, of course, the result will be just the same, as seen in (37):

(37) Gianni$_i$ *è* potuto venire t$_i$
'John has been allowed to come'

Here again, *Gianni* moves into subject position, and the θ-dependency thus established causes *essere* to be selected.

Essere is also what is selected when the matrix verb is ergative. The complex verb assigns its θ-roles to its object. Since this is not a Case-marked position, the NP must move to matrix subject position, as in (38):

(38) Gianni$_i$ gli *è* andato a telefonare t$_i$
'John has gone to phone him'

Essere is selected here just as it is in (36) and (37).

Now let us consider the cases where *avere* is selected. We saw earlier that if the complex verb reassigns two external θ-roles, then these must be assigned to its subject (i.e. the matrix subject). Thus the subject will not be dependent on another position for a θ-role, and *essere* will not be selected. This is the case in (39):

(39) Gianni *ha* voluto telefonare
'John has wanted to phone'

This is essentially the same structure as (17).

Suppose now that the matrix verb is a raising verb. The θ-role of the embedded verb may be assigned either to the subject of the embedded verb or to the subject of the matrix verb. As mentioned in the last section, this is a matter of lexical idiosyncrasy. With the verb *potere* 'to be allowed,' for instance, the θ-role is assigned to matrix subject position. There is no movement, then, and *avere* is selected:

(40) Gianni *ha* potuto telefonare
'John has been allowed to phone'

With *sembrare* 'to seem,' the θ-role is assigned to the position of the embedded subject. Movement thus results, and *essere* is selected, as seen in (41) (from Burzio 6.5.4 (104)):

(41) Maria ne *era* sembrata conoscere l'autore
'Mary had seemed to know the author of it'

Our analysis thus succeeds in predicting which auxiliary will be selected in each case. Notice, first of all, that if θ-roles were not reassigned in the way described, the principle of *essere*-assignment in (32) would not yield the correct results. In (36), for example, the matrix subject position would be a θ-position, and thus no binding relation between elements without independent θ-roles would exist. The auxiliary *essere* would then not be expected. We could of course modify (32) so that the auxiliary would be selected differently in Restructuring than in the standard cases. This is obviously not a desirable move, though, since it goes against our aim of minimizing the special properties needed for Restructuring. In the analysis developed here, θ-roles need to be reassigned simply to allow for the generation of sentences like (36) (and (29)). The fact that (36) selects the auxiliary *essere* follows from the normal operation of (32), just as it does in the standard example in (33).

Notice also that it is not sufficient to say, as we tentatively stated in section 4.1, that the complex verb selects the same auxiliary that the embedded verb would normally select.[9] This is incorrect for (38), where the embedded verb is non-ergative and hence selects *avere*. The complex verb selects *essere*, however, since its subject is in a binding relation with an NP governed by it.

We mentioned in section 4.1 that *faire* and the Restructuring verbs do not appear to pattern together in the selection of auxiliaries. This is no longer mysterious, under the present view. Consider again sentence (12), repeated here as (42):

(42) Mario lo $\left\{\begin{array}{l}\text{ha}\\ \text{*è}\end{array}\right\}$ fatto venire
'Mario has made him come'

The subject of the complex verb, *Mario*, has an independent θ-role, and is not bound to any NP in the complement. *Avere* is thus selected. This may be compared with (36), where the matrix subject is dependent on an object for its θ-role, thus allowing *essere* to be selected. This is consistent with our view that both causatives and Restructuring require parallel structures. The difference in auxiliary selection is a reflection of a more fundamental difference in θ-role assignment.

4.3.2 Passives

Another descriptive property of Restructuring which we saw briefly in section 4.1 is that the embedded verb may be passive, as in (14), repeated here as (43):

(43) Piero_i gli poteva essere presentato t_i
'Peter was allowed to be introduced to him'

Piero here moves from the position of object of *essere presentato* to matrix subject position, where it receives Case. Thus (43) is well-formed.[10]

If the matrix verb is passivized, however, the sentence is not well-formed, as seen in (44):

(44) *[Quel film]$_i$ sara voluto vedere t$_i$ (da tutti)
'That film will be wanted to see (by everyone)'
(Burzio's 6.4.3 (49b))

Sentence (44) is impossible because, as we claimed in section 4.2, Restructuring verbs are intransitive when they appear in this construction. Intransitive verbs independently do not take passive morphology.

The situation is just the reverse with causatives. As seen in (13), repeated here as (45), the embedded verb may not be passivized:

(45) *Gianni ha fatto essere picchiato Piero da Mario
'John has had Peter be beaten by Mario'

Here *Piero* is in a non-Case-marked position, and there is no Case-marked $\bar{\theta}$-position to which it may move. Hence (45) violates the Case Filter.

The matrix verb, on the other hand, may be passivized, as in (46):[11]

(46) Quei brani furono fatti leggere
'Those passages were made read'

Here the matrix subject position is not θ-marked, so *Piero* may move there and receive Case. *Fare*, unlike the Restructuring verbs, does assign Case and thus may be passivized. It is this difference in Case-assigning ability which yields the contrast between Restructuring and causatives in (43)–(46).

4.3.3 Dative clitics

A further distinction, noted by Rizzi, which separates Restructuring from causatives lies in the possibility of cliticizing PP complements of the embedded verb onto the complex verb. As noted in section 4.1, this is possible with Restructuring, but not with causatives:

(47) (=(16)) Mario *gli* vuole scrivere
'Mario wants to write to him'

(48) (=(15)) *?Mario *gli* farà scrivere Piero
'Mario will make Peter write to him'

Causative sentences like (48) were already discussed in section 3.5.4. We saw there that (48) is out because the empty category associated with *gli* intervenes between the complex verb and *Piero*. Since *Piero* is hence not adjacent to the verb, it may not receive Case.

In (47) there is nothing to which the verb needs to assign Case, so the fact that there is an empty category after *vuole scrivere* is of no particular consequence; (47) is thus allowed. This is reminiscent of causative sentences like (49):

(49) Mario *gli* farà scrivere
'Mario will make write to him'

where, just as in (47), the complex verb also need not assign Case.

4.3.4 Other clitics

We have already seen evidence, in section 4.1 and elsewhere, that the complex verb in Restructuring may assign Case. I have claimed that this is possible because the complex verb may assume the Case array of the lower verb. From this, the set of facts in (50) (noted in Aissen and Perlmutter 1976; Rivas 1977; Zubizarreta 1979) immediately follow:

(50) a. Juan quiere dár*telo*
b. Juan *te lo* quiere dar
c. *Juan *te* quiere dar*lo*
d. *Juan *lo* quiere dar*te*
'John wants to give it to you'

In (50a), the embedded verb *dar* assigns ACC and DAT to the two clitics *te* and *lo*. In (50b), this Case array is passed on to the complex verb, to which the clitics thus attach.[12] Sentences (50c) and (50d) are impossible, because these require that the embedded verb and the complex verb each assign only part of the Case array __ACC DAT. The theory of Case-assignment which we have been assuming (see section 3.3.2) states that when Case is assigned at all, the entire Case array must be assigned.

(50a) is structurally ambiguous between the parallel structures analysis, where it is the lower verb which happens to assign Case, and the normal control structure, where the lower verb *dar* is the only possible Case-assigner for its complements. (50b), on the other hand, must involve parallel structures. In essence, then, I am assuming that (50a) and (50b) may both contain a complex verb, even though in (50a) there is no direct evidence for this, in that the position of the clitics does not require an analysis with a complex verb.

In principle, we should be able to find evidence to tell us whether or not there is a complex verb when the clitics appear on the lower verb, by examining how auxiliaries are selected in sentences like (50a). If in fact it is possible to have a complex verb in this type of example, then *essere* should be able to appear. If not, *essere* should be impossible. Unfortunately, the data do not speak very clearly on this point. Rizzi (1982) provides the following example:

(51) Maria *è* dovuta venir*ci* molte volte
'Mary has had to come there many times'

Here the auxiliary *essere* is selected, indicating that there is a complex verb, since if there were not, *Maria* would not be bound to the object of ergative *venire*, and we would have *avere*. In addition, the clitic appears on the lower verb. This is just what is predicted by our analysis; the lower verb happens to be the one which assigns Case here.

Rizzi notes, however, that if the subject in (51) is not a 3rd person NP, then *essere* is not possible:

(52) *?*Siamo* potuti venir*ci* solo poche volte
'We have been able to come here only a few times'

This would seem to indicate, in our terms, that the lower verb may not assign Case just in case the subject is non-3rd person. I have no way of accounting for this.

A more plausible interpretation of the general state of affairs here is that there is some amount of indeterminacy as to whether Restructuring requires parallel structures or simply a complex verb, i.e. whether or not (53b) may be generated as an independent phrase marker:

(53) a.

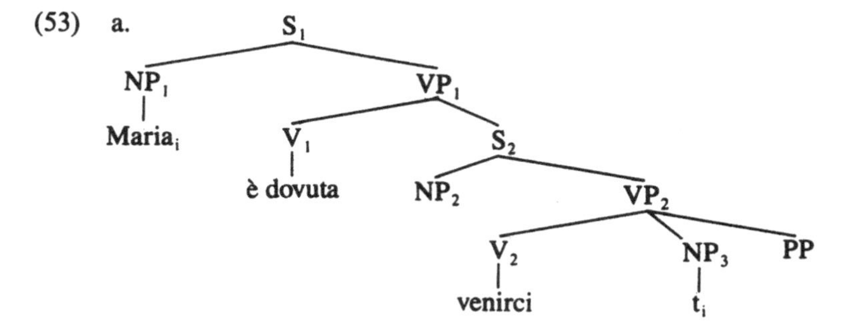

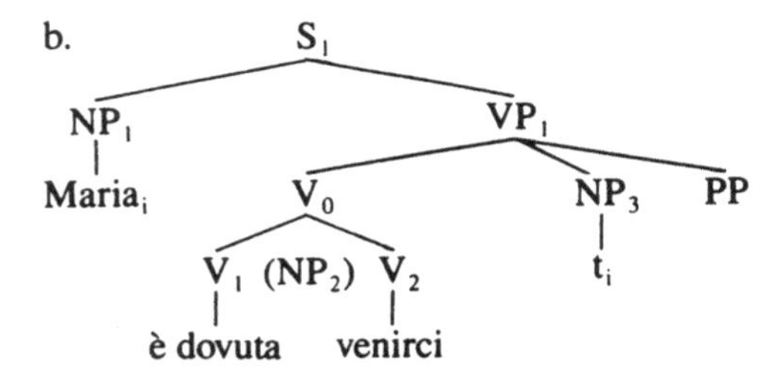

Notice that parallel structures are necessary in order to account for (51). *Venire* may take clitics only in (53a), since only there does it govern its complements as an independent verb. The fact that *essere* is selected shows that we also have the structure (53b). We might account for (52), on the other hand, by associating with it a structure like that in (53b). *Essere* is selected, just as in (51), but here the clitic *ci* must appear on the verb V_0, as in (54):

(54) *Ci siamo* potuti venire solo poche volte
'We have been able to come here only a few times'

(52) is excluded because the clitic does not govern its empty category.

Of course we still cannot explain why (51) and (52) should have different structures, as just described. The fact that such variation appears to exist should not be particularly surprising, though. As we saw in section 4.1, the evidence for simultaneous analyses in Restructuring is much less direct than in causatives. The grammar developed by the child may then leave the question of the exact structure of Restructuring partially open. This, one might speculate, could lead to the confusion of data evidenced in (51) and (52).

4.3.5 Matrix ergative verbs

Burzio (1981) observes the following contrast concerning the placement of the object of matrix ergative verbs:

(55) a. *Lo è andato *Giovanni* a prendere
b. Lo è andato a prendere *Giovanni*
'Giovanni has gone to get it'

In (55a) we see that adjacent to the verb *andare* is its object *Giovanni*, just as we might expect. This sentence is ungrammatical, however, whereas (55b), where *Giovanni* is non-adjacent, is grammatical.

This contrast falls out from the system we developed above. In sentences like (55), both θ-roles are assigned to an object of the complex verb. It is this θ-position where *Giovanni* will appear. (55b) is what we would expect, then, in that *Giovanni* appears to the right of the complex verb *è andato a prendere*, where it receives a θ-role. (55a) is impossible because there *Giovanni* appears within the complex verb, where it is not able to receive a θ-role.

4.3.6 PRO

One of the important properties of the analysis of Restructuring presented in this chapter is that the subject of the embedded verb is never PRO. Instead, it is NP-trace at S-structure if it receives a θ-role, and if it does not receive a θ-role it becomes part of the complex verb. This differs from the non-Restructuring use of some of these verbs, when they subcategorize only for $\bar{S}$. For those which are obligatory control verbs, the embedded subject is always PRO. This claim that Restructuring does not involve PRO carries with it some significant consequences, as we shall now see.

In fact, we have already seen at least one way in which the non-existence of PRO plays a crucial role. In sentences like (36), repeated here as (56), the auxiliary selected is *essere*:

(56) Gianni$_i$ *è* voluto venire t$_i$
'John has wanted to come'

This is because the subject, *Gianni*, is bound to an NP governed by the complex verb. These two NP's do *not* have independent θ-roles (the θ-roles are assigned to t$_i$), so the selection of *essere* is triggered. This may be contrasted with the control use of *volere*, as in (57):

(57) Gianni$_i$ *ha* voluto [$_S$PRO$_i$ venire t$_i$]
'John has wanted to come'

Here *Gianni* is coindexed with PRO, but PRO and *Gianni* have independent θ-roles; *avere* is thus selected, instead of *essere*.

If PRO were present in the Restructuring structure as well, then (56) should be disallowed, contrary to what we have seen. In fact, it appears that *essere* is obligatory in structures like (56). We can tell this from the fact that *avere* is disallowed when the placement of the clitic indicates that there is a complex verb. This is shown in the paradigm in (58), from Rizzi (1982):

(58) a. Maria *ha* dovuto venir*ci* molte volte
b. Maria *c'è* dovuta venire molte volte
c. *?Maria *ci ha* dovuto venire molte volte
'Mary has had to come there many times'

(58a) is the non-Restructuring case. The (b) and (c) examples, on the other hand, are Restructuring, as the position of *ci* shows. Here we see that the sentence with *avere* is excluded. This is just what our analysis predicts.

Notice that the situation does not change essentially if we say that PRO in Restructuring is made inaccessible to direct binding from the matrix subject, so that *Gianni* binds the object of *venire*, as in Burzio (1981). *Gianni* and t_i still have independent θ-roles, and (56) and (58b) would be falsely predicted to be ungrammatical. In the present analysis this problem is avoided by positing a readjustment of θ-roles. This was seen to be necessary for the generation of sentences like (56), completely independently of the question of auxiliary selection.

Another consequence of the non-existence of PRO was suggested to me by Mario Montalbetti and Carme Picallo. Suppose that the following condition on LF, from Montalbetti (1984), is correct:[13]

(59) Overt pronouns cannot be coindexed with a trace antecedent.

Let us say that if a pronoun is coindexed it will have a *bound*, as opposed to *coreferential*, interpretation. This distinction is illustrated in (61), where two possible readings of (60) are given:

(60) Many students think that they are intelligent
(61) a. (Many x:x a student) x thinks that they are intelligent
b. (Many x:x a student) x thinks that x is intelligent

(61a) is the coreferential reading and (61b) is the bound one. Now consider the LF representation of a Spanish version of (60), given in (62):

(62) [Muchos estudiantes]$_i$ t_i piensan que *ellos* son inteligentes

Here the pronoun *ellos*, according to (59), cannot be coindexed with the Quantifier Raising trace of *muchos estudiantes*. Thus *ellos* cannot have the bound interpretation, and the reading of (62) is only as in (61a), not (61b).

If *ellos* is coindexed with something other than trace, it may be interpreted as bound. Consider then (63):

(63) [Muchos estudiantes]$_i$ t$_i$ van a [PRO$_i$ convencerlo de que *ellos* son inteligentes]
'Many students are going to convince him that they are intelligent'

Ellos here may be coindexed with PRO instead of with trace. As predicted by (59), then, (63) may have a bound reading.

The contrast between (62) and (63) provides a good test for the presence of PRO. Consider the sentence in (64):

(64) [Muchos estudiantes]$_i$ t$_i$ lo van a convencer de que *ellos* son inteligentes
'Many students are going to convince him that they are intelligent'

The position of the clitic *lo* tells us that this is a Restructuring sentence. In an analysis of Restructuring where the subject of *convencer* here is PRO, then *ellos* should be able to have a bound interpretation, since it may be coindexed with PRO.[14] This is not the result which obtains, however: (64) only has the coreferential reading. Notice that this is exactly what our analysis predicts. The nearest NP with which NP may be coindexed is the trace of *muchos estudiantes*. This is impossible, according to (59), so the bound reading is disallowed.

Here again we see that the positing of PRO in Restructuring leads to undesirable results. In our system an analysis with PRO is excluded for principled reasons.

4.4 Conclusion

4.4.1 Summary

At the beginning of this chapter I pointed out some similarities and differences between causatives and the phenomenon known as Restructuring. The source of the similarities, I claimed, is that both constructions require parallel structures. That is to say, both causative and Restructuring verbs subcategorize for V and $\bar{S}$. The ultimate source of the differences is that causative verbs have a Case array (i.e. are transitive), whereas Restructuring verbs do not. This means, in effect, that the subject of an embedded verb in a causative construction may be lexical (because it will receive Case), but this will not be true of Restructuring. Null subjects (or objects, in the case of ergative verbs) of the embedded verb will not be allowed in either construction, primarily because it would result in PRO being governed. Each construction has a device, then, which allows sentences to surface in which the embedded subject is not overt. Causative verbs may delete the subject θ-role of the embedded verb. This does not work in Restructuring, though, again because of the lack of Case. If the embedded verb is ergative, or made ergative because of the deletion of the subject θ-role, the object will not receive Case. What happens instead, then, is that Restructuring verbs may readjust the assignment of θ-roles, thus allowing for the generation of Restructuring sentences. Confirming evidence for this position comes from several specific properties of Restructuring which then follow without stipulation. It is significant that the analysis of Restructuring presented here not only accounts for an interesting range of facts, but is also forced on us by the theory of parallel structures developed in the previous chapter.

4.4.2 Some speculations on *wanna*-contraction

In our discussion of Restructuring up to this point, we have concentrated exclusively on Spanish and Italian. It is worth asking now whether a similar structure is needed for English sentences like (65):

(65) John wants to eat the cake

That is, is there in the syntactic representation of (65) a complex verb *wants to eat*?

It is unlikely that we will be able to find much evidence for such a position. The tests that we have used in Romance, such as the placement of clitics, do not exist in English, so it would be difficult to show how the Restructuring analysis would be motivated.[15] Nevertheless, there does appear to be some inconclusive, yet intriguing, evidence bearing on this question. There is a well-known contraction process in colloquial English which converts the sequence *want to* into *wanna*, as in (66):[16]

(66) We wanna eat the cake

It has been pointed out (see, e.g., Pullum 1982) that the syntactic contexts in which this contraction occurs appear to be the same as those for Restructuring. In our terms, Restructuring means that a verb subcategorizes for both $\bar{S}$ and V. Thus we only see evidence for a complex verb when there is a matrix verb adjacent to the verb of its complement. Similarly with contraction, *want to* becomes *wanna* only when *to* is from the clause which *want* subcategorizes for. Postal and Pullum (1982), for example, show that contraction is impossible in examples such as the following:

(67) a. I don't *want* [*to* flagellate oneself in public] to become standard practice in this monastery
b. I don't want anyone [who continues to *want*] *to* stop wanting
c. I *want*, *to* be precise, a yellow, four-door De Ville convertible

In none of these cases is *to* from the main verb of the clausal complement of *want*. In addition, the two verbs must be strictly adjacent, just as in Restructuring. Contraction is thus blocked in sentences like (68), where a Case-marked trace intervenes between the two verbs.[17]

(68) Who_i do you *want* t_i *to* look at the chickens?

One simple way to capture this parallel behavior between contraction and Restructuring is to say that contraction is an instance of Restructuring. When *want to* V forms a complex verb, the result is *wanna* V. The facts in (67) and (68) then follow.

One interesting facet of this analysis is that we are essentially giving a syntactic solution to what is usually assumed to be a phonological (PF) problem. That is, we are claiming that the syntactic structure of (66) is importantly different from the control structure generally given. There is some indication that this is correct, however. Consider coordinate sentences such as those in (69) (from Postal and Pullum 1982):

(69) a. I *want to* dance and to sing
b. I don't need or *want to* hear about it

Contraction is blocked in these cases. The structures are given in (70):

(70)

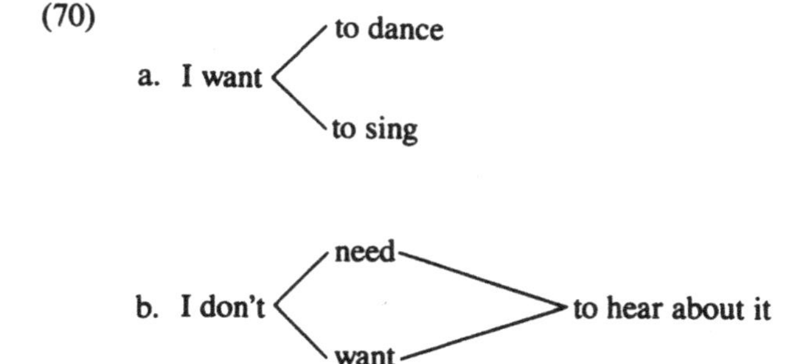

If contraction were purely a PF phenomenon, then it would be strange that it could not take place after the linearization of (70). If, on the other hand, *wanna dance* and *wanna hear* are complex verbs, with *wanna*

represented syntactically as a word, then it is clear why there is no contraction here. This would require structures as in (71):

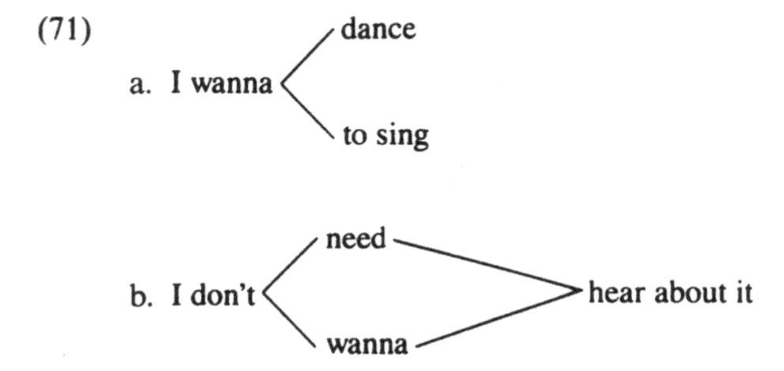

Since it is impossible to generate one of the component sentences in each of these structures (i.e. **I wanna to sing*, **I don't need hear about it*), it is impossible to generate the structure as a whole. The fact that contraction is not possible here thus supports the idea that what we see as contraction has its source in the syntax. This of course does not argue directly for the Restructuring account of contraction, but it does make it more plausible.

Thus we see that by assuming that *wanna*-contraction is an instance of Restructuring, we can account for the cases in which contraction does or does not occur. One question which naturally arises here is how the child who hears *wanna eat* would learn that this is a complex verb, and not just the result of PF contraction. Recent work by Nigel Fabb and Ian Roberts might suggest an answer.[18] Suppose that verbs, like NP's, need to be Case-marked. Infinitives receive Case from *to* and finite verbs receive Case from the tense marker. Now notice that in *wanna eat* the Case-assigner *to* is not overtly present. Suppose that this means that *eat* is not independently Case-marked. The child would then know that *eat* cannot be an independent verb, but rather must form part of a complex verb, which is able to receive Case from the tense of *wanna*. Another way of thinking of this, then, is that since *wanna eat* is a single complex verb, only one Case-assigner is necessary: *to* may then attach to *want*. In this manner, the child would predict the data in (67)–(69) after being exposed only to (66).

5 *Parallel structures*

5.1 Parallel structures and the operation of the grammar

As was stated in chapter 1, the purpose of this study has been to argue for a definition of phrase markers in which neither dominance nor precedence necessarily obtains between pairs of nodes. The form of this argument has been straightforward. Given phrase markers of the type proposed, an explanatorily appealing analysis of some recalcitrant grammatical phenomena follows without further assumptions. I have claimed, then, that we can achieve this result by altering the objects on which the grammar operates (i.e. phrase markers), without substantively modifying the grammar itself. Principles of grammar apply to the novel forms of phrase markers proposed here in the same way that they apply to phrase markers of the traditional type.

What we shall do in this section is see whether this claim in fact has been substantiated in the present study. We will attempt to separate those parts of the analysis which must be stipulated from those which may be derived independently. If my central claim is correct, the necessary stipulations will be minimal.

Let us begin with the causative and Restructuring constructions. Any analysis will have to specify what it is about these verbs that enables them to behave in their distinctive fashion. Here I have claimed that the special lexical property of these verbs is that they may (or, in the case of *faire*, must) simultaneously subcategorize for $\bar{S}$ and V, thus giving rise to parallel structures. Any analysis will also have to state what it is that distinguishes causative from Restructuring verbs in their syntactic behavior. In my analysis, causative verbs contribute a Case array to the complex verb, while Restructuring verbs do not. In addition, the causative verb may delete the external θ-role of the embedded verb, and the Restructuring verb may reassign it.

Thus we have two distinct structures for the causative and Restructuring constructions, both involving parallel structures. This much needs to be stipulated; the rest falls out from the normal operation of the grammar. Case theory plays a particularly large role here. I proposed a detailed theory of Case-assignment which is plausibly the same as that needed generally, but which when applied to parallel structures with a complex verb yields exactly the desired distribution of NP's and clitics. In addition, I show that θ-theory, similarly, operates on parallel structures just as it would on any other structures. Some complex facts, especially with regard to Restructuring, may be traced to this.

Binding theory plays a lesser role in our analysis, but it nonetheless interacts with parallel structures in interesting ways. Since this theory regulates the distance (in hierarchical terms) between pairs of elements, it does not always yield unique results when there are two simultaneous hierarchical structures separating the two elements. Thus an anaphor may be properly bound by its antecedent within one structure but not within the other. It is not clear whether a situation like this satisfies binding theory or not, and, not surprisingly then, we encountered some variation across languages on exactly this point. Notice that binding theory differs from the formulation of Case theory and θ-theory assumed here, in which a given NP may "receive" Case and/or a θ-role. Binding theory does not "mark" NP's in this sense, and thus it is not necessarily sufficient for an anaphor to be bound within only one structure.

Causatives and Restructuring thus appear to validate my claim that significant results are attainable, without making specific stipulations about how the grammar operates with these constructions. I do have to stipulate the structures associated with the constructions, but this has been minimal, in that any analysis must specify what it is that distinguishes causative and Restructuring verbs from other, more canonical verbs.

We now turn to the analysis of coordination. As with causatives and Restructuring, we want to know to what extent the properties of coordination follow from general properties of the grammar. As always, we must make some stipulations. Specifically, we must define coordination as the union of two or more phrase markers. A more accurate way of saying this is that conjunction elements subcategorize for two or more phrase markers (S's). That is, whenever a conjunction such as *and* is present in the structure, two or more sentences must also be present (in parallel).

Given this structure, we should then expect the subsystems of grammar to apply and produce the correct set of sentences. The structure is subject, for example, to the requirements of $\bar{X}$-theory. We saw how the principle that X must be dominated by XP leads to the effect that only like categories can coordinate.

Binding theory also makes some interesting predictions when applied to coordinate structures. In particular, the peculiar asymmetries in Across-the-Board extraction are the direct result of applying Principle C of the binding theory.

The use of θ-theory in coordination appears at first to be somewhat problematic. I stated in section 2.4 that the θ-criterion (and the principle barring vacuous quantification) applies separately to each component sentence of the coordinate structure. This would seem to be at odds with my general claim that grammatical principles apply to parallel structures without any special provision. Here I seem to be making just the kind of provision we would hope to avoid, in that the θ-criterion is required to apply to each part of the structure, rather than to the entire structure itself.

This problem is only apparent, however. Let us look at the θ-criterion in somewhat more abstract terms, as part of a general requirement that all elements of a sentence be syntactically licensed in some way. θ-marking is then the way argument NP's are licensed; but other categories (e.g. predicates, adverbs, quantifiers, etc.) must be licensed as well. No element in a sentence is permitted unless it is licensed in some fashion.[1]

Let us now look at coordinate structures in this light. I said earlier that *and* subcategorizes for two or more sentences. In these more general terms, however, we can say that *and* licenses the existence of two or more sentences.[2] Once these component sentences have been licensed, we can then proceed to examine the constituent elements of the component sentences themselves. These elements too must be licensed. To say that the elements of each of the sentences must be licensed is to say equivalently that each of the sentences must be well-formed according to the θ-criterion, given that this is simply a particular instantiation of the general licensing requirement. It also means that each sentence must obey the prohibition of vacuous quantification, which is most naturally seen here as a reflection of the fact that quantifiers must be licensed.

We may now return to what appeared to be a problem with regard to the application of the θ-criterion to coordinate structures. As it turns out, there is no stipulation that the θ-criterion apply separately to each component sentence. Instead, there is a general requirement that every element in the coordinate structure be licensed. The conjunction licenses the component sentences; the predicate of each of these sentences licenses its subject; the head noun of the subject NP licenses its determiner (if there is one); etc. In this manner, each component sentence must be well-formed according to these licensing requirements, and the results discussed in 2.4 and 2.5 follow without any special provision.

Thus coordinate structures, like those associated with causatives and Restructuring, substantiate my claim that parallel structures are subject to the same principles as any other type of structure. The interaction of parallel structures with the principles of grammar yields an intricate set of predictions which, as we have seen in the preceding chapters, are in large measure correct. There are, of course, pieces of the analysis which do not follow from independently needed principles (most notably, the rule of linking in section 2.6), but crucially these require additions to the grammar and not substitutions. We may say that Gapping requires the special rule of linking, for example, but not that it violates $\overline{\text{X}}$-theory, the θ-criterion, etc. This is a very strong claim, and it is interesting that it appears to be borne out.

5.2 Other versions of parallel structures

There have been a number of studies in the last few years which deal with the possibility of more than one structure existing in the same phrase marker. Despite the broad conceptual similarity among these studies, they differ greatly in their technical implementation. All of these proposals utilize structures distinct from the ordinary phrase markers representable as trees, but they each pick out a different class of non-trees which are to be incorporated into syntactic theory. In this section I will examine these approaches and see how they differ from the system proposed here. I will concentrate mainly on the formal aspects of these proposals, leaving aside for now any extensive comparison of the empirical evidence which has been put forth in favor of each of them. Our discussion will be concerned only with phrase markers containing a simple terminal string, since the proposals to be examined do not deal with coordination.

The first explicit proposal for parallel structures of which I am aware had its roots in Jaeggli (1978), and was later elaborated in Chomsky (1982) and Goodall (1985). In this analysis, parallel structures are formed by adding a monostring to an otherwise normal RPM. The resulting set is identical in type to the new RPM's I defined in chapter 1, but the way it is interpreted is different. The set is divided into two smaller sets, one with the added monostring and one without it, each of which is a well-formed

RPM, in the original Lasnik and Kupin (1977) sense. Suppose, for example, that we add the monostring Dc to the set in (1), yielding (2):

(1) {A, Bbc, aC, abc}
(2) {A, Bbc, aC, abc, Dc}

Notice that the pair aC–Dc in (2) does not satisfy *dominates* or *precedes*. The set in (2) is then split into two subsets, one as in (1) and the other as in (3):

(3) {A, Bbc, abc, Dc}

The final representation thus consists of the pair of RPM's (1) and (3), which constitute the parallel structures in this model.

There are some important properties which distinguish the above system from the one developed in chapter 1. First, a single representation consists of two separate structures, e.g. (1) and (3). The two structures act autonomously, in the sense that principles affecting an element in (1) (e.g. government, Case-assignment, etc.) do not necessarily affect the same element in (3). It is possible, for example, for an empty NP to be a variable in one structure and an anaphor in the other (see e.g. Chomsky 1982: 57). In the system in chapter 1, on the other hand, (2) is well-formed, and it is not split into (1) and (3). There is thus no sense in which a single element could have two incompatible properties, since there is only one structure. We say that there are parallel structures here only because there is no dominance or precedence between the non-terminal nodes C and D.

Another interesting property of the system under discussion here is that the pair of sets (1)–(3) is derived from the set (1). This is accomplished by adding the monostring Dc to the set in (1). Monostring addition, resulting in parallel structures, is then a process or rule, usually referred to as "reanalysis" or "restructuring". We may presume that this kind of reanalysis takes place in the mapping from D-structure to S-structure, and thus may interact with movement operations. In this view, then, a simple D-structure may become reanalyzed in the course of the derivation, in which case the original structure is preserved along with the reanalyzed one. This picture is quite different from that presented in this study, in which parallel structures are not created by rule within the transformational component, but rather are the result of the subcategorization properties of certain lexical items and, as such, are present at D-structure.

Another proposal for parallel structures is presented in Zubizarreta

(1982). The core of this proposal is that nodes in the phrase marker may be parenthesized, as seen in (4):

(4)
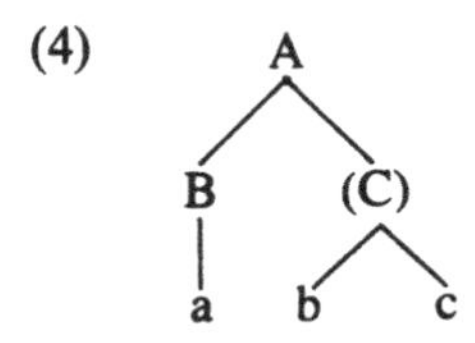

Two projections (i.e. parallel structures) may be read off this: the virtual projection, which contains the parenthesized nodes, and the actual projection, without the parenthesized nodes. Such phrase markers are needed in order to satisfy the subcategorization forms of some lexical items.

Notice that these structures are not representable in terms of the RPM's that I have proposed here. Consider (4), for example, where b and c are immediately dominated by both A and C simultaneously, in two different projections. It is impossible to state this configuration as an RPM. In a set such as (1), for instance, there are no parallel structures. The terminal elements b and c are immediately dominated by C, not by A.

RPM's with parallel structures, on the other hand, are not representable in Zubizarreta's system. Consider the set in (2). In my system, nodes C and D form parallel structures, since neither one dominates or precedes the other. The terminal element b is thus simultaneously dominated by both D and C. This may be visualized as the pair of structures in (5):

(5)
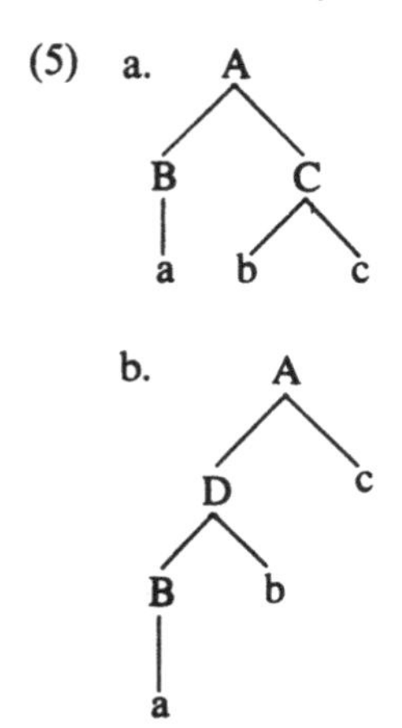

There is no parenthesized phrase marker, however, which has (5a) and

(5b) as projections. A tree such as (6), for example, has an actual projection as in (7), not as in (5a) or (5b):

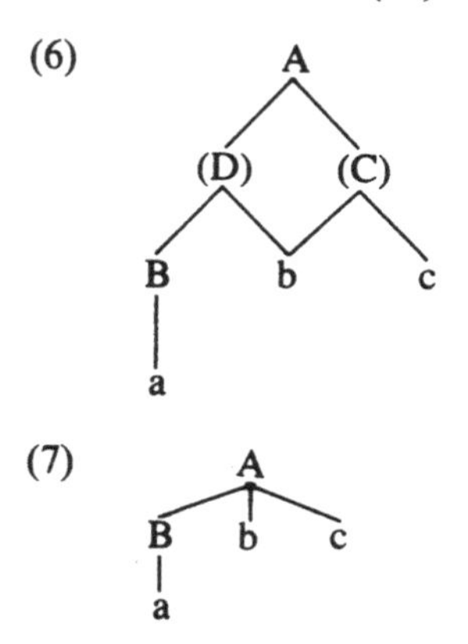

Zubizarreta points out that one of the consequences of the above proposal is that terminal elements are unordered at D-structure. The reason for this may be seen in the D-structure for the Restructuring sentence in (8), which Zubizarreta gives as in (9):

(8) Juan puede visitar a Maria

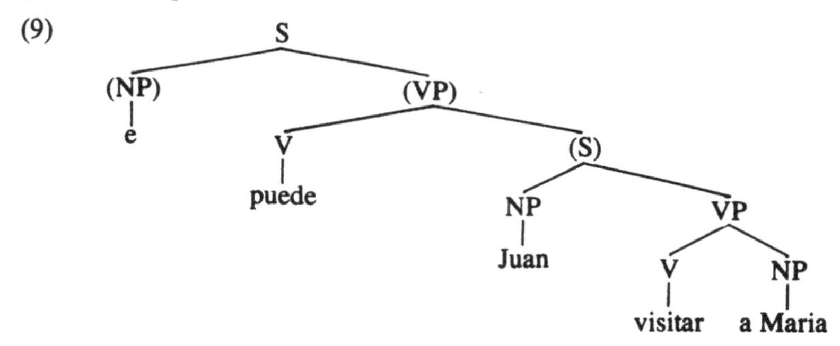

Zubizarreta states that nodes dominating lexical material, such as the NP above *Juan* in (9), may not be parenthesized. *Juan* thus does not move into the parenthesized matrix NP position. In the actual projection of (9), the NP *Juan* is dominated by the matrix S, but the ordering, of course, still does not correspond to (8). Zubizarreta suggests that ordering is not relevant until S-structure, at which point the correct order is imposed.

Finally, we examine the analysis of parallel structures presented in Manzini (1983). In purely configurational terms, Manzini's system is very unconstrained in comparison to the other approaches we have seen. A phrase marker with parallel structures is simply a pair of trees, with terminal strings which may or may not be identical. Any pair is acceptable as long as each member is itself well-formed as an ordinary tree. This contrasts with the previous approaches we discussed, which all imposed configurational restrictions on what could count as possible parallel structures.

Although Manzini's theory of phrase markers allows for an extremely large set of possible parallel structures, she subjects them to a syntactic constraint which requires that the two trees in the pair be relatable by either movement or deletion. Thus if one tree may be syntactically derived from the other, then the pair is allowed. In a sense then, these phrase markers are really a pairing of an S-structure phrase marker with a phrase marker from an earlier stage in the derivation. However, both structures must be subcategorized for by a specified lexical item and hence both structures are present at D-structure. Manzini's analysis is thus distinctive in that the two structures existing in parallel are related by derivational notions rather than by phrase structural ones.

In summary, we have briefly analyzed three definitions of phrase markers which allow for what might be thought of as parallel structures. All three proposals differ in important ways from the approach advocated here. My main interest has been in the formal systems themselves and not in the empirical bases supporting them, so I have not attempted to demonstrate the superiority of any particular analysis. Arguments in favor of the analysis proposed here have already been presented in the preceding three chapters.

5.3 Parallel structures and linguistic theory

A further question which we can ask at this point is whether the introduction of parallel structures into linguistic theory, as seems to be necessary, is a desirable result. One might worry, for example, that the structures we have posited are far removed both from the surface string immediately available to us and from the types of analyses which traditionally have been proposed. It is important to keep in mind, however, that there is no reason to assume that constraints on surface strings will be the same as those on syntactic structures. The surface output is presumably subject to limitations of the vocal and auditory mechanisms, at least, which do not affect syntax proper. Thus the fact that surface strings are linear does not automatically mean that syntactic structure is similarly configured. Likewise, the fact that it is convenient to represent syntactic structure in the form of tree diagrams should not be taken as evidence about the nature of syntactic representations.

A more serious issue bearing on the question of the desirability of parallel structures is that of restrictiveness. Lasnik and Kupin's original definition of RPM's has the advantage of being more restrictive than the one proposed here. That is to say, the set of RPM's allowed by their definition is a proper subset of the set of RPM's allowed by a definition without *dominates* and *precedes*. On the assumption that the more restrictive theory is the more desirable one, it would seem that the introduction of parallel structures is a step backwards, rather than an advance. Within the narrow domain of the theory of phrase markers, this is true. Within the theory of grammar as a whole, however, this appears to be false. A theory in which phrase markers satisfy *dominates* and *precedes* is able to account for the phenomena described in the previous chapters only with significant additions to the rule-types which are otherwise needed. This leads to a large expansion in the class of possible grammars, contrary to our ultimate goals. With the theory of phrase markers presented here, however, the phenomena in question follow from a limited set of independently needed devices. Thus the addition of parallel structures into syntactic theory is compensated for by an overall reduction in the class of possible grammars. In the end, this is the criterion by which the introduction of parallel structures must be judged.

Notes

Chapter 1

1 Our discussion of "trees" here may be taken to apply as well to the phrase markers formalized in Chomsky (1955).

2 As Lasnik and Kupin state, "... we could have defined the predicate [*dominates*] so that neither of the two was true, but no definition could make one of them true and the other false."

3 My formulation thus contrasts in this respect with proposals by McCawley (1968, 1982) and, more recently, Higginbotham (1983, 1985) and Zubizarreta and Vergnaud (1982). This issue is independent of the main claim presented in this study, however.

Chapter 2

1 It has long been noted that coordination might work in this way. See Chomsky (1982) for discussion.

2 I will be looking at broad trends in the treatment of coordination, rather than at specific analyses. The mention of an article in connection with a certain approach does not imply that my discussion of the approach is a summary or portrayal of that article. Stockwell, Schachter and Partee (1973) provides a good summary of the earlier articles on this topic.

3 As we shall see in section 2.4, it is not clear that (3) is a problem if we assume S-structure semantic interpretation (as is now standard). In any event, the argument presented here is what historically motivated the phrasal analysis discussed below. Strangely, some supporters of phrasal analyses (e.g. Gazdar *et al.* 1985) still cite this argument approvingly, without mentioning that it crucially depends on assumptions which are no longer widely accepted.

4 Dougherty (1970, 1971) is the most comprehensive defense of this approach.

5 It is immaterial here whether we take Passive to be an independent transformation, as in traditional analyses, or an instance of Move α.

6 Recall that examples such as (6) argue for the existence of these underlying sentences.

7 I ignore here the question of what types of categories may be conjoined; hence, I rely solely on terminal elements in (12). A complete formulation would need to be stated in terms of non-terminals.

8 Notice that if (12) imposes precedence relations different from these, the

structure will not be linearized. If we say that b precedes g and d precedes f, for example, this is inconsistent with the precedence relations already present. If we say that b and d both precede g, then b and f are still unordered.

9 I am assuming for now that a conjunction (in this case *and*) must be placed before *Alice*. More about this later.

10 (18) also has a "Gapping" output, to be discussed in section 2.6.

11 In fact, letting y_i/y_{i+1} be *Jane*/*Alice* and *saw*/*kissed* allows both (24a) and (24b), since in both cases *Jane* precedes *saw* and *Alice* precedes *kissed*.

12 Of course (43′) will turn out to be an inappropriate tree diagram, since I argue that truncation is not union of phrase markers.

13 Truncation is not unrestricted. It seems that it may only affect non-subcategorized complements of the verb. Compare (38) with (i):

(i) *John cooked the steak and Mary devoured

14 The reader should be careful to avoid the reading where the second conjunct is an afterthought, as in (ii):

(ii) The bouncer was muscular – and a guitarist (too)!

15 The main motivation for choosing this formulation comes from the c-command facts in 2.5.4. There are some restrictions on c-command, however, which do not fall out from this particular formulation (or from any other that I can think of, in this or any other model of coordination). Essentially, we need to disallow c-command between nodes x and y when x and y belong to different component sentences of a union of phrase markers. The motivation for this is given in 2.4.3. However, this restriction may be ignored when x and y are in the same linear position (i.e. when they are conjoined). This is what happens, for example, in 2.5.4, where we have c-command from one conjunct to another, leading to a violation of Principle C. C-command in this configuration, though, appears to be subject to some curious constraints, as pointed out to me by Leslie Saxon. In the Athapaskan language Dogrib, NP's containing a reflexive possessive may be conjoined with an NP coreferential with the possessive (as in *John*$_i$ *and his*$_i$ *wife*) in subject position but not in object position. It seems, then, that c-command from one conjunct to another is limited to subject position in Dogrib. I have no explanation for this.

In summary, c-command between x and y is allowed when they are both in the same component sentence or (sometimes) when they belong to conjoined constituents. C-command is disallowed when x and y are in different component sentences and are not conjoined. It is not clear how to make this generalization fall out from the phrase structure configuration associated with coordination. I will nonetheless assume it for the rest of this chapter.

16 To save space, I am omitting the second instance of S here.

17 According to the original Lasnik and Kupin definition, (r) does satisfy *dominates*, since John VP_1 *dominates* John VP_2 and John VP_2 *dominates* John VP_1. I modify the definition of *dominates*, however, so that mutual dominance such as this does not count as dominance:

(iii) φ *dominates* ψ in P if $\psi = x\chi z$, $\chi \neq \emptyset$, $\chi \neq A$, $\chi \notin N$

18 Irrelevant details of structure are omitted.
19 Much of what I have done in this section would not have been possible without George's insightful discussion of LCL effects. He is one of the few who give an explicit formulation of it.
20 See Williams (1983), however, for an opposing view.
21 See Sag *et al.* (1985) for a more explicit proposal along the same general lines.
22 The sentences in (92) are also out because the position of the conjuncts does not allow NP's in the (a) version or AP's in the (b) sentence, as seen below:

(iv) *That a liar man is my brother
(v) *Proud of it lives next door

23 As Stowell explains, this result follows even if we say that Case-assignment is optional.
24 I am grateful to Ed Blansitt for bringing these facts to my attention.
25 This last possibility is of course the one used by standard English. By saying that it is ungrammatical in the dialect under consideration, I mean that it sounds affected or unnatural in this dialect.
26 Archangeli states that "this kind of conjunction is, according to the informants, real conjunction, not the sequential ordering that the English gloss might imply."
27 For a more precise discussion of the nature of this requirement, see chapter 5.
28 The empty category in this sentence presumably causes the sentence to be ruled out by the ECP as well.
29 Recall that NP's conjoined with *or* are not like plurals. Thus neither (vi) nor (vii) is possible:

(vi) *John or Mary met in the park
(vii) *John or Mary saw themselves

Example (viii) is also impossible, but this time for a different reason:

(viii) *John or Mary saw himself

Himself requires a masculine antecedent, and *John or Mary* is neither masculine nor feminine. This may be contrasted with (ix), which is grammatical:

(ix) John or Bill saw himself

John or Bill here is masculine. Note that for some non-standard dialects *themselves* (or *themself*) may function as a gender-neutral, singular anaphor (cf. *One of the students hurt themselves*). In these dialects, then, (vii) is grammatical.
30 The following discussion owes much to Guy Carden (personal communication) and Chametzky (1984).
31 We saw in section 2.2 that the ordering of the component sentences in a union of phrase markers is indicated in the syntax. The operation needed to allow for a Gapping linearization (see section 2.6) might also plausibly occur in the syntax. Thus the "filtering out" of coreference in sentences like (159) could be a function of either PF or LF. I take no stand on this issue here.
32 The operation of Principle C will be examined in 2.5.4.

33 This forbids extraction of a category A which is dominated by A.

34 Whether it should or not depends on the particular formulation of coordination.

35 The facts in English seem to be somewhat different. Consider a sentence such as (x), where *they* is a resumptive pronoun:

(x) ?*Those are the people who the police don't know where they live, but John spotted __ on campus yesterday

Each of the component sentences is better than (x):

(xi) a. ?Those are the people who the police don't know where they live
b. Those are the people who John spotted __ on campus yesterday

Since resumptive pronouns are fairly marginal in English, it is probable that the kind of binding involved is different from ordinary quantifier-variable binding, and that the *wh*-phrase in (x) is not able to perform both types of binding simultaneously.

36 Georgopoulos (1984, 1985) and recent work by Peter Sells (1984) discuss these types of facts in much greater detail.

37 I thank Hagit Borer and Dan Finer for suggesting the possible relevance of Principle C to me. See Finer (1982) for a similar treatment under a somewhat different set of assumptions.

38 I am assuming here that the two strings *saw* t and *thinks* t *is handsome* do not share common material, in the sense discussed in 2.3.2, and hence constitute distinct VP's. The two traces are not in the same position, and thus do not count as the "same material" for our purposes.

Notice that if the VP's were non-distinct, the trace in the upper conjunct would c-command the other, as occurs in the structure in (188b).

39 More recently, Gazdar *et al.* (1985) have attempted to do the same, although in their account (unlike the others mentioned here) there is no discussion of the contrast between (191) and (193). It is otherwise very similar to Gazdar (1981) and is subject to the same objections (to be outlined in what follows).

40 This can be easily translated into Gazdar's (1981) system, although he takes a different option, suggesting instead that Spanish does not obey the GLBC. This will not affect the point I am trying to make here.

41 As Osvaldo Jaeggli has pointed out to me, conjoined sentences in which the subject has been inverted in only one of the sentences are stylistically somewhat odd even without extraction:

(xii) Comió Juan y María besó al niño
'Juan ate and Maria kissed the child'

However, this does not appear to be the source of the ungrammaticality of (195), since many speakers find a clear contrast between the awkwardness of (xii) and the relative unacceptability of (195). Note that (xii) is not ruled out on any known syntactic grounds, the CSC and parallelism not being relevant here.

42 See Huybregts and van Riemsdijk (1985), Bennis and Hoekstra (1985), and Haïk (1985) for a much more comprehensive discussion of the relation between parasitic gaps and Across-the-Board extraction.

43 In fact, Gapping with *but* yields strange results for most speakers:

(xiii) ?Mary eats apples, but John oranges

44 (208a) will also be ruled out by a constituenthood requirement which we will examine later.

45 Incidentally, these facts constitute a strong argument in favor of deriving the LCL from union of phrase markers. It is hard to see how a phrasal conjunction analysis, for example, could handle these facts.

46 It was noted later, in Sag (1976), that the material to the left of the gap is also limited to one constituent.

47 See, e.g., Hankamer (1971); Jackendoff (1971); Kuno (1976); Sag (1976).

48 Notice that it doesn't really matter whether we say in (216) that both x and z and v and w are linked or just x and z. Parallelism guarantees the same result.

49 Linearization may also produce (xiv):

(xiv) Ted's wine from New York and Bill's from California startled our friends from France and pleased them (respectively)

This is grammatical, although awkward.

50 Here again, the version in (xv) is possible:

(xv) The French drink wine and the Germans beer at 6:00 and at 8:00 (respectively)

51 In (227) and (228) it is, of course, the Gapping reading which I am referring to.

52 One might expect to find examples similar to (227) and (230) with $\bar{N}$-Gapping, but as far as I can tell, these are always grammatical:

(xvi) Ted's wine pleased our guests last week and Bill's disgusted them this week

I have no explanation for this.

53 See, however, Neijt (1979), who argues that Gapping is constrained by Subjacency.

54 This distinction is not normally necessary for the Locality Principle, since the two elements being operated on are always coindexed.

55 However, the Locality Principle seems to have no effect when α_{i+1} is not NP. Witness (xvii).

(xvii) At home we have soup and at work sandwiches

Here there is an intervening subject, but the sentence is good. It is not clear what the Locality Principle has to say about examples like these.

56 Strictly speaking, (237) makes no predictions about the grammaticality of individual sentences, being a tendency rather than a principle. Kuno's system as a whole, of course, does make interesting predictions.

57 Kuno gives examples of sentences which violate the Tendency for Subject–Predicate Interpretation and hence the more restrictive Locality Principle:

(xviii) 50% of his constituents asked the Senator to vote for the bill and 25% to vote against it

This only seems to be possible, though, when, as in (xviii), the Gapping reading is forced. In a neutral context, a sentence structurally identical to (xviii) is ungrammatical (with the Gapping reading):

(xix) *One of my neighbors asked the mailman to vote for the bill and my sister to vote against it

58 Isabelle Haïk has pointed out to me, however, that this restriction is not completely general. Compare (241) with (xx).

(xx) That Harry is a fool is true and that Bill is a fool false

59 Notice, however, that this is somewhat controversial in the case of (245b).

60 Chinese uses no overt conjunction in these cases.

61 There are many interesting questions which I do not pursue here; for example, I at present have no explanation for the oddness of (xxi):

(xxi) ?*Every Sunday, John and Mary shave himself and wash herself, respectively

This should be grammatical, from what we have seen so far. On the other hand, I can explain the ungrammaticality of (xxii):

(xxii) *Every Sunday, John and Mary shaves himself and washes herself, respectively

Here the subject–verb agreement is wrong – cf. (264). We would expect that (xxii) would be worse than (xxi), and I believe that this is true.

62 McCloskey (1986) argues that with RNR in Modern Irish, the right node is simultaneously governed by a governor in each conjunct. This strongly suggests that in Irish, unlike what we have just seen for English, RNR is an instance of union of phrase markers. Further evidence for this view comes from the fact that in Irish and in other languages with similar properties with respect to RNR, the equivalent of English (xxiii) is ungrammatical:

(xxiii) John spoke to, but Mary ignored, the new boss

If RNR in these languages does in fact arise through the union of phrase markers, then (xxiii) appears to be a predictable LCL violation.

Clearly, the issue needs to be explored further, but McCloskey's data are exactly what we would expect if RNR were from union of phrase markers. The English data, as we have seen, are just the opposite, and an analysis of them remains elusive.

Chapter 3

1 I will be for the most part ignoring many interesting questions of dialectal variation within each of these languages. Almost all of the data from French come from Kayne (1975) and Rouveret and Vergnaud (1980), while those from Spanish come mostly from Zubizarreta (1982). I am grateful to Isabelle Haïk and Mario Montalbetti for informant help when the published literature was insufficient.

2 In section 3.4.1 we will see an exception to this generalization, where the subject of an apparently intransitive clause acts like an indirect object.

3 For clarity, I ignore the distinction between S and $\bar{S}$, the COMP node not being relevant to our discussion. "S" may be read as "$\bar{S}$" here.

4 Unlike *laisser*, for instance:

(i) Marie a laissé l'enfant manger la tarte
'Mary let the child eat the cake'

I must assume, then, that *laisser* may be either an Exceptional Case Marking verb or a *faire*-type verb. In other words, *laisser* subcategorizes either for a clause or simultaneously for a clause and a verb. When it subcategorizes for a clause only, it must be able to govern across the clause boundary.

5 For interesting discussion of this point, see McCloskey (1985), who argues in favor of optional Case-assignment.

6 Some of these verbs, e.g. *téléphoner*, do not appear ever to be overtly transitive. Thus it seems that the ability of a verb to take an implicit object does not always correlate with the ability to take an overt object.

Gibson and Raposo (1982) claim instead that the verbs which allow the (45b) pattern are those which (may) take an indirect object. Moreover, they attempt to show that the (45b) pattern is only possible when an indirect object is present, as seen in the contrast in (ii):

(ii) a. On lui laissera parler à son avocat
'We will let him speak to his lawyer'
b. *On lui laissera parler (seule)
'We will let him speak'

Kayne's examples too are all the type shown in (iia). If Gibson and Raposo's generalization is correct (implying that (45b) is ungrammatical as is), then we might modify our analysis so that an implicit direct object is present if and only if there is an indirect object. In other words, an indirect object complement requires the presence of a direct object, whether overt or implicit.

7 I am assuming here in (46) that *écrire* subcategorizes for a PP complement. We could also assume, however, that *écrire* takes an NP complement, to which it assigns dative Case. This NP would then be eligible to receive ACC from the complex verb, while *l'enfant* would be assigned DAT. The resulting sentence is ungrammatical, though, under the intended reading:

(iii) *Marie a fait écrire sa mère à l'enfant
'Mary made the child write to his mother'

This can be accounted for in the following way. Suppose that the complex verb assigns θ-roles to its objects, as will be proposed in chapter 4. The direct object of a complex verb containing an intransitive verb such as *écrire* is assigned the θ-role corresponding to the subject θ-role of *écrire*. In (iii), this is *sa mère*, and hence the grammatical reading of (iii) is that the mother writes to the child.

In order to get a well-formed output from (iii), we must say that the NP *sa mère* is extraposed to the right of *l'enfant*, as in (iv):

(iv) Marie a fait écrire l'enfant à sa mère
'Mary made the child write to his mother'

Here *l'enfant* receives the θ-role equivalent to the subject θ-role of *écrire*. It is also assigned ACC, while *sa mère* is assigned DAT.

8 These facts are noted in Rouveret and Vergnaud (1980).

9 Note that I do not assume that what I am here calling PP Extraposition is a result of movement. If the analysis given here is correct, then in fact it cannot be movement, since this would leave a trace which would block Case-assignment from the verb onto NP_2.

10 Some other verbs in Spanish which display this property are *ayudar* 'to help', *accompañar* 'to accompany', *llamar* 'to call', *saludar* 'to greet', *invitar* 'to invite', *escuchar* 'to listen', *castigar* 'to punish', *acostar* 'to put to bed', *vestir* 'to dress', *perdonar* 'to pardon', and *matar* 'to kill'. There is some variation among speakers concerning exactly which verbs fall into this class, but the important point is that the class is very large.

This phenomenon should not be confused with the existence of "*leísta*" dialects, in which *le* is the human masculine accusative clitic and *lo* is the non-human one. The dialect being described here is "*loísta*" (i.e. the masculine accusative clitic is always *lo*), and the alternation between *lo* and *le* in these examples represents a distinction between accusative and dative, not between human and non-human. Thus with verbs such as *ver* 'to see', for example, which does not belong to the above class, only *lo* is possible.

I am very grateful to Jesús Armando Vargas Matus for enlightening discussion on this matter.

11 The extraposed version, equivalent to French (48), is acceptable to some, but not all, speakers:

(v) María hizo escribir al niño a su mamá
'Mary made the child write to his mother'

12 In (52a) I assume that *la tarte* has not moved into subject position, but I could equally as well assume that it has, since under either option it will not receive Case from V_2. The empty subject position in (52a), which receives neither Case nor a θ-role, is absorbed into the complex verb.

13 For clarity, I am ignoring the subject position in S_2. Nothing hinges on this. See section 3.4.5 for discussion of the embedded subject.

14 There will be a binding theory violation here even if *la tarte* moves first to the subject position of S_2 before raising to NP_1. The trace in subject position then will not be properly bound, since, being in an ungoverned position, it has no governing category.

15 The French facts are discussed in Kayne (1975: 248) and the Spanish facts are discussed in Zubizarreta (1985).

16 An alternative account of the Italian facts is given in Zubizarreta (1985). In her analysis, only French and Spanish have parallel structures; Italian causatives use the complex verb analysis alone. If we then say that anaphors must be bound in all their governing categories, the contrast between (57) and (58) is

accounted for: (57) is bad because, as we have seen, the trace is not bound in one of its governing categories; (58) is good because there the trace has only one governing category, in which it is bound. I will not attempt to decide between the two accounts here. Both of them seem to be possible within the general framework I am adopting.

17 The lack of an equivalent lexical anaphor in French and Spanish makes it difficult to compare these languages here.

18 I will be using the term "deletion" here in a relatively non-technical sense, since I will only be concerned with the claim that the subject position of the lower verb is not θ-marked. The precise status of this unassigned θ-role is a separate question. For interesting discussion, see Zubizarreta (1985), who uses the term "blocking" where I am using "deletion".

19 We might say, instead, that NP_3 is not present when it has no θ-role. The Extended Projection Principle (Chomsky 1981) requires clauses to have subjects even when the subject is not θ-marked, but it is not clear how this affects causative structures. With the complex verb, there is only one clause, and hence there need be only one subject. There is thus no need for NP_3 to be present.

I will continue to speak of the embedded subject being "absorbed into" the complex verb, as in (62b), but it should be kept in mind that this means essentially that the embedded subject does not exist.

20 This is also possible when the embedded verb independently assigns no θ-role to its subject, as in (vi) (from Rouveret and Vergnaud 1980):

(vi) Cela a fait pleuvoir
'That made it rain'

We can also get embedded intransitive verbs, as in (vii) (from Zubizarreta 1985):

(vii) Ce médicament fait dormir
'This medicine makes one sleep'

In both (vi) and (vii), the embedded verb has no syntactically realized θ-position.

21 See Zubizarreta (1982) for a discussion of why these idioms have this property.

22 Clitics in French appear to the left of their verb. Clitics which are attached to the complex verb will appear attached to the left of *faire*.

23 The ungrammaticality of sentences like (70) is noted in Kayne (1975: 270).

24 This is noted in Kayne (1975: 269).

25 The data in (72)–(73) are discussed in Kayne (1975: 230); Rouveret and Vergnaud (1980); Zubizarreta (1982).

26 This fact is noted in Rouveret and Vergnaud (1980).

27 My remarks here assume that the empty category associated with the dative clitic is adjacent to the verb. We also get an ungrammatical result, though, if we assume that the empty category is "extraposed", in the sense discussed in section 3.4.2, since in this case the empty category is not governed by the clitic.

28 Facts like (79a) are noted in Kayne (1975: 291). Sentences such as (79b) are

listed as ungrammatical in Kayne (1975: 291) and Rouveret and Vergnaud (1980: fn. 62), but my own informants have told me that although (79b) is worse than (79a), it is not fully ungrammatical. I thus count it as grammatical here and leave open the question of why there is a contrast between the (a) and (b) sentences.

29 It will in addition be coindexed with the subject of the verb to which it is attached.

30 It is not completely clear what prediction this system makes for sentences which are like (87) but where the complex verb governs an indirect object instead of a direct object. This may be a good result, since (as Kayne 1975 points out) the grammaticality of such examples depends on the lower verb. This is seen in the contrast between *connaître* 'to know' and *embrasser* 'to kiss' in (viii):

(viii) a. Jean se fera connaître à Marie
'John will make Mary know him'
b. *Jean se fera embrasser à Marie
'John will make Mary kiss him'

Thus the uncertainty of the grammar with respect to this type of pattern seems to be mirrored by an uncertainty in the data. Sentences such as (87), though, which are ungrammatical no matter what verb is chosen, are clearly ruled out by this analysis.

31 Spanish also differs from French in that clitics attach to the left of finite verbs but to the right of infinitives.
Se and *le* in (90) are both dative clitics.

32 For unknown reasons, sentences like (90a) are only possible in Spanish when *lo* is inanimate. See Bok-Bennema (1981) for a possible analysis.

33 Note that it is not possible to say simply that the difference between Spanish and French is that Spanish allows clitics on the lower verb while French does not. If this were true we should also see a difference between French and Spanish with *faire-par*. We do not, however. Compare (ix) with (84b):

(ix) *María hizo comer*lo*
'Mary had it eaten'

34 The grammaticality of sentences like (93b) is reported in Zubizarreta (1979). My own informants have told me of the contrast between this sentence and (93a).

35 The ungrammaticality of sentences of this type has been noted in Zubizarreta (1979) and Rouveret and Vergnaud (1980).

36 Here I have only examined the interaction of clitics and Case-assignment. There are other clitics, notably French *y* and *en*, for which the relationship to Case is not as clear, and I do not discuss them here for that reason. Their behavior in causatives is notoriously complex (see Rouveret and Vergnaud 1980).

37 It should be pointed out that in Zubizarreta (1985) this position is no longer taken.

38 We would naturally expect that this analysis would apply to causatives in some other languages as well. The implications for languages with "morphological" causatives are not entirely clear, however, in that here I have heavily relied on the fact that the causative morpheme in French is morphologically a separate word.

Chapter 4

1 I use the term "Restructuring" as a descriptive label only, as I will not claim that there is any process of restructuring involved.

2 Examples (1)–(3) are from Rizzi. It should be noted that whatever Restructuring is, it is optional. When we see the special properties exemplified in (1)–(3), though, we know Restructuring is involved.

3 Restructuring exists in both Spanish and Italian. I will be using examples from both languages in what follows.

4 Example (11) is marginal, presumably, because the Case-marked *wh*-phrase *che* is within the complex verb.

5 Zubizarreta (1982) has also proposed this. Strictly speaking, we should say that these verbs subcategorize *either* for $\bar{S}$ or for $\bar{S}$ and V, since Restructuring is optional.

6 It has also been argued (e.g. in Burzio 1981) that (20) is out because passivization disrupts subject control, but I reject this here. See Stowell (1981) for discussion.

7 When some of these verbs appear in non-Restructuring environments (i.e. only (19a), not (19b)), then NP_3 must be PRO.

8 This is a shift from the more traditional analysis of the θ-criterion, in which the one-to-one correspondence is between *θ-roles* and arguments. It has been argued independently (in, for example, Chomsky 1986) that such a shift is necessary.

9 This is essentially the analysis of Zubizarreta (1982).

10 As Burzio (1981) notes, structures like (43) do not select the auxiliary *essere*:

(i) Mario gli $\left\{\begin{matrix}\text{ha}\\ \text{*è}\end{matrix}\right\}$ voluto essere presentato da Gianni
'Mario wanted to be introduced to him by John'

This is counter to what we would expect, since (i) seems to be parallel to (37). As Burzio suggests (p. 644), this may be because the past participial phrase is a small clause complement of *be*. Binding across clause boundaries only idiosyncratically triggers *essere*.

11 This is not true for Spanish, as we saw in section 3.4.4. There I claimed that in Spanish, binding theory must be satisfied in both parallel structures. This appears to be true for causatives, but not for Restructuring. Consider (ii):

(ii) Juan_i le quiere ser presentado t_i
'John wants to be introduced to him'

Here binding theory is only satisfied in one structure. Since I claimed that the choice is arbitrary, this is not necessarily a bad result.

12 Further evidence for the view that the complex verb assigns Case comes from the sentences in (iii) (with thanks to Armando Vargas for supplying these data):

(iii) a. ?*Juan *lo* compró y cocinó
'John bought and cooked it'
b. ?*Juan *le* mandó un regalo y compró un coche
'John sent a present and bought a car to/for her'
c. Juan *lo* quiere comprar y cocinar
'John wants to buy and cook it'
d. Juan *le* quiere mandar un regalo y comprar un coche
'John wants to send a present and buy a car to/for her'
e. *Juan *lo* va a comprar y quiere cocinar
'John is going to buy and wants to cook it'
f. *Juan *le* va a mandar un regalo y quiere comprar un coche
'John is going to send a present and wants to buy a car to/for her'

In the (a) and (b) sentences of (iii) we see that verbs which are conjoined cannot share the same clitic. This is presumably because each verb has its own Case array, and the clitic, as an overt manifestation of Case, cannot belong to both Case arrays simultaneously. In the superficially similar sentences in (c) and (d), the single clitic is allowed, because there is only one complex verb with its associated Case array. There are two complex verbs in (e) and (f), so there are two distinct Case arrays. The clitic cannot belong to both arrays and thus the sentences are out, just as in (a) and (b).

If complex verbs did not have their own Case array, then we would expect (c) and (d) to be ungrammatical in the same way that the others are.

13 To simplify the exposition I am using the more familiar notion of coindexing here, rather than Montalbetti's "linking." In what follows, "coindexation" will mean "local coindexation" in every case.

14 To save such an analysis, one could say that PRO is somehow inaccessible to binding here (e.g. because of a lack of c-command between PRO and *ellos*).

15 This does not, of course, always come out positive: French, for instance, has clitics but apparently does not have Restructuring:

(iv) *Jean *le* veut manger
'John wants to eat it'

16 See Postal and Pullum (1982) for a listing of the relevant literature.

17 Some dialects apparently accept (68).

18 See, for example, Fabb (1984) and Roberts (1985).

Chapter 5

1 This principle, called Full Interpretation in Chomsky (1986), expresses the intuitive idea that sentences do not contain meaningless elements. See the above work for further discussion.

2 This is roughly equivalent to Pesetsky's (1982) proposal that *and* θ-marks its conjuncts.

References

Abbott, B. 1976. Right Node Raising as a test for constituenthood. *Linguistic Inquiry* 7: 639–42.

Aissen, J. 1974. Verb Raising. *Linguistic Inquiry* 5.3: 325–66.

Aissen, J. and D. Perlmutter 1976. Clause reduction in Spanish. *Berkeley Linguistics Society* 2.

Anderson, C. 1983. Generating coordinate structures with asymmetric gaps. *Chicago Linguistic Society* 19.

Anderson, S. and P. Kiparsky (eds.) 1973. *A Festschrift for Morris Halle*. New York: Holt, Rinehart, and Winston.

Archangeli, D. 1983. Coordination in Malayalam. Unpublished MIT paper.

Bennis, H. and T. Hoekstra 1985. A parameterized gap condition. Paper presented at GLOW Colloquium on Parametric Typology, UFSAL, Brussels.

Bierwisch, M. and K. Heidolph (eds.) 1970. *Papers in linguistics*. The Hague: Mouton.

Bok-Bennema, R. 1981. Clitics and binding in Spanish. In R. May and J. Koster (eds.) (1981).

Bordelois, I. 1974. The Grammar of Spanish causative complements. MIT Ph.D. dissertation.

Borer, H. 1983. *Parametric syntax*. Dordrecht: Foris Publications.

Bresnan, J. 1982. *The mental representation of grammatical relations*. Cambridge, Mass.: MIT Press.

Burzio, L. 1981. Intransitive verbs and Italian auxiliaries. MIT Ph.D. dissertation.

Chametzky, R. 1984. Anaphoric dependencies and coordinate structures. Unpublished University of Chicago paper.

Chomsky, N. 1955. *The logical structure of linguistic theory*. New York: Plenum Press (1975).

Chomsky, N. 1965. *Aspects of the theory of syntax*. Cambridge, Mass.: MIT Press.

Chomsky, N. 1973. Conditions on transformations. In S. Anderson and P. Kiparsky (eds.) (1973).

Chomsky, N. 1981. *Lectures on government and binding*. Dordrecht: Foris Publications.

Chomsky, N. 1982. Some concepts and consequences of the theory of government and binding. *Linguistic Inquiry*, monograph.

Chomsky, N. 1986. *Knowledge of language: its nature, origins and use*. New York: Praeger.

Dougherty, R. C. 1970. A grammar of coordinate conjoined structures I. *Language* 46: 850–98.

Dougherty, R. C. 1971. A grammar of coordinate conjoined structures II. *Language* 47: 298–339.

Fabb, N. 1984. Syntactic affixation. MIT Ph.D. dissertation.

Finer, D. 1982. A parametric approach to Across-the-Board extractions. Paper presented at LSA meeting in San Diego, Dec. 1982.

Gazdar, G. 1981. Unbounded dependencies and coordinate structure. *Linguistic Inquiry* 12.2: 155–84.

Gazdar, G., E. Klein, G. Pullum and I. Sag 1985. *Generalized phrase structure grammar*. Cambridge, Mass.: Harvard University Press.

George, L. 1980. Analogical generalizations of natural language syntax. MIT Ph.D. dissertation.

Georgopoulos, C. 1983. Trace and resumptive pronouns in Palauan. *Chicago Linguistic Society* 19.

Georgopoulos, C. 1984. Resumptive pronouns, syntactic binding, and levels of representation in Belauan. *North Eastern Linguistic Society* 14.

Georgopoulos, C. 1985. Variables in Palauan syntax. *Natural Language and Linguistic Theory* 3.1: 59–94.

Gibson, J. and E. Raposo 1982. Clause union, the Stratal Uniqueness Law, and the chômeur relation. Unpublished University of Hawaii and Universidade de Lisboa paper.

Gleitman, L. 1965. Coordinating conjunctions in English. *Language* 41. 260–93.

Goodall, G. 1983. A three-dimensional analysis of coordination. *Chicago Linguistic Society* 19.

Goodall, G. 1985. Notes on reanalysis. *MIT Working Papers in Linguistics* 6: 62–86.

Grosu, A. 1973. On the nonunitary nature of the Coordinate Structure Constraint. *Linguistic Inquiry* 4: 88–91.

Gueron, J. 1980. On the syntax and semantics of PP Extraposition. *Linguistic Inquiry* 11.4: 637–78.

Haïk, I. 1985. The syntax of operators. MIT Ph.D. dissertation.

Hankamer, J. 1971. Constraints on deletion in syntax. Yale University Ph.D. dissertation, circulated (under the title 'Deletion in coordinate structures') by Garland Publishing.

Higginbotham, J. 1983. Linguistic relations. Paper written for a meeting of the Cognitive Science Seminar, MIT, Oct. 25 1983.

Higginbotham, J. 1985. A note on phrase-markers. *MIT Working Papers in Linguistics* 6.

Huybregts, R. and H. van Riemsdijk 1985. Parasitic gaps and ATB. *Tilburg Papers in Language and Literature* 76; also appears in *North Eastern Linguistic Society* 15.

Jackendoff, R. 1971. Gapping and related rules. *Linguistic Inquiry* 2: 21–35.

Jackendoff, R. 1977. *$\bar{X}$-syntax: a study of phrase structure. Linguistic Inquiry*, monograph.

Jaeggli, O. 1978. Spanish infinitivals. Unpublished MIT paper.

Jaeggli, O. 1981. *Topics in Romance syntax*. Dordrecht: Foris Publications.

Kayne, R. 1975. *French syntax: the transformational cycle*. Cambridge, Mass.: MIT Press.

Koopman, H. and D. Sportiche 1982. Variables and the Bijection Principle. *The Linguistic Review* 2: 139–60.

Koster, J. 1978. *Locality principles in syntax*. Dordrecht: Foris Publications.

Kuno, S. 1976. Gapping: a functional analysis. *Linguistic Inquiry* 7: 300–18.

Kupin, J. 1978. A motivated alternative to phrase markers. *Linguistic Inquiry* 9.2: 303–8.

Kuroda, S.-Y. 1965. Causative forms in Japanese. *Foundations of Language* 1: 20–40.

Lakoff, G. and S. Peters 1966. Phrasal conjunction and symmetric predicates. In D. Reibel and S. Schane (eds.) (1969).

Lasnik, H. and J. Kupin 1977. A restrictive theory of transformational grammar. *Theoretical Linguistics* 4.

Li, M.-D. 1985. Reduction and anaphoric relations in Chinese. UCSD Ph.D. dissertation.

McCawley, J. 1968. Concerning the base component of a transformational grammar. *Foundations of Language* 4.

McCawley, J. 1982. Parentheticals and discontinuous constituent structure. *Linguistic Inquiry* 13.1: 91–106.

McCloskey, J. 1985. Case, movement and Raising in Modern Irish. Paper presented at Fourth West Coast Conference on Formal Linguistics, UCLA.

McCloskey, J. 1986. Right Node Raising and preposition stranding. *Linguistic Inquiry* 17.1: 183–6.

Manzini, M. R. 1983. Restructuring and reanalysis. MIT Ph.D. dissertation.

May, R. and J. Koster (eds.) 1981. *Levels of syntactic representation*. Dordrecht: Foris Publications.

Mohanan, K. P. 1982. Grammatical relations and clause structure in Malayalam. In J. Bresnan (ed.) (1982).

Montalbetti, M. 1984. After binding. MIT Ph.D. dissertation.

Neijt, A. 1979. *Gapping*. Dordrecht: Foris Publications.

Perlmutter, D. 1978. Impersonal passives and the Unaccusative Hypothesis. *Berkeley Linguistics Society* 4.

Perlmutter, D. 1983. Personal vs. impersonal constructions. *Natural Language and Linguistic Theory* 1.1: 141–200.

Pesetsky, D. 1982. Paths and categories. MIT Ph.D. dissertation.

Postal, P. and G. Pullum 1982. The contraction debate. *Linguistic Inquiry* 13.1: 112–38.

Pullum, G. 1982. Syncategorimaticity and English infinitival *to*. *Glossa* 8: 109–20.

Reibel, D. and S. Schane 1969. *Modern studies in English: readings in transformational grammar*. Englewood Cliffs NJ: Prentice-Hall.

Rivas, A. 1977. A theory of clitics. MIT Ph.D. dissertation.

Rizzi, L. 1982. *Issues in Italian syntax*. Dordrecht: Foris Publications.

Roberts, I. 1985. Agreement parameters and the development of English modal auxiliaries. *Natural Language and Linguistic Theory* 3.1: 21–58.

Ross, J. 1967. Constraints on variables in syntax. MIT Ph.D. dissertation.
Ross, J. 1970. Gapping and the order of constituents. In M. Bierwisch and K. Heidolph (eds.) (1970).
Rouveret, A. and J.-R. Vergnaud 1980. Specifying reference to the subject. *Linguistic Inquiry* 11.1: 97–202.
Sag, I. 1976. Deletion and logical form. MIT Ph.D. dissertation, circulated by Garland Publishing.
Sag, I., G. Gazdar, T. Wasow and S. Weisler 1985. Coordination and how to distinguish categories. *Natural Language and Linguistic Theory* 3.2: 117–71.
Schachter, P. 1977. Constraints on coordination. *Language* 53: 86–103.
Sells, P. 1984. Syntax and semantics of resumptive pronouns. University of Massachusetts, Amherst Ph.D. dissertation.
Sjoblom, T. 1980. Coordination. MIT Ph.D. dissertation.
Sportiche, D. 1983. Structural invariance and symmetry in syntax. MIT Ph.D. dissertation.
Steedman, M. 1985. Dependency and coordination in the grammar of Dutch and English. *Language* 61.3: 523–68.
Stillings, J. 1975. The formulation of Gapping in English as evidence for variable types in syntactic transformations. *Linguistic Analysis* 1: 247–74.
Stockwell, R., P. Schachter, and B. Partee 1973. *The major syntactic structures of English*. New York: Holt, Rinehart, and Winston.
Stowell, T. 1981. Origins of phrase structure. MIT Ph.D. dissertation.
Strozer, J. 1976. Clitics in Spanish. UCLA Ph.D. dissertation.
Wehrli, E. 1984. On some properties of French clitic *se*. Paper presented at Fourteenth Linguistic Symposium on Romance Languages, USC.
Williams, E. 1978. Across-the-Board rule application. *Linguistic Inquiry* 9.1: 31–43.
Williams, E. 1981a. Transformationless grammar. *Linguistic Inquiry* 12.4: 645–53.
Williams, E. 1981b. Argument structure and morphology. *The Linguistic Review* 1: 81–114.
Williams, E. 1983. Syntactic vs. semantic categories. *Linguistics and Philosophy* 6: 423–46.
Zubizarreta, M. L. 1979. Restructuration thematique II. Unpublished MIT paper.
Zubizarreta, M. L. 1982. On the relationship of the lexicon to syntax. MIT Ph.D. dissertation.
Zubizarreta, M. L. 1985. The relation between morphophonology and morphosyntax: the case of Romance causatives. *Linguistic Inquiry* 16.2: 247–89.
Zubizarreta, M. L. and J.-R. Vergnaud 1982. On virtual categories. *MIT Working Papers in Linguistics* 4: 293–303.

Index of names

Index of topics